HA80/5329

£12-00

£l

D1614401

SCOTTISH HISTORY SOCIETY

FIFTH SERIES

VOLUME 6

———

Clerk's *History of the Union*

A

Detail from portrait of Sir John Clerk by William Aikman

(collection Sir John Clerk, Bt.)

History of the Union of Scotland and England

by

Sir John Clerk of Penicuik

━━

Extracts from his MS 'De Imperio Britannico'
translated and edited by
Douglas Duncan

★

★

EDINBURGH

printed for the Scottish History Society *by*

PILLANS & WILSON LTD., EDINBURGH

1993

British Library Cataloguing-in-Publication Data:
A catalogue record for this book is available
from the British Library

ISBN 0-906245-15-x

Printed in Great Britain

CONTENTS

—

vi

PREFACE

This volume departs from the Society's usual practice by not reproducing original documents (except in the appendices). I was glad to agree with Council's recommendation that the space needed to print the original Latin of Sir John Clerk's sixth book (dealing with the union debate) could be more usefully devoted to translated extracts from his earlier books, so as to give a broader impression of his character and scope as a historian. To make it easier to check my translation against the originals, I have throughout given references to the folio numbering of the manuscripts used. I have printed, in notes or within square brackets in the text, the Latin terminology used by Clerk to denote his most central concepts. Latin is also given at a few points where alternative translations seem to me possible. Further, though only in the case of Book 6, I have noted where my version departs from the readings of one or both of the surviving manuscripts.

A further difference from usual practice is that this volume is not the work of a professional historian. I have brought to it patience and a good deal of interest but no detailed knowledge of Scottish history or the union period in particular. My aim has been to offer an accurate translation which historians can read in the light of their own expertise. I have therefore confined my introduction and notes to matters which caught my attention or came readily to hand without extraordinary research, and not tried to provide the mass of information or reference to published works of scholarship normal in editions of this kind. I apologize to students who would have found that useful, and ask pardon from scholars, especially those from whom I have learned.

In the choice of extracts for translation from Books 1-5 in Part One I had no option but to use my own judgement. The general principle I followed was to choose passages which would illustrate (in order of priority) Clerk's main preoccupations, his rhetorical methods, and his idiosyncratic viewpoints. More passages are included from Book 4 than from earlier books because there, as he arrives at the seventeenth century, Clerk ceases to follow authorities closely and expresses himself more freely than before.

Of the appendices, the first two explain themselves. The third, the long 'Testamentary Memorial', overlaps the *History* and Clerk's previously publish-

viii

ed writings at several points, but room has been made for it to let him speak here on union in his own words. It should be noted, however, that he wrote it aged sixty-eight, about fifteen years after finishing the *History*. It is an undisguised exercise in self-justification, addressed to family and friends.

I am grateful to Sir John Clerk of Penicuik, Bt. for permission to use materials from the Clerk archives on deposit at the Scottish Record Office, Edinburgh, and to Lady Clerk and himself for their interest and hospitality. The first stages of my work were aided by the award of a Visiting Research Fellowship at the Institute for Advanced Studies in the Humanities, University of Edinburgh and travel grants from the Arts Research Board of McMaster University, Hamilton, Ontario. While in Canada I received friendly encouragement and help from Professor Roger Emerson, University of Western Ontario. More recently, I owe thanks to Bishop Alastair Haggart and the Principal and staff of Coates Hall Theological Institute for making visits to Edinburgh pleasant and financially feasible, and to Mr Warren McDougall for answering a query. My chief debts are to Dr Iain Gordon Brown of the National Library of Scotland, who generously shared with me the knowledge and enthusiasm that will soon be reflected in his full study of Clerk and his circle now in preparation, and who suggested my approach to the Society; to the late Dr Ian Rae for early guidance; and to Dr Julian Goodare, who has dealt with my antiquated typescripts with exemplary forbearance, courtesy and care. Neither he nor Dr William Ferguson, who kindly agreed to read the introduction, should be charged with defects that remain.

Finally, I dedicate my share in this volume to my wife Susan, *sine qua nihil*.

D.D.

Kinloch House, Lochcarron
June 1993

ABBREVIATIONS

—

APS *Acts of the Parliaments of Scotland*
HMC Historical Manuscripts Commission
NLS National Library of Scotland, Edinburgh
SHS Scottish History Society
SRO Scottish Record Office, Edinburgh

Anderson, *Historical Essay*: James Anderson, *An Historical Essay, showing that the Crown and Kingdom of Scotland is Imperial and Independent* (Edinburgh, 1705)

Brown, 'Sir John Clerk': Iain Gordon Brown, 'Sir John Clerk of Penicuik (1676-1755): Aspects of a Virtuoso Life' (Cambridge University PhD thesis, 1980) (copy in NLS)

Brown, 'Modern Rome and ancient Caledonia': Iain Gordon Brown, 'Modern Rome and ancient Caledonia: the Union and the politics of Scottish culture' in *The History of Scottish Literature*, vol. ii, ed. A. Hook (Aberdeen, 1987)

Buchanan, *Ruddiman*: *Georgii Buchanani Opera Omnia, curante Thoma Ruddimanno* (2 vols., Edinburgh, 1715)

Clerk, 'Letter to a Friend': [anon] 'A Letter to a Friend, Giving an Account how the Treaty of Union has been Received here &c.' (Edinburgh, 1706)

Clerk, 'A List of the Books I made use of': see Appendix B

Clerk, *Memoirs*: *Memoirs of the Life of Sir John Clerk of Penicuik ... extracted by himself from his own Journals*, ed. J.M. Gray (SHS, 1892)

Clerk, 'Memorandums': see Appendix A

Clerk, Notes on Lockhart: see 'Lockhart' below. Clerk's annotated copy (SRO, GD18/6080)

Clerk, *Observations (1730)*: 'Sir John Clerk's Observations on the present circumstances in Scotland, 1730', ed. T.C. Smout, *SHS Miscellany*, x (1965)

Clerk, 'Testamentary Memorial': see Appendix C

Defoe, *History*: [anon] *The History of the Union of Great Britain* (Edinburgh, 1709). Sections separately paginated

Hume, *Diary*: Sir David Hume of Crossrig, *A Diary of the Proceedings in the Parliament and Privy Council of Scotland, 1700-1707*, ed. J. Hope (Bannatyne Club, 1828)

Lockhart, *Memoirs*: [anon] *Memoirs Concerning the Affairs of Scotland, from Queen Anne's Accession to the Throne to the Commencement of the Union* (London, 1714)

Stukeley: The Family Memoirs of the Rev. William Stukeley, M.D. and the Antiquarian and other Correspondence of William Stukeley, Roger and Samuel Gale etc., ed. W.C. Lukis (3 vols., Surtees Soc., 1880-5)

INTRODUCTION

Three reasons can be offered for raising the wreck of Sir John Clerk's *History*. The first concerns the stature of the author. At least since his *Memoirs* were published by this Society in 1892 he has won enough respect to justify enquiry into his principal literary undertaking, a work of some 360,000 words which occupied his mind for forty years. The second, partly accidental, reason is that recent growth of interest in the history of Anglo-Scottish relations vests him in the garb of a pioneer, since that was the topic on which he focused exclusively for all but a few of his pages, becoming (*pace* Mair) Scotland's first international historian. And third is the fact that his sixth and final book ✗ contains the longest surviving account by a participant of an affair that, at least in the mind of the public, refuses to be denied controversial significance—the debate on union in the last session of the last Scottish parliament.

These rather portentous claims on our attention may shrivel on the discovery that Clerk's skills as a historian were limited and that even his last book, though written with authority, tells us little that we do not know already and steadfastly overlooks much that we do. None the less, we are left with a major curiosity, a work doomed to fail from the moment of its conception but of interest, perhaps chiefly, as a record of contradictions, some of them inherent in the author himself, others reflecting the Scotland of his time. We encounter a writer who could be variously painstaking and lazy, naive and hard-headed, tolerant and dogmatic, orthodox and eccentric, North Briton and Scot; a Janus-faced history that sought to infuse the British peoples with an optimistic faith in their destiny while employing a mode of discourse, rooted in the past, that ensured its future unreadability. We shall not make the mistake of taking Clerk's work quite as solemnly as he took it himself, but our knowledge both
✗ of him and of Whig views of union may be increased by bringing it to light.

Biographical.

John Clerk was born in 1676.[1] His paternal grandfather, a merchant from the North-East, had made a fortune in Paris buying works of art for the Scottish

---

[1]   The following outline of Clerk's life, which emphasizes aspects relevant to the *History* and neglects many others, derives chiefly from *Memoirs*. On his cultural interests see Brown, 'Sir John Clerk' and 'Modern

nobility and set up as a gentleman in the 1650s, purchasing the barony of
Penicuik, seven miles south of Edinburgh. His father, made baronet in 1679,
was not only a sober Whig member of parliament and elder of the kirk but a
shrewd manager of his estates who assured their prosperity by developing
coal-mines. On his mother's side Clerk could claim descent from the royalist
poet and historian, William Drummond of Hawthornden. After schooling in
Latin and Greek at Penicuik he was sent at sixteen to Glasgow University
where he stayed two years, but 'never felt any benefite' from his study of Logic
and Metaphysics: 'it cost me as many years to unlairn what I had learnt at
Glasgow'.[1] That unlearning process, and the opening of his mind, occurred at
Leyden. There he studied civil law under Philip Reinhard Vitriarius, then
recently acclaimed for his book on the Law of Nature and Nations, a
consolidation of Grotius and Pufendorf.[2] He also took 'colleges' on Roman
history from Leyden's celebrated professors of Rhetoric, Jacob Perizonius and
Jacob Gronovius, scholars whose interests had shifted from textual criticism
toward the study of 'antiquities', or ancient civilization.[3] But it was characteristic of Clerk to devote most of his energy to extra-curricular studies:
mathematics,[4] philosophy, music, drawing and the French and Italian languages. These last were a preparation for his travels of 1697-9, chiefly in Italy,
undertaken without his father's approval or support and vividly described in
Memoirs. Encouraging a wide range of his future cultural interests—in antiquities, painting, architecture, music and especially perhaps the pleasures of
patronage—these showed how a spirited and likeable young man could
achieve a Grand Tour on the cheap without letters of introduction. But
stock-taking on his return to Scotland he had one negative item to record:
that he had 'spent at least 600 lib. Str. more than my Father knew of, which
gave me a very great deal of truble for many years after'.[5]

The problem was not solved by admission to the Faculty of Advocates in
1700, and certainly not by marriage a year later to a lady who was sister to the
5th earl of Galloway and cousin to the 2nd duke of Queensberry. Debt, or the
fear of it and his father's displeasure, influenced Clerk's choice of a political
career, for which he seems to have had no inclination. By the standards of the
time his vote was not sordidly bought. When his wife's death in childbirth left
him sick and disoriented, her powerful relatives treated him kindly. Galloway

Rome and ancient Caledonia'; also his 'Critick in antiquity: Sir John Clerk of Penicuik', Antiquity, li
(1977), 201-10. On Clerk as economist see T.C. Smout's introduction to Observations (1730).
1   Memoirs, 12.
2   Institutiones Juris Naturae et Gentium ... ad methodum Hugonis Grotii conscriptae (Leyden, 1692).
3   Rudolf Pfeiffer, History of Classical Scholarship from 1300 to 1850 (Oxford, 1976), 129, 163.
4   His skill with figures was to prove crucial to his professional career, a fact easily forgotten by readers of
     Memoirs.
5   Memoirs, 36.

arranged his election to parliament as member for the burgh of Whithorn. But lucrative office had to come from Queensberry, whose favours carried strings attached. *Memoirs* records initial suspicion of Queensberry's promises ('His Grace was a compleat Courtier ... I knew his charecter') but lets us infer that what proved irresistible was the fact that his promises were kept.[1] Clerk, who was later to rejoice in independence, earned it in his twenties by becoming Queensberry's man.

In parliament he worked hard to meet his obligations. His first session, 1703, was an exciting one, dominated by the Act of Security and Fletcher of Saltoun's limitations, against which he dutifully wrote two pamphlets.[2] It was not the Court party's finest hour, however, and Fletcher's attacks on its subservience to England impressed Clerk deeply.[3] But he was kept too busy for wavering. Appointed almost at once to serve on a commission 'to enquire into the publick accompts and debts of the nation', he was one of four out of fifteen members who did all the work, and it was he who drew up the commission's reports, twice receiving £200 for his pains.[4] His diligence brought him recognition. The duke of Argyll, High Commissioner in 1705, backed his election to the Council of Trade, and later that year we find the earl of Stair[5] and Lord President Dalrymple, Stair's brother, persuading his father to let him accept a more important appointment, as a commissioner to negotiate a Treaty of Union.[6]

According to *Memoirs* Clerk was himself reluctant to accept, having 'observed a great backwardness in the Parliament of Scotland for an union with England of any kind whatsoever' and fearing that the negotiations would be a waste of time. Only when 'the Duke of Queensberry threatned to withdraw all friendship for me, I suffered my self to be prevailed upon'.[7] But his letters to his father from that period show him eager to make the trip to Whitehall

1 Ibid., 44.
2 'One against diminishing the antient prerogatives of the Crown, the other an Essay upon the intended Limitations' (Ibid., 49). (Copies of the latter in NLS and SRO, GD18/3129.) Clerk envisages four courses Scotland might take on the death of Queen Anne: acceptance of the Hanoverian succession, separation of the crowns, union with England, or establishment of a republic. He argues pragmatically that in each case the proposed limitations would be unnecessary or counter-productive. In the crucial first case he asserts that the Scottish parliament's arrogation to itself of the right to make peace and war would be 'cutting our own king's throat' by inviting alliance with France.
3 See below, pp. 22-3.
4 His growing confidence in economic matters is shown by his pamphlet, *The Circumstances of Scotland consider'd, with Respect to the present Scarcity of Money: together with some Proposals for supplying the Defect thereof, and rectifying the Ballance of Trade* (Edinburgh, 1705). Copy in SRO, GD18/3129.
5 Son of first Viscount Stair; Secretary of State, 1691-5; disgraced following enquiry into the Glencoe massacre but restored to favour and created earl, 1703.
6 Letter, Clerk to his father, 14 Dec. 1705, SRO, GD18/3131/25.
7 *Memoirs*, 58.

and subsequently enjoying his work there.[1] He was made a member of a joint committee for the Minutes and, more responsibly, of a Scottish committee on the Equivalent, where the knowledge he had acquired of Scotland's finances could be applied to those of England. Later he was to be given the task of explaining and defending the Equivalent to the Scottish public.[2]

He was active for the cause: how deep was his commitment to it? Such evidence as we have from his letters at that time suggests a young man, still only thirty, excited by participating in great events in the company of the great statesmen of his day, but unlikely to question what they were doing or why they were doing it. If Fletcher had impressed him, so now could Stair and the amazing 'condescension' of the English.[3] He was too honest to support a cause in which he did not think he believed, yet he did, in 1706-7, let himself drift on a powerful tide, one which he hoped would lead to preferment. The wholehearted commitment to union proved by the *History* and other documents was a later phenomenon.

His account in Book 6 of the debate on union in the Scottish parliament generates just enough conflict to suggest that he experienced some at the time. All we know is that he regularly voted with the government. He was elected to the British House of Commons, and to the body responsible for managing the Equivalent, but his reward came in 1708 with his appointment on Queensberry's recommendation as a judge (titled 'Baron') in the newly-formed Scottish Court of Exchequer. Releasing him from politics, this provided income, professional prestige and a great deal of leisure[4] for the remaining forty-seven years of his life.

His multifarious activities during those years can only be summarized here. He remarried and begat a large family. He improved and extended his father's estates, starting new coal-seams and embarking on a vast programme of plantation and landscaping. Inheriting the baronetcy in 1722, at the age of forty-six, he began to assert his own interests and especially his character as a 'virtuoso'. The old interest in antiquities came to life in his excavation, study and collection of Roman remains, a field in which he quickly acquired a reputation that brought him election as a Fellow of the Society of Antiquaries of London.[5] As an architect he designed for himself, with William Adam's help, the Palladian villa of Mavisbank, Loanhead, to complement the old house at Penicuik as a setting for his distinctively Roman ideal of cultured,

1   SRO, GD18/3131.
2   *An Essay upon the XV. Article of the Treaty of Union, wherein the Difficulties that arise upon the Equivalents, are fully cleared and explained* ([Edinburgh,] 1706). Copy in SRO, GD18/3129.
3   Letter, Clerk to his father, 23 May 1706, SRO, GD18/3131/12.
4   Clerk took his duties seriously (see 'Testamentary Memorial', Appendix C, pp. 204-5 below) but the Court sat for only about twelve weeks a year.
5   See especially his letters to the English antiquary, Roger Gale, printed in *Stukeley.*

gentlemanly leisure.[1] He resumed travel: to the north of England to study coal-works and Hadrian's wall; to London to renew acquaintance with the nobility, to view the earl of Burlington's villa at Chiswick and the earl of Pembroke's collections at Wilton. On a more modest scale than they, he became a leading patron of the arts in Scotland,[2] but also encouraged scientific enquiry, himself giving papers to the Edinburgh Philosophical Society and communicating with the Royal Society in London as a Corresponding Fellow. And throughout, by virtue of his work in the Exchequer, he kept a close eye on the Scottish economy, helping to set up, and himself serving on, the Board of Trustees for Manufactures and Fisheries established by royal charter in 1727.

Long before his death in 1755 Clerk had become a self-assured figure of consequence in Scotland, very different from the able but raw aspirant who had signed the draft Treaty of Union. As a new kind of Scottish gentleman—cosmopolitan and secular in outlook, devoted to the cultural and economic improvement of his country—he is deservedly seen as a forward-looking figure, a precursor of 'Enlightenment'. We shall find that view complicated, as well as endorsed, by examining his *History*.

Composition.

About its writing he tells us much in *Memoirs*, 'Memorandums',[3] and notes on the manuscripts. The idea came to him 'but a few years after the union' ('Memorandums'), about 1714 (*Memoirs*, 84). The date of 1711 heading a notebook of excerpts from Livy[4] suggests that the idea had been formed by then, but it was certainly reinforced in 1714 by the pirated publication of George Lockhart of Carnwath's *Memoirs*.[5] As well as setting himself to read 'all the Histories and all the Memoirs and Pamflets that related to the affaires of England and Scotland'(*Memoirs*, 84), Clerk embarked on a programme of reading Roman authors to improve his style which lasted 'at least Eghteen years' ('Memorandums'). This is acceptable on the likely assumption that he continued to read after starting to write, which he tells us that he did about

1　See his poem, 'The Country Seat' (SRO, GD18/4404) and the fanciful but revealing Latin letter to Hermann Boerhaave (extracts translated in *Memoirs*, 236-40).
2　Among those he patronized were the poet Allan Ramsay, the painter William Aikman, the musician and antiquary Alexander Gordon, the scholars James Anderson and Thomas Blackwell, and the architects William and Robert Adam.
3　See Appendix A.
4　SRO, GD18/5078/51.
5　Clerk's heavily-annotated copy of this survives (SRO, GD18/6080). Strongly opposed in politics, Clerk and Lockhart were on fair terms as neighbouring landowners. See Lockhart's numerous letters to him in *Letters of George Lockhart of Carnwath, 1698-1732*, ed. D. Szechi (SHS, 1989).

1725.[1] In that year, however, Robert Wodrow heard through the clerical grapevine that he had already 'come some lenth'.[2] Since copying and revision of all six books had begun by 1731-2,[3] we can reasonably date composition to around 1724-30, the most active period of Clerk's middle life.

Manuscripts multiplied over the next fifteen years. Clerk's principal amanuensis, his chaplain William Ainsley, wrote neatly but with poor comprehension of Latin, so that correction of his errors, added to the author's obsessive revisions of his own style, soon led to new fair copies being needed, which in turn had to be corrected and revised.[4] Then in 1745, as the Pretender's army reached Edinburgh and Clerk prepared for flight into England, he destroyed all his original holographs and all but one copy of each of Books 4, 5 and 6, which presumably he thought the most politically sensitive. These were 'lodgd in a coal hole' and 'spoiled with black water'.[5] Further revisions to all books were made in 1746 and again in 1749-51, but no new fair copies were made until, in April 1751 (at the age of seventy-five), he himself began a copy of Book 6, handing over to an amanuensis after twenty sheets. This remains uncorrected. The result of the whole process is that three copies survive of Books 1 and 2, two of 3 and 6, and only single, coal-stained copies of 4 and 5.[6]

The questions of why Clerk wrote, why he wrote in Latin, and why he never published are matters for conjecture, since all touched on areas of private sensitivity about which he was reticent. At the start of 'Memorandums' he lists four 'motives' for writing: to correct the widespread view, based on 'silly' accounts such as Lockhart's, that union was 'brought about by compulsion & corruption'; to explain its necessity by setting it in historical context; to provide an example to foreigners of the benefits of uniting with their neighbours; and finally to vindicate his own conduct, "tho amongst wise people, especially such as deal in matters of State it will need no appology'. The first and last of these, plainly connected and of central importance to the author, are reflected in the text only by haughty denials of Lockhart's charges, which are side-stepped and made to look petty through a lofty vision of union supporters as disinterested patriots fulfilling God's will. Such evasiveness was typical of Clerk, who, as smaller instances will show, habitually resorted to silence or dogmatic assertion when he felt challenged on matters that touched him closely. Having acted on union in good faith, and benefited in a then-normal way from political patronage, he was no doubt disturbed by the allegations

1   Note on Book 1, MS C.
2   *Analecta*, iii (Maitland Club, 1843), 236.
3   Notes on Books 5 and 6 (MS 1).
4   Every revision is recorded and dated on the MSS.
5   SRO, GD18/5116.
6   SRO, GD18/3202/1-6.

that circulated,[1] and as a member of the commission that managed the Equivalent may have known that some were well-founded.

Further, as the *History* will show, he so vehemently endorsed Andrew Fletcher's attack on the political system by which Scotland was managed to suit English interests that he must have become aware that he himself and his fellow-commissioners under Queensberry could be seen to have co-operated with just that system. The sincerity of his life-long defences of union can hardly be doubted, but behind them lay an uncomfortable, unacknowledged sense of the need for self-justification. Of this the clearest proof is the composition of the *History* itself. Nothing else can explain the drudgery he endured over forty years in preparing, writing and revising it, drudgery unparalleled in his life and totally at odds with his sense of what befitted a gentleman.[2]

In history such as he wrote, however, apologetic motives are soon overlaid by rhetorical objectives. He wrote, he tells us, 'that the people of Britain should lairn to know how to value the union'.[3] Internal evidence puts beyond doubt that Clerk wrote to persuade British readers, with 'foreigners' only an added bonus provided by his Latin medium. Why, then, the choice of medium? Here again he is silent on a controversial issue; the decision, once taken, was never to be discussed. Presumably he thought Latin the only medium worthy of so great a subject; it would give his work the *gravitas* needed to sink Lockhart.[4] He may also have mistrusted his English prose style, which never aspired to dignity or polish. Latin also flattered the 'Roman' aura with which he liked to surround his private life, and had the practical advantage of cutting out ignorant readers. But it brought its own problems. He himself acknowledged the difficulty (though not the absurdity) of latinizing the more technical aspects of the union negotiations.[5] A more sensitive, and again unacknowledged, problem was his command of the language itself. Clerk's long work is an astonishing linguistic feat for a gentleman amateur, but publication would have shown that he was no George Buchanan.[6] The long process of stylistic revision

1   Clerk's father objected from the start to the commissioners' being paid from the Equivalent: 'to seek a decreet of p[t] for y[e] commissioners expenses to be rais'd' in Scotland by way of cess is just but to be taken off y[e] equivalent looks very scandalous in my opinion & I shoud beg for my own part befor I either sought or took it y[t] way for it will lay a foundation of aspersing the treaters for ever' (note on his son's letter of 25 Jan. 1707, SRO, GD18/3135/1).

2   *Memoirs* significantly conceals much of the drudgery: 'I finished the work at last, but it was so tedious and the success of it so doubtful that I never had the courage nor the time to revise it' (84). Brown, 'Sir John Clerk', 136ff. discusses at length how the gentlemanly ethos excused Clerk from writing and publishing, and acquits him of indolence mainly on the strength of the *History* (154).

3   Note on Book 3, MS B.

4   Clerk was scornful of Lockhart's style, 'below the dignity of either History or memoirs' (Clerk, Notes on Lockhart, 33).

5   'The Romans were acquainted with few things that became the subject of the Treaty of union' (note on Book 5).

6   Grammatical faults are not uncommon in Clerk's Latin, his use of tense and mood particularly uncertain.

which he proudly describes as perfectionism—adding the *ultima manus*, or 'finishing hand'—resulted from anxiety made worse by isolation: he seems not to have been willing to show his work to anyone other than copyists. Among the threats to his cherished peace of mind which always made him chary of publishing, the prospect of criticism of his Latin may have daunted him as much as the embroilment in political controversy he feared in 'Memorandums'.[1]

But conflicting impulses made him waver over publishing almost to the end. A copy, or more likely draft,[2] of a letter survives, dated 25 March 1751, in which he offers the manuscripts to the booksellers, Hamilton and Balfour. The tone is off-hand: 'if you think them worth your trouble you may publish them when you will'.[3] For Clerk's sake one hopes that the letter was not sent. It is an index of how fashion had changed in Edinburgh that in the previous year Hamilton and Balfour had brought out their edition of *L'Esprit des Lois*.

Subject; title; preamble to Book 1.

The subject of the *History* is well described in *Memoirs* (84) as 'an account of all the attempts that had been made to unite Britain under one Head, from the days of Julius Caesar down to the accomplishment of this great work in 1707'. This reveals the inadequacy of the title, borrowed from Defoe, which Clerk always used when referring to his work in English. Defoe's *History of the Union* (1709) had contained a section called 'A General History of Unions' (from Edward I to 1670), followed by another tracing Anglo-Scottish relations up to 1706, but together these comprised only about one-tenth of his volume. Clerk's emphasis is different. Of his six books the first four deal with pre-union history, illustrating his wider concern with what he calls the *fata Britannica*— the long, complex, destined process which the Treaty of Union completed.

His interests are therefore better reflected by his Latin title, '*De Imperio Britannico*'.[4] This would be used for the present volume if it were easier to translate, but no English word has the range of *imperium*, which embraces both

As for style, his claims to have imitated Caesar ('Memorandums') or Livy and Sallust (*Memoirs*, 84) must be taken with salt. He shows some skill in varying the style of speeches but his narrative style is monotonous (see below, p. 26).

1   When in 1747 Clerk sent his short *Dissertatio de Monumentis quibusdam Romanis* to the Ruddiman press, the grammarian Thomas Ruddiman covered 'two or three Leaves of Paper' with suggestions for stylistic improvement (SRO, GD18/5108).

2   At the start, the letter implies that it accompanies the manuscripts; at the end it gives instructions on where they may be found at Penicuik House.

3   SRO, GD18/5116.

4   This is the commonest form but the title varies between manuscripts. Also found are '*De Imperiis Britannicis*' and '*De Imperiis Britannicis eorumque ortu & progressu*'. The title '*Historia Coalitionis Angliae & Scotiae*' occurs once only, in the 1751 copy of Book 6.

the subject and object of rule.[1] Thus the title's primary meaning, 'concerning rule over Britain', implies the concept of Britain as a unit to be ruled as well as the concept of a single ruler. Also evoked is the constitutional meaning which *imperium* acquired in the Renaissance: autonomous sovereignty. All fused together in Clerk's belief that Britain was intended by Nature to be an autonomous entity under a single government.

Introducing the whole work, the preamble to Book 1 (#A[2]) is the only place where Clerk gestures even faintly in the direction of philosophical history. So rapid is his survey of the origin of society and government that it can hardly be traced to particular sources. On this much-trodden ground he harks back to Buchanan and opposes Hobbes in stressing God's purposes, while his allusions to the Laws of Nature and Nations show him following in tracks marked out for him at Leyden.[3] There, too, he may first have imbibed the notion that the larger a political unit, the greater its security.[4] Since political security emerges as Clerk's main reason for valuing union, the principle of 'the bigger the better' was important to him, and it is uncharacteristic to find him conceding the contrary principle that 'a plurality of small states ... may permit a more even distribution of wealth and commerce'. Where he found this idea cannot be determined, but the fact that Andrew Fletcher had advanced it in his forecast of how the wealth of a united Britain would be concentrated in London[5] could be significant, since it will later be argued that the clash between Fletcher's thinking and his own contributes to conflict in Book 6.

Clerk certainly has his own time in mind when he goes on to distinguish between societies entered into voluntarily and those formed under constraint. That he should then give so much prominence, in a general introduction, to the society of Rome and the Caledonians' resistance to it ceases to surprise when one has read Book 1. Finally, it is worth noting that at the end of his preamble he uses the 'rise and progress' formula to introduce the later books. Evolutionary and providential interpretations of history will co-exist throughout.

---

1   'Dominion' and 'command' are the nearest but unsatisfactory equivalents. Several distinct meanings of *imperium* are illustrated in the preamble to Book 1, #A, p. 33 below.

2   Letter-references are to the translated extracts in Part One.

3   See above, p. 2. Vitriarius, following Grotius, defined the Law of Nature as 'the law with regard to good and evil which God requires all men to follow through the right use of reason' (*Institutiones Juris Naturae et Gentium*, 5, translated). Thus for Clerk's age the term 'Nature' meant God in philosophical disguise: 'the way God means things to be' in every aspect of creation. Since it included physical nature, the fact that Britain was an island could be evidence that it was meant to be united.

4   Samuel Pufendorf, *De Iure Naturae et Gentium* (Lund, 1672), Bk. 7, ch. 2, 2.

5   Towards the end of *An Account of a Conversation concerning a right regulation of Governments* (Edinburgh, 1704).

Book 1: from the Romans to 1066.

To the four major *imperia* of Romans, Saxons, Danes and Normans Clerk is tempted to add a fifth, that of Scots and Picts dominant in Britain before the Saxon invasion (#H, p. 39 below). More than half the book's 128 sheets deal with the Roman period, because authoritative sources for this were available.[1] Although Clerk followed Eachard and anticipated Robertson and Hume by beginning with the Romans for that reason, in other respects his practice was traditional: his narrative, like that of the humanist historians, mainly repeats what he found in his sources with little or no shaping comment.[2] After the Romans he admits to groping in darkness. He uses Gildas and Bede where he can, Geoffrey of Monmouth with deep mistrust, and mostly Buchanan, who leads him to give long circumstantial accounts of persons and events no longer mentioned by historians.

Because the Dark Ages could most easily be moulded to his design, Clerk's first book yields striking eccentricities. Most obviously, he projects his idea of Britain back into the past. While it is true that the Romans thought of Britain as a unit, and fair comment that the British peoples succumbed to invasion because of their disunity, it is another thing to suppose that these peoples shared a sense of being British. This Clerk regularly does, urging for example that British fellow-feeling would have impelled the Scots and Picts to assist their southern neighbours against the Saxons (#I, p. 39 below). Coldly uninterested in the separate English and Scottish myths of national origin, Clerk substitutes the unionist myth of primeval Britishness.

More astounding is his back-projection of the Scots. In assuming that the Romans met resistance from Scots as well as Picts (#A, p. 34 below), he followed the traditional Scottish history of Fordun, Boece and Buchanan which held that the Scots and their kings had been resident in Scotland since the fourth century BC.[3] But not even that early date satisfied Clerk: he insists that the Scots were indigenous to Scotland and never came from Ireland at all (#F, p. 38 below). This idiosyncratic conviction—which he characteristically claims to be the majority view, in accord with Nature and Truth—sprang in part from Clerk's need to identify himself and fellow-Lowlanders racially with the Caledonians who stemmed the Roman tide, but had a deeper root also. He makes passing reference in the *History* (fo. 114) to a theory he developed

---

1   See 'A List of the Books I made use of' (Appendix B below).

2   This dominant characteristic of the first three books is for obvious reasons not much illustrated in the extracts translated.

3   Clerk was unmoved by the *raison d'être* of that history, to prove the antiquity of the Scottish royal line (see #B, p. 35 below). At fo. 77 he expresses indifference as to whether Fergus was the first king, the fortieth king, or not a king at all.

in 'An Enquiry into the Ancient Languages of Great Britain'[1] that the common language of Britain before the Romans came was not Celtic but Saxon, introduced by earlier Saxon settlers. This enabled him to argue that all the indigenous British peoples (Scots, Picts and Britones[2]), though politically divided, had been 'naturally' united by speaking variants of that common Saxon language that most of them still spoke.[3] Thus Clerk's belief that the common language of English and Scots in his own day was a sign that the island was originally intended by Nature to be united made it necessary for him to dissociate the early Scots from any connexion with Ireland.[4] Clerk's extraordinary hypothesis is an example of how unionist propaganda tried to suppress the facts of Scotland's Gaelic-speaking past and present. His tenacity in maintaining it also shows up his much-vaunted revisions. Thomas Innes's *A Critical Essay on the Ancient Inhabitants of the Northern Parts of Britain* (London, 1729), though it appears in his library catalogue,[5] receives no mention in his text.

Clerk preaches union by relentlessly exposing the evils of division. Hadrian is slighted for abandoning Scotland and dividing Britain with his wall (fo. 50); Constantine's division of his empire caused its collapse (fo. 65). The Picts deserve favour only so long as they ally with the Scots, and win obituary praise for contributing to the 'fair union of Caledonians' (#J, p. 40 below). But the Scoto-Pictish union was enforced by conquest, and is compared to Egbert's contemporary domination of the Saxon heptarchy: such unions, involving the suppression of free peoples, are normally to be deplored as 'unnatural'. In what appears to be a parable for his times Clerk justifies both these enforced unions because the *salus populi*—the welfare of all the Caledonians in one and all the Saxons in the other—demanded an end to internecine strife. 'In such cases wounds can be quickly cured and true freedom spring from what was thought to be slavery.' The Danes, however, who proceeded to exploit the resentment of disaffected Picts and Saxons, had no better motive than ambition for forcing them into alliances. That evident allusion to the French exploitation of Jacobitism lays bare the rest of Clerk's parable. His countrymen (here somewhat infelicitously equated with long-forgotten Picts) had been forced into union for Britain's greater good.

---

1   'A Paper intended for the Philosophical Society at Edenborough', 1742 (*Stukeley*, i, 339-57).

2   Clerk regularly uses this form to denote the 'British' tribes of England and is at pains (fo. 87) to distinguish it from *Britanni*, meaning all the inhabitants of the island.

3   When and how the Welsh and Gaelic languages reached Britain he does not say, but manages to embrace them in his linguistic unionism by suggesting more sensibly that they shared with Saxon a common Celtic root.

4   Throughout the *History* Ireland is ignored as far as possible. Colonized by Scots, then conquered by England, it is an offshore island irrelevant to the destiny of Britain.

5   NLS, MS Dep.187/5.

But his practice of reading the present into the past is most interesting in his treatment of the Roman *imperium*. Clerk's ambivalent feelings about the English—his admiration for their superior wealth and culture, his resentment of how they had treated his own people—underlie the division of his sympathies between civilizing Romans and freedom-loving Caledonians.[1] Regret for what Scotland had lost by its rejection of Roman society is set against pride that his ancestors had forced Rome to wall them out (#E, p. 36 below), and generals like Agricola, though offering the benefits of *pax Romana*, are criticized as invaders fired by ambition and intolerant of other peoples' freedom (#B, p. 35 below). Clerk's summation of this matter (#G, pp. 38-9 below) is a small masterpiece of concentrated ambivalence. It is his chief, perhaps only, strength as a historian that he could recognize such conflicts of response within himself and build his *History* around them.

Book 2: 1066-1363.

Describing 'the attempts of Anglo-Norman kings to acquire the *imperium Britannicum*' (#A, p. 43 below), Book 2 could not fail to bring patriotic issues to the fore. It is remarkable, however, chiefly for its pacifying rhetoric, as Clerk tries to reconcile the attitudes of Scots and English readers to the most contentious period of their countries' relations. He has a clear run at the start, finding common ground not only in an idealized view of Malcolm III's relations with the Saxon court and marriage to Margaret (#B, pp. 43-4 below),[2] but also in hostility to the French invaders who drove the Saxons north. Later in the book he objects on religious grounds to blanket condemnations of entire peoples (#E, p. 52 below), but throughout the *History* ignores that principle with regard to the French. Unlike the Romans, the Normans are credited with no civilizing influence; feudalism is the object of recurrent attacks right up to the union debate; and by associating it in medieval times with England rather than Scotland, Clerk can ascribe the unacceptable behaviour of 'Anglo-Norman kings' in part to the workings of a French virus.

Much space is devoted to the matter of homage by Scottish to English kings (#C; see also Book 1, #K; pp. 44-8, 41-2 below). Just as the assertion of Scotland's sovereignty had been a crucial preliminary to union negotiations, so English readers of the *History* must be left in no doubt that they had entered into a union with an independent people. The Scottish parliament's authorized spokesman on this subject, James Anderson, had been patronized by Clerk

---

1   The importance of this topic for Clerk extends far beyond the bounds of his *History*. It is admirably treated in Brown, 'Modern Rome and ancient Caledonia', to which readers are referred.

2   Clerk admits (fo. 12) that hostility to Saxon incomers prompted Donald Ban's usurpation, but stresses the resumption of good relations with England under Edgar (#C, pp. 44-5 below).

in the early 1720s,[1] a fact which may explain why Clerk felt entitled to use Anderson's *Historical Essay* more often than he acknowledged. Like Anderson, he strengthens the Scottish case for English readers by citing English chroniclers and documents wherever possible, and from Anderson he derives several of his arguments: on the insignificance of homage done for lands in England, the invalidity of homage extracted under duress, and the reminder that Richard I and John had signed away their kingdom as much as any king of Scots.

But his indebtedness should not be exaggerated. Clerk has studied, not indeed original charters or manuscripts as Anderson had done, but a wide range of printed collections of documents and printed editions of medieval chroniclers.[2] These have the salutary effect of weaning him away from mechanical reliance on Buchanan. He does, however, often use one argument drawn from Buchanan which Anderson had carefully avoided. This is that a king's actions—including acts of homage on behalf of his kingdom—do not bind the nation or affect its honour unless backed by parliament. On occasion (Book 1, #K, pp. 41-2 below), Clerk will assert this for Britain as a whole, but more commonly applies it to Scotland, thus supporting Buchanan's claim that the Scottish monarchy had always been limited (#E, p. 51 below). As a corollary of this, he admits the notion of periods of national degeneracy when one or more of the estates connive to prostitute the national honour. These occur under Malcolm IV and William I (#C, pp. 45-6 below) and again when the Competitors swear loyalty to Edward I (#E, p. 50 below). Clerk is careful to balance these concessions by insisting that England, too, had periods (and longer ones) of national disgrace. Thus it was the degeneracy of the Saxons in 1066 (Book 1, #L, p. 42 below) that invited the imposition of feudalism, and although the English people asserted their rights under John and Henry III (#D, pp. 48-9 below), they submitted to tyranny again under Edward I.

Interludes of peace between Scotland and England are emphasized; Richard I's friendship with William (#C, p. 48 below) and Henry III's fatherly treatment of the young Alexander III (fo. 60) are unctuously described, as though Clerk thinks it 'natural' that the stronger kingdom should foster the weaker. But Edward I's imperial ambitions posed a challenge: this was a king still remembered with pride by the English and 'with pain' by the Scots (#E, p. 49 below). In keeping with his overall British design, Clerk starts with the conquest of Wales (fos. 64-7). He pays elegiac tribute to the old Britones—freedom-loving savages again—but justifies Edward by stressing their treachery and brutality and praises him for following Roman example by admitting them into fellowship with England. Gradually, however, in the

---

1   SRO, GD18/5020. See also Brown, 'Sir John Clerk', 109.
2   See Appendix B below, and marginal notes (given here as footnotes) in the MSS.

course of his dealings with Scotland, Edward is changed from a responsible statesman seeking dynastic union into a power-hungry tyrant and monster of vanity. Because it prompted that change, the Maid of Norway's death is described as disastrous for the whole of Britain, England as much as Scotland suffering from Edward, who used Scotland as a power-base from which to tyrannize his own subjects. Ingeniously, then, the long wars which stemmed from the death of the Maid are shown to have united both peoples in common suffering under feudal oppressors.

Such an approach clearly damps down the fires of Scotland's pride in its 'wars of independence', and in unobtrusive ways Clerk carries this further, seeking to adjust his countrymen's attitudes. A preliminary case is his treatment of Macduff's appeal to Edward against the judgement of Balliol (fos. 86-7). Buchanan had slanted this story against Edward for summoning the king of Scots to defend his decision before the parliament of England. Clerk uses it to illustrate the degeneracy of the Scottish nobility, since this Macduff was a descendant of the one who had supported Malcolm III. About the severity of Edward's measures in Scotland no punches are pulled, but they are presented as an example of how *not* to achieve an effective union. If only Edward had treated a conquered people as the Romans did! This note of regret (#E, p. 52 below) implies that Scotland's later achievement of independence was a second-best outcome.

Clerk maintains conflict by warmly endorsing the traditional Scottish accounts of Wallace and Bruce as champions of national freedom; their exploits, however, are kept in critical perspective. Wallace, though a hero of classical proportions (fo. 138), is essentially a throw-back to the Caledonian savage, playing Galgacus to Edward's Agricola: his 'inveterate hatred of the English' (fo. 96), his 'slaughter of prisoners with awful cruelty like enemies of the human race' (fo. 98) are not to be admired. Nor is Bruce magnified quite as Scottish readers would expect. 'His *imperium* was based on the murder of his kinsman and the utmost treachery to Edward' (fo. 136). 'His success was due more to faction in England than to the battles he fought' (fo. 146). Surprisingly, at his death, there is no summing-up of his character and achievement such as Clerk normally accords to major figures.

One of the most astonishing moments in the *History* occurs in the course of an intimidating address delivered by Bruce to his troops before Bannockburn (#F, p. 55 below):

> All Britain awaits the outcome of this day, for no part of this island can be enslaved without damage to the whole, and the destinies of the British peoples are so intertwined that what happens to one affects all.

For Clerk, freedom and slavery are important concepts—only 'union' is evoked more often—and he transcribes in full (from Anderson's appendices) the Declarations of Dundee and Arbroath that state freedom as a cause worth dying for. He can therefore praise Bruce for rekindling a flame which the tyranny of the Edwards had extinguished elsewhere in the island. But history taught Clerk to mistrust the equation of Scotland's freedom with independence from England. When he writes (#E, p. 52 below) that the Scottish estates were 'enslaved' under Edward I's Ordinance in the same way as they later were under English ministers before the union, he shows willingness to face the objection levelled against his fellow-unionists in Book 6 that they were unworthy of their ancestors by reacting to a similar situation quite differently from Bruce. He closes Book 2 with a rueful account (#H, p. 56 below) of how Edward III's generous peace-proposals to David II were emphatically rejected by the Scottish parliament. 'Patriotism prevailed, or more probably one should say that it was inveterate hatred of the English'. Patriotism barely distinguishable from anti-English feeling was in Clerk's scheme of things not enough.

Book 3: 1363-1603. •

This book opens without preamble, the introduction to Book 2 having served for the whole period from 1066 to the union of crowns. But between the two books the point of division has been carefully chosen. Scotland's rejection of Edward's proposals fittingly concludes a book which had begun with Malcolm's welcome of the Saxon exiles; now, with the accession of the House of Stewart, the issue for Scotland will be less her independence than her political alignment. Accordingly, Scotland's choice between English and French alliance will be the binding theme of Book 3.

Strongly as Clerk felt on this subject, it was not one which aroused in him tensions of the sort that lend interest to the first two books. On three separate occasions—following the lead of Buchanan twice and Drummond of Hawthornden once[1]—he states the rival claims of England and France in the form of a debate. That these debates were meant as nodal points in the book is plain from the fact that they are the only long passages of reflective writing it contains. But they were primarily a challenge to the author's rhetorical skill: how to state a finite number of arguments three times over without exactly repeating either himself or the writers he followed, and, still more difficult, how to state the French case well enough to make its triumph credible each time. Since this was a kind of exercise in which students of rhetoric and

---

1   See #B, pp. 58-60 and 60-1 below. The third debate, fos. 155-6, concerns the proposed French marriage of Mary queen of Scots. Like the second, it is modelled on Buchanan.

law-students in particular were commonly trained—arguing *in utramque par-
tem*, on both sides of a question—Clerk acquits himself competently in a
manner which foreshadows his practice of it on a much larger scale in Book
6. Here, however, his failure to simulate pro-French (as distinct from anti-
English) sentiment renders his achievement somewhat coldly technical. The
intended element of conflict in Book 3 never sparks into life.

Buchanan remains the chief narrative source; other Scottish writers occa-
sionally mentioned are Boece, Mair, Leslie, Drummond and Abercromby.[1]
Rymer is regularly cited on treaties. Clerk's tactical need to give prominence
to English historians becomes less urgent in this book, but he frequently claims
support from Eachard. And towards the end there are references to De Thou.
But such gestures are of little significance. The 315 sheets of Book 3—it is the
longest of the books—consist almost entirely of conscientious but mindless
chronicling, the author's comments on issues and other writers' opinions rarely
extending beyond a summary, one-sentence judgement. It is here that Clerk's
drudgery, as he forced his way through what was plainly uncongenial material,
becomes most conspicuous. One might say that he was depressed by his
countrymen's failure to make the right choices: time and again he laments the
Scots' inability to enjoy the fruits of peace with England, their restless habit of
provoking their neighbours or each other.[2] But what Book 3 chiefly conveys
is the boredom of hack-work pursued to masochistic lengths in the interest of
a grand design.

And hack-work, as often, leads to mental laziness. Near the start, for instance
(#A, p. 57 below), Clerk loftily alludes to the extensive literature on Robert
III's legitimacy but in doing so makes clear that he had not read it,[3] and at the
same point comes close to inconsistency in his comments on 'title' with regard
to Robert and Henry IV. His limited interest in ecclesiastical matters and
Reformation theology leads him (#C, pp. 61-2 below) to pass over very
sketchily indeed a major binding-agent in Anglo-Scottish relations. More
lamely still, he records the deposition of Mary queen of Scots with no
comment at all (fo. 206). He could perhaps have claimed that it was outside
his brief, but as one who has let himself be guided by Buchanan in full
awareness of his bias,[4] he is evasive on this topic to the point of cowardice.
The last hundred sheets of Book 3, from Mary's captivity in England to the

---

1   He does not use Lindsay of Pitscottie, available among the Advocates' MSS but not printed until 1728.
     An added note (fo. 189) mentioning Robert Keith's *History of the Affairs of Church and State &c* (1734) is
     almost unique as a reference to a book published after the *History* was originally written.
2   #A, pp. 57-8 below; #C, p. 61 below. See also fos. 65-7.
3   The case for Robert III's legitimacy rested on a papal dispensation legitimating the relationship and
     children of Robert II and Elizabeth Mure, not, as Clerk says, on his parents having been secretly married.
4   Buchanan 'takes every least opportunity to undermine royalty' (fo. 67); 'sided with the regent Moray in
     all things, reviling the poor Queen with harsh and impudent eloquence' (fo. 216).

death of Elizabeth, show Clerk at his perfunctory worst, drifting from episode
to episode with no sense of direction, the fragments glued only loosely
together with occasional references to mutual understanding between Elizabeth and James VI.

In a note on one manuscript, Clerk apologizes for 'the long Episode I have
made in relation to Queen Mary',[1] and elsewhere explains that such episodes,
'pieces of our History that may seem to be not altogether to the main purpose',
were intended 'to divert my Readers, otherways I supposed that my History
wou'd be very heavy & dry'.[2] That Clerk relaxed his normally firm sense of
relevance over Mary is understandable, and the 20-odd sheets he devotes to
her personal drama are certainly less 'dry' than the rest of the book. They do
not, however, show him in an attractive light. Professing to soften Buchanan's
portrait and doubt its veracity, he in effect accepts it and renders it harsher
through simplification. From comparison of the extracts on Mary's return to
Scotland (#D, p. 62 below), one sees how Clerk closely follows Buchanan
but coarsens his comment on her French education and substitutes vague
commiseration for adverse but intelligent character-analysis. On all the essential points of controversy—her affair with Riccio, her adultery with Bothwell
during Darnley's life, her complicity in his murder and authorship of the
Casket Letters—Clerk's practice is to refuse to commit himself, whisper the
worst, and then proceed on the assumption of its truth. We have seen that
elsewhere he could sometimes hold conflicting viewpoints in a cool balance.
Here, however, the emotions aroused in him by the lustful woman and the
tragic queen are in most uncomfortable accord.

Book 4: 1603-1706.

Few extracts from Book 3 are given in the present volume because in that
book Clerk rarely dwells long enough on any topic to say anything worth
reproducing. In Book 4 the situation is different. Although showing for the
seventeenth century even greater distaste than for earlier periods, Clerk writes
about it with fluency and conviction. From the start—his brief introduction
could still yield quotations for unionists—we sense that his mind is more
actively engaged with his material. Confident touches of irony further that
impression. There is no more reliance on rhetorical exercises to give relief
from perfunctory narration, and the citing of sources soon ceases as Clerk
comes to deal with matters with which he feels at home. This is not to say that
he has read nothing: Clarendon, for instance, has clearly been digested, but

1   Note at end of MS B.
2   SRO, GD18/5116.

Clarendon had become part of a familiar scene and so did not need to be acknowledged.

Increased confidence does, it is true, encourage Clerk's vices of laziness and dogmatism. Thus he conspicuously fails to investigate the Cromwellian union; on the union negotiations of 1670 and 1703 he is content to translate what he found in Defoe; and he uses his aversion to James II and VII as a pretext for ignoring him almost totally. But faults of impatience can be pardoned in writing which at times conveys urgency, even involvement. Book 4 is a reminder of how close men of Clerk's generation felt themselves to be to the events of the seventeenth century, inheriting and often reacting against the memories and opinions of their fathers and grandfathers. More and longer extracts are given from it here, not on account of their historical worth, but because they are readable and show very clearly what the author believed.

For those reasons, too, they can be left to speak for themselves. One may note, however, that as well as exposing the disastrous results of an incomplete union Clerk is interested in explaining the period's religious commotions. He finds their root cause in the pacifism of James I and VI. Peace, or *otium*, which has always brought out the worst in the Scots, bred 'corruption of manners' in both kingdoms and encouraged 'the natural fickleness of the British peoples' (#C, p. 69 below). Clerk's is a rationalist's view of national psychology. In times of ease, reason is overwhelmed by passions, the most damaging and nearest to madness of these being *dira superstitio*, religion carried to irrational extremes. It was this 'disease of the mind', from which even a king could suffer (#D, p. 74 below), that disordered all Britain and broke down the proper divisions of responsibility between clergy and laity, monarch and parliament (#D, pp. 73-4 below).

With regard to Anglo-Scottish relations, the whole book is governed by the premiss that they went from bad to worse throughout the period until, under Anne, nothing but full political union could set them to rights. In this gathering darkness there are few chinks through which light can be allowed to shine; there are plenty of victims but no heroes. Rhetorically, with his Scottish and English readers still in mind, Clerk's main concern is to distribute blame even-handedly. This he does from start to finish, but one suspects that the exceptionally heavy stress he lays on the Scots' culpability for instituting rebellion in 1638[1] was meant as a counterweight to the almost Fletcherian

---

1   This is said to have incurred God's anger (#D, p. 72 below). Clerk's support for Charles I is remarkable since he admits that he was guilty of curtailing his subjects' religious freedom, a crime which he has earlier envisaged as grounds for rebellion (Bk. 3, #A, p. 58 below). After tacitly acquiescing in Buchanan's justification of the revolt against Mary, Clerk seems to become more monarchist the closer he comes to Queen Anne. This may explain why he is anxious to draw a veil over James II and VII.

virulence with which he attacks England's treatment of Scotland from 1660 onward.

Book 5: negotiation of the Treaty of Union, 1706. ๑

An even greater change comes over the *History* in its last two books. Narrative becomes almost entirely confined to the exchange of words, as the treaty is negotiated at the Cockpit, Whitehall, then debated in the parliament of Scotland. Clerk's pride in having been 'an Eye and Ear Witness'[1] of these events raises hopes that he will communicate new information. These are only meagrely fulfilled.

Book 5 (124 sheets) does little but translate available documents: the position papers exchanged by the commissioners[2] and the text of the treaty they drew up.[3] Turning this often technical material into Latin caused Clerk difficulty,[4] and exposes him today to bemused ridicule, but clearly he thought he was giving dignity and permanence to a climactic achievement.[5] He adds some linking matter and editorial comment, but these for the most part repeat what he wrote in the surviving journal that he kept throughout the proceedings.[6]

An exception is the extract provided. The Scottish commissioners, alarmed by the English proposal that only thirty-eight of their members should sit in the British House of Commons, requested and obtained a 'conference' on the matter, the only occasion when negotiations were conducted through face-to-face discussion. This was not recorded in the Minutes, nor did Clerk treat it fully in his journal.[7] His more ambitious summary of the arguments in Book 5, though probably accurate, was written long after and is therefore chiefly valuable as a 'dramatic' presentation of the Scots' predicament.

Lockhart's comment on this is often quoted: 'At the separate meetings of the Scots Commissioners, if a Difficulty was at any Time started, or an Objection made to what they were concluding, all the Answer you receiv'd was to the Purpose, 'tis true it had better be so and so, but we must not be too

1   'Memorandums', Appendix A, p. 175 below.
2   These papers, edited by a joint committee on which Clerk sat, became the 'Minutes of the Proceedings of the Commissioners', published after the Scottish parliament met in Oct. 1706 and incorporated, with 'observations', in Defoe's *History of the Union* (1709).
3   The translated text appears again, in its amended form as approved by both parliaments, in Bk. 6, fos. 220-42.
4   'Memorandums'; endnote on MS of Book 5.
5   Cf. 'the union ... will be found so beneficial to posterity that some of the articles deserved well to be written in Letters of Gold' (SRO, GD18/5116).
6   'A journall of the proceedings of the Scots & English Commissioners &c' (SRO, GD18/3132).
7   'Indeed there were but very ordinary things said & put in a very ordinary dress for upon y^c English side the great speakers said nothing' (p. 78). The debate produced 'more heat than reasone' (p. 79).

stiff; the English won't agree otherwise.'[1] Less often quoted is Clerk's rejoin-
der: 'Some people had reasone to talk so who in their consciences believed
the union to be the *summum bonum* of their countrey.'[2] His account of the
conference succeeds in suggesting the veiled insults and blatant injustices that
the Scots had to stomach in pursuit of that goal, as their arguments based on
'national dignity' succumb to economic *realpolitik* and they experience the grip
(*tenacitas*) beneath the velvet glove (*suavitas*) of their counterparts. Though
unable to forget or forgive a peculiarly ill-timed sarcasm from Harley, Clerk
could not, in the context of his *History*, openly criticize English attitudes.
Instead he lets them stand self-condemned. Through this irony he re-lives and
transmits the strain felt by patriotic Scots as they learned to accept their destiny
as Britons.

Book 6: the debate on union in the Scottish Parliament, 1706-7. •

Shortage of information about this debate[3] scarcely troubles those who see it
as a three-month charade, the outcome predetermined, the voting influenced
not by speeches in the house but by prior inducements. Clerk's contrary
assumption—he barely mentions management and posits a triumph of rea-
soned argument—will change no one's view, but few will disagree with him
that (apart from some passages of drudging) this is 'the most interesting part'[4]
of his *History*. Where the interest lies is for historians to determine. Two
matters only will be dealt with here: the value of Clerk's account as evidence
of what was said, and the way it appears to have been shaped in part by a
conflict of personal loyalties.

It differs radically from Defoe's by emphasizing speeches.[5] In classical and
humanist historiography the definition of speeches as 'plausible fictions'

1   Lockhart, *Memoirs*, 210.
2   Clerk, Notes on Lockhart, 210.
3   *APS* prints formal addresses by the Chancellor and Commissioner but no debating speeches; it records
    motions, protestations, votes and voters' names. Defoe's *History* reprints most of the official record, adds
    'observations' on each day's debate, and gives the text of four speeches: by Lord Belhaven on Articles 1
    and 2 and William Seton younger of Pitmedden on Articles 1 and 3. The other main sources of
    information on speeches are Hume's *Diary*, Lockhart's *Memoirs* and Mar's letters to Sir David Nairne.
4   Note inserted in MS 1.
5   Clerk's use of Defoe's *History* is not problematic. As well as quarrying in the four printed speeches, he
    uses the book as a standby on matters of fact (compare his praise of it in *Memoirs*, 64: 'there is not one
    fact in it which I can challenge') and falls back on it at times when his own interest is flagging. That the
    two writers often express the same views is to be expected, since they worked together as propagandists
    before and during the union debate: see Paula R. Backscheider, 'Defoe and the Clerks of Penicuik',
    Modern Philology, lxxxiv, 4 (May 1987), 372–81. They also often differ: Clerk, for example, is more critical
    of the ministers, and never uses Defoe's argument that the treaty would be unalterable by the British
    parliament. His sense of having 'contributed a good deal of assistence' to the publishing of Defoe's
    account ('Memorandums', Appendix A, p. 176 below) probably explains why he does not acknowledge

covered anything from fantasy to careful reconstruction of what the author
had heard and perhaps taken notes on. So Clerk, having earlier fantasized
freely, could switch without notice in Books 5 and 6 to practise something
closer to the latter extreme. But how close is difficult to say. Book 6 is
'literature', not reportage. Here, on a grand scale, article by article, Clerk
argues 'on both sides of the question' as he had done in the miniature debates
of Book 3, writing all the speeches like a dramatist. Usually he simplifies,
dividing the contestants into 'Hamiltonians' and 'union supporters' and writing 'composite' speeches to summarize the former's objections, then the
latter's replies. Even when speeches are ascribed to individuals, this is no
guarantee of authenticity. Court-party speakers will say what Clerk wants
them to say; opposition speeches may be caricatured as emotive.[1] Signs of
fictional reshaping range from the unlikely pretence that major closing addresses were made before the final vote[2] to the small but telling fact that, in
mining the four speeches printed by Defoe, Clerk twice moves detail from its
original context to another.[3]

But it is likely that his account is more reliable than this may suggest. Partisan
always, sometimes deluded, and probably disingenuous on the matter of
inducements, he was otherwise not bent on wilful misrepresentation: he
impresses as a writer who has at least aimed to bear faithful witness. He swears
in 'Memorandums': 'As to such facts which fell within my own proper
knowledge, these I affirm to be true.' And later:

> As to the Speeches I mention to be made in the parliament of Scotland when the Articles
> of the Union were under review: they are given with all the force & energy on both sides
> as they were delivered & 'tho some of them may seam to contain very rude & unpolished
> Expressions yet they were such things as were spoken with great freedom of speech....

Writing twenty or more years after the event, Clerk could have reconstructed
the debate solely on the basis of memory and knowledge of the issues. But he
was a life-long diarist. His *Memoirs* were 'extracted from Journals I kept since
I was 26 years of Age', i.e. 1702.[4] It is hard to believe that he did not keep

        it in his own (see comment on his treatment of James Anderson, pp. 12-13 above). Much as he respected
        Defoe's work, it will be clear that he regarded his own as quite different in kind.

1   This caricature is achieved through stylistic parody of Ciceronian bombast. Extreme examples are
        Annandale's speech (pp. 105-6 below), the attack on the Equivalent (pp. 148-50) and the lament for
        Scotland's ancient nobility (p. 168).

2   See n. 4, pp. 169-70 below.

3   See n. 2, p. 105, and n. 1, p. 162, below.

4   *Memoirs*, 3. He had earlier kept a full journal of his continental travels. (Seen by J.M. Gray when editing
        Memoirs, this may have perished in a fire at Penicuik House in 1899.) With the single exception of his
        'Journal of the Commissioners' (kept as part of his duties) Clerk allowed only politically-innocuous travel
        journals to survive his lifetime. Almost certainly he refers to his destruction of the remainder in a
        memorandum dated 2 May 1747 (SRO, GD/5105) where he writes of having burned the original MSS

some record of the union debate, and some evidence that he did is his ability to name large numbers of speakers on the major articles.[1] So, as well as names, he may have noted arguments, even expressions, used by those speakers who impressed him most. It is needless to say that any such journal, however scrappy like Hume's, would have benefited historians far more than highly-wrought Latin orations. Its absence leaves us tantalized by probabilities that resist conversion into fact.

We can none the less ask why Clerk chose to give prominence to certain speakers. Of those previously spotlit by Defoe, he says little about Seton of Pitmedden (though he uses his arguments), but makes shrewd remarks on Belhaven.[2] His ascription, with obvious satiric intent, of a highly rhetorical speech to Annandale reflects his negative view of a statesman whose ability as a speaker he acknowledged.[3] But these figures are marginal compared to Stair. Three major speeches, on Articles 1, 3 and 6, are assigned to Stair, who is also named as the main source of a composite speech on Article 22. His skills as an orator—'he was indeed the finest speaker I ever heard in my Life either in England or Scotland'[4]—probably led Clerk to listen to his speeches with particular attention and to try to recreate them. But a deeper cause of admiration appears in the notice of his death (fos. 187-8) which identifies Stair as the principal architect of union and therefore, by implication, the hero of the *History*. Counteracting Lockhart's terrible indictment,[5] Clerk's tribute also commemorates a family friend[6] who had become the second and greatest political influence on his early life.

The first, in 1703-5, had been Andrew Fletcher. That can be inferred, not from the distant estimate in *Memoirs*, 49, but from the *History* itself[7] and earlier

---

of the *History* in Sept. 1745 'with about 800 sheets which I was unwilling should fall into bad hands'. The journal material admitted into *Memoirs* generally avoids political controversy. Thus readers are referred to a separate MS (which has not survived) for an account of the 1703 session of parliament and to Defoe for an account of the union debate (*Memoirs*, 47, 63).

1   Thirteen opposition speakers on Article 1; five opposition speakers and nine court-party speakers on Article 3.

2   Pp. 108, 121-3 below.

3   Pp. 105-6 below; Clerk, Notes on Lockhart, 179-80.

4   Ibid., 97, agreeing with Lockhart's view that Stair was 'so great a Master of [eloquence], that he expressed himself, on all Occasions and Subjects, with so much Life & Rhetoric, and that likewise so Pointedly and Copiously, that there was none in the Parliament capable to take up the Cudgels with him'.

5   Lockhart, *Memoirs*, 95-8. Clerk's full notes on this passage deny Stair's responsibility for Glencoe, but mainly answer criticism of his political behaviour with praise of his private character. 'He was the pleasantest best humour'd & best conditioned Man I ever knew in all my Life & was open-minded to a Fault for a politician. The Author never knew him wheras I have lived with him and been much in his company.' Clerk probably 'lived' with the Dalrymples during the treaty negotiations in London, 1706.

6   Stair's wife was first cousin to Clerk's father. Correspondence between Stair and Clerk's father is in SRO, GD18/3121 and 3126.

7   Pp. 79, 111-12 below.

writings.[1] Even in late life Clerk was proud to record that he had heard Fletcher's speeches in those years.[2] Like many of his generation, he had been stirred by Fletcher's harsh diagnosis of the nation's sickness, though he rejected his proposed cure. Moreover, his clear perception that the Act of Security had precipitated England's insistence on incorporating union meant according Fletcher a major role in the ironic workings of the *fata Britannica*. And it is reasonable to guess, though there is no evidence for this, that Fletcher's fervent and disinterested patriotism set a standard by which Clerk had to measure his own conduct. Although much less conspicuous in Book 6 than Stair, the opposition between them can be felt as an undercurrent almost throughout.

Fletcher's only specified 'appearance' (under Article 1, p. 112 below) is, although vivid, almost too symbolic of Clerk's interest in him to be true, being prompted by a misapplication of his arguments to support the unionist cause. His passionate outburst is followed by a cool speech from Stair. That pattern is repeated under Article 3, where the opposition speech is said to be drawn chiefly from Fletcher. The case for maintaining separate parliaments under a federal union is presumably his, but is very incompletely made. Since Clerk insists that no one had managed to explain how a federal union could be made to work under a shared mixed monarchy, one hardly expects this speaker to be able to do so. But our sense that Fletcher is being used here as a target for Stair to shoot at becomes strong when the speaker proposes that Scotland should follow the example of Holland, thus releasing the bogey of republican-ism[3] which Stair goes on to exploit. Fletcher's later presence in the book must be read between the lines. It is probably detectable in the attack on Article 4, on which we know that he spoke at length and was answered by Stair's brother, Sir David Dalrymple.[4] The great row between Fletcher and Stair on 17 December is not described, but is not forgotten either.[5] And when Clerk regrets that Scotland's exemption from the malt tax had been voted, not

1 In a letter to his father, 28 May 1703, Clerk records gleefully Fletcher's triumph in having the Cess Act deferred until national grievances had been addressed. "Tho I have a great respect for Queensberrie yet I thank God for what has hapned, the Court being pretty well humbled.... it was cast up to the commissioner & the rest of the courtiers that they did nothing without the advice of the treasurer of England, that in former parliaments many things had been promised from the throne which were not granted, but that now the house would not trust either to their promises, proposals or advices any more' (SRO, GD18/3127/1). Three years later ('Journal of the Commissioners', pp. 10-11) Fletcher's theme of how Scotland's welfare was jeopardized by the nobility's self-interest became Clerk's reason for opposing federal union. Apparently he thought that Scottish affairs would suffer less interference from mercenary magnates when run from London. This argument disappears from the *History*, replaced by Stair's objection to a federal union as constitutionally impracticable.
2 'Testamentary Memorial', Appendix C, p. 187 below.
3 Clerk describes Fletcher in *Memoirs*, 49, as 'a Man of Republican principles, who had spent his youth in Holland'.
4 See n. 1, p. 133 below.
5 See n. 1, p. 146 below.

B

perpetual, but for the duration of the war, he is remembering that Fletcher had been right on that issue, Stair wrong.[1]

In those three instances, Clerk's subtextual references are clarified for us by Hume of Crossrig, who showed interest in the same two speakers. But in January Hume fell sick, and Mar's correspondence is also interrupted,[2] so that Clerk becomes a principal source for the debate on the final articles. On Article 22, although only Stair's voice is acknowledged, we can probably hear Fletcher's also, especially in the attack on the commissioners. But it is on Article 23, dealing with the minor matter of the privileges of peers, that Clerk surprisingly brings his antagonists together through a series of linked, Ciceronian allusions. First, in a 'ferociously'[3] sarcastic move to have the Scottish peers renounce the privilege of immunity from prosecution for debt, a speaker who sounds extraordinarily like Fletcher compares the pro-union magnates to the Roman aristocrats who, through Catiline during Cicero's consulship, had conspired against the republic to advance their own interests. Secondly, in a speech which Clerk clearly satirizes as an expression of outdated values, the 'old' Scottish nobility lament their loss of precedence to English 'upstarts' (*novi homines*, the taunt levelled at Cicero on the same occasion). Finally, the unionists remind the house that the Scottish peerage too contains new creations, and that such 'new men' were the saviours of Rome. This compliment to the newly-ennobled Dalrymples leads up to the notice of Stair's death. The effect is neat. What is not clear is whether Clerk knew that he had achieved it by prolonging Stair's life by five days.[4]

Whereas Stair could be used to speak for the unionists, Fletcher was too independent to be given equal prominence as a representative 'Hamiltonian'. Clerk's view of the essential conflict between the two sides is clearest in the (probably fictional) final speeches. Style, more obvious in the Latin, heightens the distinction between anguished emotion and rational forbearance. The opposition's outrage at what Scotland is losing—its sovereignty, honour, dignity and freedom—is answered by pragmatic reminders that these had been lost long ago and by optimistic faith in their recovery through union. Appeals to the memory of Wallace and Bruce are shown to spring from a narrow and outmoded patriotism. Where the opposition sees a tyrannical and treacherous parliament riding roughshod over popular sentiment, the government, again

1   See n. 2, p. 148 below.
2   Noted by Paul H. Scott, *Andrew Fletcher and the Treaty of Union* (Edinburgh, 1992), 203.
3   The word itself almost points to Fletcher. Clerk, in his excerpts from Livy (SRO, GD18/5078/51, fo. 171), writes 'Sa—n' in the margin against Livy's description of a Roman envoy (trans.): 'a man of harsh temperament, who increased the savage effect of his remarks by his grim looks and accusatory voice.' His description of Fletcher in *Memoirs*, 49, as 'a little untoward in his temper' is a nice example of ironic understatement.
4   See n. 3, p. 169 below.

pragmatically, sees itself as bowing to political necessity. It is 'wiser than the people' because it accepts that, although neither people wants incorporating union, circumstances enforce it, therefore Nature can be said to decree it. When the courtiers disclaim hopes of personally profiting from union, the effect may be the opposite of what Clerk intended: protesting too much, he risks suggesting a hypocritical cover-up. Otherwise, however, he can hardly be convicted of either sabotaging the opposition's case or idealizing the government's. If we still feel some conflict as we read these speeches, the credit is his.

Clerk as historian: some conclusions.

Clerk rarely changed his mind about anything bigger than a use of the subjunctive. He could waver, as about publishing, but stubbornly adhered to decisions once taken, convictions once formed, and so became, in all his many fields of interest, a famous rider of hobby-horses, some of which trot across the pages of his *History*. A result of his unwillingness to reconsider is that the substance of what he wrote in the late 1720s remained sacrosanct, not to be affected by anything he read later or the stylistic tinkerings of the 30s and 40s. We can similarly be sure that what he wrote after long years of preparation remained true to the original concept of the work he had formed around 1710-14. At that time the plan of a 'British' history, reinterpreting Anglo-Scottish relations in a manner that would justify union, was bold and from a Whig viewpoint timely. There was a Tory ministry in London, and in Edinburgh a near take-over of historical publishing by Jacobites. Union remained deeply unpopular—attempts were made in parliament to dissolve it in 1713—and the widespread suspicions of how it had been achieved became public scandal through Lockhart a year later. Had Clerk acted swiftly, he could have made some stir, and injected some much-needed life into Scottish Whig culture.

But a stir was what he did not want to make. He wanted to give judgement from an unchallengeable height and justify his conduct without risk of cross-examination. The guess has been offered that the massive, self-imposed labour of the *History* means that he was less complacent about his role in union than he liked to appear. More certainly, his private sensitivities contributed to the fact that he brooded over his project in secret for the rest of his life, preferring finally to present himself 'before the great judicature of posterity' through the medium of selective memoirs and an undeniably complacent 'Testamentary Memorial'. Such secretiveness deprived him of the criticism and support that might have encouraged him to publish, and resulted in his work being largely unread until now.[1]

Also a retreat from the public arena was the move into Latin. This was a calamitous error of judgement. Granted that dignity and polish were never the hallmarks of Clerk's English prose, the style of his published pamphlets was rapid and lively, flexible enough to accommodate the turns of a practical mind and express a lot of meaning in a down-to-earth way. This his Latin could not do. A limited range of stiff syntactical structures not only makes his narrative monotonous—this is particularly obvious when he is paraphrasing Buchanan—but confines his intelligence in a linguistic straitjacket, promoting repetition and simplification. Latin also exposed him to the temptation of eloquence. Though he was well aware that history demanded a plain style, his fondness for empty and grandiose turns of phrase is by no means restricted to speeches where they might be appropriate. If Clerk can be said to have 'Latinized' British history, it was not through the influence of Roman historians, or the drawing of classical parallels, or even through his use of Rome as a standard of 'empire', but rather because Latin released in him a strain of sententious rhetorical moralizing which he would never have allowed himself in English. Had he cared for his message more than his vanity, he could have made his points better in English in a sharper and much shorter book.

It is also of course Latin that aligns him most closely with the humanist historians. Since he used Buchanan so much in his first three books, and Boece and Mair sometimes, he must have been conscious of following a Scottish tradition, but of this he says nothing. Unlike most historians of his day, he provides no preface discoursing on how history should be written. His practice is our principal guide. Certainly humanistic, if not medieval, is that dismal feature of the early books, the undirected chronicling of events taken over on trust from previous narratives. It is only in Book 4, when he comes to write more spontaneously on the basis of his own thinking, that he sometimes uses argument, or cause and effect, as an organizing principle.

Other features, however, cannot be so easily dismissed as outmoded. Even speeches, though frowned on by Rapin as false and unnatural,[2] could still be defended by Adam Smith in the 1760s as a useful means of introducing ideas into impartial narration.[3] Clerk's interest in the past was, like the humanists', radically determined by his political views, but *histoire à thèse* still had plenty of life in it, so long as the thesis was new and up-to-date, as his was. Still flourishing, too, was the humanist concept of history as rhetoric. Clerk's

1   It was not among the Clerk papers used by Thomas Somerville for his *The History of Great Britain during the Reign of Queen Anne* (London, 1798).
2   *The Whole Critical Works of Monsieur Rapin* (London, 1706), ii, 300.
3   *Lectures on Rhetoric and Belles Lettres*, ed. J.C. Bryce (Oxford, 1983), 103.

blatant didacticism, and his careful efforts to reconcile English and Scottish readers, reflect a view of the historian's function still orthodox when he wrote, if hardly avant-garde.

Without showing any awareness of the fact, Clerk straddles the gulf between humanist history and the 'polite' history in vogue in England since the Restoration. Addressing 'Advices to my Sones' in 1725, he made the humanists' point that learning was worthless unless combined with the active life.[1] But for himself it mattered more that the scholar should be seen to be a gentleman. He makes several assumptions of the polite historian. He must value the evidence of manuscripts such as charters, but need not examine them himself. He must acknowledge his sources, but lightly, without a vulgar parade of authorities.[2] Minutiae are not his concern:

> as for some trifles which little folks value themselves on such as telling minutely each day moneth & year when things were done or whose father's brother's cousin's sister's Grandmother's sone or daughter such a one was, or whether certain actions were done in this or that house or field I heartily renounce them & recommend them to others.[3]

Above all, Clerk knew that the polite historian should avoid 'as much as possible ... party prejudices'.[4] Since the design of his book made that barely possible, he compensated by showing a lofty lack of interest in the party disputes that raged around him in the Edinburgh presses: on the historicity of Scotland's early kings, the hereditary or elective succession of its monarchy, the legitimacy of Robert III, and so forth. Where distance from controversy suited him best was on religious matters. He shared Dryden's view that 'the things we must believe are few and plain'.[5] Late in life he wrote: 'I have ... no reasone to wish my self one bit more inclined to Religion than I am. Enthousiastick notions, superstition, and singularity in Religious points are my utter aversion'.[6] Reacting against the legacy of the seventeenth century (and perhaps his father), he treats religious disputes with disdain, tempered by pity for the 'tender consciences' of the weak-minded mob and respect for freedom of worship. He harps on the point he attributes to William Carstares, that the church should confine itself to the cure of souls and leave politics to the politicians (pp. 98-9 below). But he is hardly to be hailed as a leading presbyterian Moderate. The degree of his commitment to the Kirk is suspect,

1 SRO, GD18/2330 (section 15).
2 He allows himself once, as a lawyer, to parade authorities on feudal law regarding the claims of Balliol and Bruce to the Scottish crown (p. 51 below), but the list derives at second hand from Thomas Craig, *Scotland's Soveraignty Asserted*, trans. G. Ridpath (London, 1695), 365.
3 Note at end of Book 3, MS A.
4 Ibid.
5 *Religio Laici*, 432. Compare 'Testamentary Memorial', Appendix C, pp. 197-8 below.
6 *Memoirs*, 21.

and his writings are pervaded by a half-suppressed note of anticlerical irritation. Ministers and bishops, cardinals and monks, even his own long-suffering chaplain, rarely escape it.

The patina of English politeness in Clerk was by no means false. It was backed, we must remember, by genuine achievements that have barely been mentioned in these pages: in the arts, in patronage and friendship, in the successful cultivation of the Roman ideal of civilized, purposeful leisure. But it never quite covered the traces of older culture. Clerk's training as a lawyer gave him a firm grasp of fact which he turned to good account as an economist, but it also made him literal-minded: much as he enjoyed his *idées fixes*, he lacked the enjoyment of ideas *per se* required for philosophical history. To the spirit of French scepticism he was totally immune, and despite his interest in scientific experiments and his friendship with Colin Maclaurin seems not to have grasped the first principle of Newtonian method: his whole *History* springs from *a priori* reasoning in his belief that a united Britain was pre-or-dained. Whether Calvin contributed more than Virgil to his notion of the *fata Britannica* may be doubted, but it is clear that in Clerk's scheme Providence and Destiny, sometimes rationally disguised as the workings of Nature, are in full control of events.[1] His disapproval of religion encroaching on politics did not stop him from assuming divine support for his political views.

Providentialism, however, was no bar to the production of secular Whig history, and of this Clerk's faith in the destiny of Britain enabled him to produce a remarkable early example. The familiar outline is present: a long and mysterious evolutionary process, full of false starts, setbacks and failures, its successful outcome finally assuring a prosperous future in empire and commerce, provided the workers will work. On to that pattern Clerk grafts an idea equally characteristic of his age, seeing history in terms of the conflict between order and freedom. His early comments on Romans and Caledonians show him fully aware of how the rage for order can lead to aggression and tyranny, but he concludes that, where titular freedom means chronic insecurity, cultural deprivation and crippling poverty, order may need to be imposed so that 'true' freedom can flourish. Local patriotisms must yield to larger, as considerations of trade and security (not to mention God's will) call for the formation of larger political units.

Linked to the polarity of order and freedom was the simpler one of reason and sentiment. It is an exercise of reason to accept the force of circumstance calmly and to focus on the future benefits to accrue from passionately-resented sacrifices: hence Clerk's conviction that the *salus populi*, the welfare of the

---

1   References to direct divine intervention are rare. For one which seems to be intended literally see p. 72 below. Both Montrose and Cromwell are seen as 'scourges of God' punishing Scotland for rebellion against the throne.

people of Scotland, depended on a union which, as he acknowledged, ninety-nine per cent of them did not want. It should be emphasized that he saw this paternalism as authorized by reason, not rank. Whether writing about feudal superiorities or the privileges of royal burghs, he is consistently hostile to the notion of title as conferring rights over individual freedoms. And as with freedom, so also with patriotism, it is still more important to emphasize that Clerk's love of Scotland and pride in it ran deep. His consciously rational aim in the *History* was not to override sentimental attachments but to redirect them. Thus he set himself a challenge which Scots as Britons have been grappling with ever since.[1]

1   Clerk's efforts to promote a sense of 'British' identity receive mention, and are placed in a much wider context, by Colin Kidd in *Subverting Scotland's Past: Scottish Whig Historians and the Creation of an Anglo-British Identity, 1689-c. 1830* (Cambridge, 1993). Kidd's book appeared after this introduction was written.

PART ONE

From BOOKS 1-5

BOOK 1
From the Romans to 1066[1]

A. Introductory

[1[2]] God,[3] among other benefits, has bestowed on mankind a social instinct [*socialis animus*], the source of much pleasure and practical advantage [*utilitas*]. This innate longing we have for society can rightly be called the origin of all just systems of rule, for it was Nature's purpose that governments [*imperia*[4]] should be established to regulate and preserve society.

The security of sovereign states [*imperia*] is determined by their size—not of course by the size of their armies but by the number of people who combine to form them. A plurality of small states is relatively weak, for although they may permit a more even distribution of wealth and commerce,[5] they tend to encourage animosities and rivalries which undermine social stability. It was therefore well said by Gravina that the Roman empire [*imperium*] was introduced for the good of mankind, and that its disintegration destroyed a civic bond which had enabled peoples to live charitably together.[6]

The earliest unit of government [*imperium*] was the family. As the longing for society led to marriages, so it naturally followed that mothers and children came under the power of the fathers. Originally, then, there were as many units of government on earth as there were families, tied only to such laws as were dictated by the fathers or by Nature herself. Later, however, when neighbours began to threaten each other and the weaker were unable to resist the strong, recourse was had to various kinds of social contract, in which [2] the Law of Nations has its source. But when families preferred to settle their

---

1 For a survey of the content of Books 1-5 and commentary explaining the choice of extracts see Intro., pp. 8-20 above.

2 Reference to the folio numbering of SRO, GD18/3202/1A.

3 *Deus Optimus Maximus*, significantly the first words of Clerk's *History*. He follows Buchanan among others in attributing the origin of society to God, not human self-interest (*utilitas*): *lex illa divina, ab initio rerum nobis insita, conveniendi in unum coetum* (*De Jure Regni apud Scotos*, Ruddiman, I, 5).

4 The semantic range of *imperium* is well illustrated in these opening lines. See Intro., pp. 8-9 above.

5 On the consciousness possibly displayed here of Andrew Fletcher's preference for small states see Intro., p. 9 above.

6 Giovanni Vincenzo Gravina, *De Imperio Romano*, in *Opera* (Leipzig, 1717), 465.

disputes by force of arms, then the vanquished came under the power of the victors, and the danger arose that these new societies would revert to their earlier state. So different systems of rule were devised. For just as societies had been formed under different conditions—sometimes uniting for mutual defence, sometimes being forced into union by conquest—so some chose to obey kings while others obeyed other kinds of lawful magistrate.

Among all alliances of peoples under a single government, that of Rome takes pride of place, for whether we regard the vastness of its achievements or the qualities of its people, its equal is not to be found. So the fact that Britain was once admitted to that empire is something of which she can be proud. For the peoples who lived in this island at that time began to experience new benefits: some became more sociable, some more civilized, some indeed more free; and all were taught to manage arms. Opinions may differ about the names they were known by, and about which were or were not conquered, but on one point all men of sense have agreed, that only the Romans were worthy of the task of uniting and ruling Britain [*solos Romanos Imperii Britannici dignos fuisse*].

So the first government of any name over the British peoples was established by the Romans. But its authority could never be complete so long as the Caledonians, fiercer than the rest, were eager to retain their own rough freedom. For the Caledonians, divided into Picts and Scots,[1] comprised two distinct sovereign states, and with persistent warfare they harassed the Romans and their allies the Britones as the common enemies of the island. Neither armed force nor treaties could induce them to accept the society the Romans offered.

When the Romans left Britain, [3] the Saxons won control of most of the island but were at length overcome, first by the Danes and then by the Normans. All of these began to establish different governments in Britain and did their best to combine the other British peoples into one. But without success, for before the year 1604, when James VI of Scotland succeeded by right of birth to the kingdom of England, the British were never united under a single rule. Nor was even that a union except in name, for the only bond holding British society together was the fact that England and Scotland had a king in common, and since he was besieged by the conflicting counsels, interests and factions of his two realms, the result was the kindling of anger among his subjects and the sowing of seeds of mutual hostility. For a whole century this state of affairs continued: the successors of James kept struggling to unite their peoples until the time of Queen Anne. Then, as quite often before,[2] a woman's leadership proved auspicious for Britain. Queen Anne

---

1   Clerk's insistence on the Scots as an indigenous people is illustrated below, #F, p. 38.
2   Margaret and Elizabeth will later be praised as queens who promoted Anglo-Scottish union. Compare,

brought about what no ruler before her had been able to achieve by force or diplomacy. In the year 1707 she completed the union begun by her ancestor, effectively founding the *imperium Britannicum*.

We must now deal in turn with the rise and progress of those governments in Britain just mentioned, so that readers may more clearly perceive the efforts that were made to bring Britain by stages to that present proud state which is the envy of her neighbours.

B. Agricola and Galgacus

[39] The boundaries of Roman-British rule had been extended thus far.[1] Most of Britain would have been brought under the Roman yoke, and Agricola himself would have done enough to assure his own fame and even secure Rome's practical interests, if only he had known how to limit his ambition. But he nursed the hope of ruling the whole island and refused to share it with others. Much less could he endure that its northern inhabitants should breathe the air of freedom defiantly.

[45] Before we go further[2] a word should be said about this Galgacus, the Caledonian leader. Buchanan and other Scottish writers identify him with Galdus, the 23rd king of Scots. But Tacitus gave him only the title of 'leader' [*dux*], which I find more plausible, because surely if Agricola had vanquished a king, his son-in-law would have given him credit for the fact in a book so full of boastful and flattering additions. My reading of Tacitus has often led me to suspect that there were no kings in Caledonia when the Romans arrived but only leaders or tribal chieftains. Depending on their stature or the size of their following, these were called 'leaders' or 'chieftains' and eventually 'kings' but did not differ much in point of dignity or wealth from those so-called kings now found among the peoples of America.

C. The *imperium* of Christ

[51] It was about this time [the reign of Hadrian] that the empire of Christ had its beginning in Britain. It was as if God wished to demonstrate the pre-eminence among men of his power and authority. Peoples so dissident that no arts of peace or war could bring them to submit to the rule of one man, peaceably

---

on Boadicea: 'So, even then, Britain had her Elizabeths and Annes who transmitted to posterity the glorious memory of their acts' (1, 29).

1   In a section where Clerk follows Tacitus closely this passage replaces a laudation of Agricola's honesty.

2   This passage occurs between the speeches of Galgacus and Agricola, transcribed *verbatim* from Tacitus's account of the battle of Mons Graupius.

and calmly began to bear the yoke of Christ, an auspicious prognostic of union
to come.... But to the credit of the Romans it may be said in passing that it
was through them that Britain first imbibed such Christian and humanistic
culture as the whole island is known for today.

D. The vicissitudes of history

[53] Nor is the popularity of such a man[1] surprising, for the Romans had
exchanged the most ample freedom for shameful tyranny, and after boasting
with good reason of being lords of the earth now found themselves frequently
forced to bow the knee to the vilest of men as their emperors. But in human
affairs such changes occur in every age and to almost all nations, enabling us
to see that contradictions and anomalies have often determined the pattern of
history[2] and that the fate of every empire is ruled by God's providence, not by
the councils of men.

E. Antiquarian digressions

[57] Armies that retire behind fortifications show little faith in their security
in the open. But in his *Life of Severus* Spartianus, vainly anxious to interpret
everything to his hero's advantage, affirms that 'the greatest glory of his reign
was that he fortified Britain with a wall from coast to coast...'. The greatest
shame, I would much rather say, because such a defence would have been
erected more appropriately by a Caledonian chief than by a Roman emperor.[3]
Spartianus's tribute should be held to apply only to the wall's construction: its
remains to this day show that it was a fine piece of work.

I am familiar, too, with the disputes of learned men[4] about the meaning of
the word *murus* [wall] and whether it should be distinguished from *vallum*
[palisade, rampart, entrenchment]. I shall not prolong them, for in Latin the
words are interchangeable ... and shall touch only briefly on a point which is
a knotty one for antiquaries. When Severus had withdrawn his troops to their
former frontiers, he repaired the emperor Hadrian's fortifications, made of turf

---

1   Clodius Albinus, who turned the army in Britain against the emperor Commodus and became popular
     at Rome.
2   ... *mundum saepe per contraria & repugnantia stabilitum esse* (lit. 'the world has often been ordered through
     opposites and contradictions'). *Contraria* and *repugnantia* are synonymous terms of rhetoric.
3   Compare letter to Roger Gale, 19 August 1739: 'I cannot but take notice ... why the Scots' Historians,
     vain enough by nature, have not taken more pains to describe this wall, a performance which did their
     ancestors more honor than all trifling storys put together, which they have transmitted to us. 'Tis true
     the Romans walled out humanity from us, but 'tis as certain they thought the Caledonians a very
     formidable people, when they, at so much labor and cost, bilt this wall...'. (*Stukeley*, ii, 95-6).
4   Clerk's marginal note (trans.): 'see Eutropius and Aurelius Victor.'

and stakes. But finding them insecure he added those beautiful structures which can now be seen between the Tyne and the Solway Firth. Later, as Bede attests and other historians confirm, a stone wall was built on the site.... As for the *castra* and other fortifications with which the wall was strengthened, anyone inspecting them can easily see that they were added at different periods, some by Hadrian, some by Severus, some by other generals and emperors as occasion demanded. That is why the inscriptions and decorations to be seen on the same sites are so various. [58] But where two walls can be seen, we should not, in my view, ascribe one to Hadrian and the other to Severus. A single argument is enough to prove that they were built at the same time. The interior wall runs on low ground, the other on higher. Since garrisons could easily have been driven from the lower wall unless there was a higher one to protect them, no emperor in his senses would have built the lower one alone. If only one is to be attributed to Hadrian, he was far too good a general to choose the low ground, but assuming he chose the high, it would have been pointless for Severus to add a lower wall.[1] Of the entire construction one may say, however, that it seems to have rivalled or surpassed Rome's proudest monuments.

[61] Carusius is thought by some to have built that circular structure[2] which stands on the far bank of the Carron river, and indeed to have given the river its name—an unlikely tale, as it seems to me, since to my mind the building does not date from his invasion. Some[3] suppose it was a temple dedicated to the god Terminus and infer from its beauty that it was built when Roman architecture was still in its prime. I myself incline to think it was a tomb, but whatever it was it has been honoured through the ages as a holy place. Wars have wrought countless ruins around it, but still to this day it preserves its original beauty.

Clerk's marginal addition [?1750]:
Scotsmen had regarded that building with the utmost reverence, taking pride in it as a monument to the bravery of the early Caledonians who had there forced the Romans to set a limit to their empire. It was a frequent source of pleasure, not to me only, but to every lover of antiquities. All the more sad, then, that a Gothic landowner has torn it down to make farm-buildings out

---

1   Focusing exclusively on the threat posed by the Caledonians, Clerk fails to guess that the lower structure was a defence against raiders from the south.

2   The building known as 'Arthur's Oven' or 'O'on'. For Clerk's account of its destruction by Sir Michael Bruce of Stonehouse see *Stukeley*, iii, 428ff. The stones were used to repair a mill and dam, destroyed in turn by storm in 1748.

3   Clerk's marginal note (trans.): 'see Buchanan Book 4.' The building is twice referred to in Buchanan's *History* (*Ruddiman*, I, 9, 65).

of its stone. The people of Scotland suffered this misfortune around the year 1743. The day the building fell should be reckoned a black day in their calendar.

F. The indigenous Scots

[66] It was around this time, AD 360, that the Romans themselves in speaking of the Caledonians began to distinguish between Scots and Picts. It was not that their names had been hitherto unknown, but rather that the Romans did not think it worthwhile to inquire into their separate dominions and kingdoms, preferring simply to designate as 'barbarians' those whom they had failed to control. Moreover, for their part, those nations did not wish to be distinguished by separate names, being united in a common cause against Rome: they refused absolutely to deal with a people whom they saw as a threat to their freedom. This has caused error among modern writers, even distinguished ones, who, either from malice or to show off their learning, assert that the Scots were not indigenous to Britain but were migrants from Ireland (once known as Greater Scotia) or from Scythia. This attempt to detract from the antiquity of the Scottish race flies in the face not only of majority opinion but also of Nature and Truth. For just as today most inhabitants of northern Ireland are of Scottish origin, so in the past Scotland shed its surplus population over adjacent parts of Ireland further south. It has moreover been established as a general truth that, ever since the Flood, the migration of European peoples seeking room to expand has always been from east to west. But this well-worn and fruitless dispute should detain us no longer....

G. Romans and Caledonians: a summation

[82] The Romans had launched many expeditions against Britain, with great loss of life, to satisfy their immoderate ambition or (as they claimed) to unite the British people along with themselves in a single well-grafted society. But Fate was against them, for the Caledonians, either through love of liberty or from a deep-seated hatred of the Romans, continually rejected the society offered as though it were intolerable slavery. Nor ever after could they be induced to submit to a foreign king or a foreign people for longer than it took them to collect their strength and set themselves free. So the Romans could scarcely acquire Caledonia, much less keep it, a fact due in part to the bravery of its people and in part to its rugged terrain. Rugged mountains breed tough defenders, and the morale of an invading army weakens when booty is scarce and nothing but glory can be won. But the descendants of those Caledonians today should take care not to boast of their resistance too much, for to be proud

of their refusal of Roman rule means admitting that one's ancestors were barbarians with no claim to civilization whatever.

H. A Scottish *imperium Britannicum*?

[90] These events[1] are distant and uncertain, but if in such cases probabilities may be accepted as facts, I think it fair to say that, either by right of conquest or by the terms of some treaty, the Scots and Picts won the *imperium Britannicum* and held on to it precariously until the coming of the Saxons.[2]

[92] In this war with the Saxons Eugenius is said to have perished. After him, no member of the Scottish royal line ever hoped to win the *imperium Britannicum* by force. Providence had ordained that it should pass to his posterity, not by force of arms or human devices, but by right of birth and legitimate succession ... in 1604.

I. British unity against the Saxons

[94] The Britones were forced to fall back on the resource that God and Nature had provided, namely the aid of other British peoples by seeking an alliance with the Scots and Picts. A hopeful plan, indeed, if they had adhered to it firmly, for the Scots and Picts would have agreed to any peace-terms to protect the independence and freedom of British races against foreigners. And so the whole of Britain joined forces and prepared to do battle with the Saxons....

[98] The advice he received[3] from his friends contributed not a little to settling the dispute. They said that internal divisions would spell the overthrow of Christianity, whereas agreement would give all parties in Britain the religious and civil security they wished and deserved. There were two reasons why the British peoples should unite: because they were Christians, and because they were British. Any other course of action would soon be found to fail as being contrary to Nature and the will of God.

---

1   The defeat of the Britons by the Scots and Picts under 'Eugenius' in the fifth century. The quoted sentences are added to a close paraphrase of Buchanan's narrative.

2   Clerk's marginal note (trans.): 'see Sir George Mackenzie, *The Antiquity of the Royal Line of Scotland.*'

3   Lothus, king of the Picts, is advised to drop his opposition to Arthur's succession as king of the Britons. Like the previous passage, this is Clerk's interpretative addition to Buchanan's narrative.

J. The ninth century: justification of enforced unions

[103] It had been a time when Britain suffered wretchedly from too many governments and kings. Saxon kings, Scottish kings, Pictish kings, chieftains of the Britones, all at each other's throats: a condition of elemental chaos. [110] Finally,[1] when the Picts sued for peace yet again and the Scots still adhered to their earlier demands, the day had clearly come that must settle the fate of one people or the other.... So the Scots destroyed the kingdom of the Picts, who had often watched the power of Rome, unbowed and undismayed. The less hardy of the survivors joined with the Scots; others fled destitute to England. This memorable turn of events took place about AD 840. In England, meanwhile, [111] the Saxon Egbert was too busy establishing his monarchy to meddle in Caledonian affairs. He hoped that the union he had forged from the Heptarchy would enable him to vanquish the rest of Britain at a later date. But in this he was mistaken, for the forging of his union had cost so much blood that his tributary kings refused to be reconciled and tried every means to recover their freedom. Foreigners soon saw a hopeful opportunity in their resentment.

So the Danes, a fierce and savage race, began to harry the coasts of Britain. They knew they would meet no obstruction in a country whose inhabitants were at odds with each other. I agree with those writers who say that the English even welcomed the invaders, for what else could one expect from men threatened by slavery who were continually plotting rebellion? And the same can be said of the Picts, who were seriously unhappy with their servile lot and preferred to surrender to any foreigners rather than to the Scots. This shows what bitterness and hatred result from unions that are enforced rather than willingly negotiated, for Nature herself abhors a dominion to which the free are compelled to surrender. Yet there are times when enforced unions may be necessary, when the motive is not a conqueror's ambition but the welfare of the people [salus populi]. In such cases wounds can be quickly cured and true freedom spring from what was thought to be slavery. The English long ago, under Egbert's rule, deplored a state of affairs which their descendants today can look back on with pride. And the Picts today are for nothing more famous than that their downfall made possible that fair union of Caledonians which was to distinguish the north of Britain for many hundreds of years.

---

1   This follows a long account of Scoto–Pictish wars.

K. The homage of Kenneth II of Scotland to Edgar of England

[120] The memory of this seems to give much pleasure to bilious, illiterate and spiteful monks, who include it in their accounts of various sorts of homage paid by Scottish kings. They affirm that this Edgar, attended by the king of Scots and seven other kings, took ship on the river Dee near Chester and was rowed by them in triumph to the abbey of St John the Baptist and back again. They add that in the course of a boastful speech he remarked that his successors could well be called kings of England if they were attended by as many royal vassals as he.[1]

This little tale has bred major contention between English and Scottish historians, the former losing no opportunity to repeat it while the latter call it false and say the history of those times was either lost or never written. Recent writers show no agreement on the number and names of those kings, and some say that Kenneth never set foot in England. For myself, I remain neutral: the matter is uncertain, though changes of fortune can happen to anyone and to emperors and kings most of all. But with regard to Edgar's lordship over the Scots, those who assert this neglect the rule that historians should relate either facts or probabilities. Before trying to make us believe in such a thing they should have told us much else: when did Edgar invade Scotland, and with how many men? how many casualties did he inflict? what mountains and moors, [121] what forests and rivers and dangerous firths did he cross? Fair-minded readers will not easily accept that the Scots, without putting up a fight, would surrender to an English king who was hemmed in by Danes on one side and Britones on the other. It is indeed, humanly speaking, inconceivable that a people who had outfaced Agricola and Severus and the combined strength of Rome and the Britones would have yielded to the English. So this story of Edgar's dominion is a fable, on a par with that other that his navy numbered 4,800 ships. Such a figure, if not nonsense, must have included every rowing-boat in England, for a fleet of even one-tenth that size could have conquered the whole island. One wonders, too, how such a fleet could have been manned, and why, if it was, the Danes were so soon able to occupy the whole English seaboard and overthrow the Saxon monarchy. But leaving these trifles aside, what would it matter if kings of Scots, like Roman consuls often before them, were subjugated by their enemies? What if, like some kings of England, they subjected their kingdom to the Pope? What if, following the same example, some solemnly paid homage to the proud king of France? None of these actions would have diminished the honour of the kingdom or the dignity of a free people. For in Britain a country is impaired by the actions of its people,

1   Clerk's marginal note (trans.): 'see Echard, Milton, *etc.*'

not of its kings, and the wrongs a king commits without his people's consent can be wholly discounted.

L. 1066

[127] It would be superfluous to ask by what right or title William of Normandy claimed the throne of England. He came, saw, conquered, and showed just how little entitlement is needed when a people is divided. The English (if William of Malmesbury can be trusted) had grown factious and dissolute, heedless of all laws of God and man. [128] They appeared so ripe and ready for destruction that no enemy from abroad was needed to destroy them; they had one within their gates.

BOOK 2
1066 to 1363

A. Introductory

[1[1]] I have spoken so far of the various kingdoms and governments established in Britain by the Romans, the Picts and the Scots, the Saxons, the Danes and the Normans. We have heard how the Romans abandoned our island when their fortunes tottered, how the Britones were driven from their lands to take refuge in the hills of Wales, how the Scots destroyed the kingdom of the Picts and seized all Caledonia, and how the Normans took over such power as was left to the Saxons and Danes within Britain.

So 1066 found Britain divided between the Britones, the Scots and the Normans. The first two, its long-time residents, were chiefly concerned to enjoy freedom undisturbed in their rugged and mountainous countries. The Normans, however, had no sooner conquered England than they planned to drive out the Britones and the Scots, relying on their wealth and their vast armies to enable them to do so. This led to endless slaughter and a long series of wars, which resulted in the wretched Britones being finally worn down and overpowered by the Anglo-Normans, while the Scots had more varied fortunes, now defending a state that seemed ready to fall, now restoring it after its collapse, until quite unexpectedly through a union of the crowns the government of all Britain devolved by right of birth on the Scottish royal line in the person of King James VI, as will later be related.

My task in this book is to describe the attempt of Anglo-Norman kings [2] to acquire the *imperium Britannicum*. I shall treat wars briefly but treaties at greater length, since the form of government that Britons now enjoy owes more to the terms of peaceful alliances than to injuries inflicted in war.

B. Malcolm III and the English

[3] The survivors of the Saxon royal family found safe refuge with Malcolm, who was so taken with the virtuous character of Edgar's younger sister that he

---

1   Reference to the folio numbering of SRO, GD18/3202/2A.

married her.[1] [4] Thus new bonds of friendship were strengthened by ties of kinship and the Scottish royal house came to be thought of as next in succession to the Saxon throne.

Furthermore, Malcolm also gave a welcome to other English fugitives, remembering that for about fifteen years he had been brought up in England thanks to Edward, and that it had finally been with English aid that he had routed the tyrant Macbeth and recovered his ancestral kingdom. So, in view of Malcolm's many acts of gratitude and kindness toward the English, Matthew Paris testifies that it was Scotland that 'upheld the right of the English crown and became the home of England's true nobility'.[2]

[6] Apart from Edgar the Atheling, few fugitives returned to England, most choosing freedom in exile in Scotland, [7] though it may well be true, as some writers allege, that they cared less for freedom than for Scottish hospitality. The great amount of land they were granted by Malcolm led Craig, the famous Scottish jurist, to assert that their descendants in his day owned more land than lies between the Tweed and the Humber.[3] Worth remembering, too, is Craig's remark in his book, *De Unione Regnorum*: 'if the English care so much about retaining their name, the Scots can take pride in it no less than they, for the Scots have almost as many families of English descent as do the English themselves, who today trace their ancestry rather to the Normans.'[4]

C. The homage question: Edgar, Malcolm IV, William I

[14] After being made king to the great joy of his countrymen, Edgar ruled so wisely and successfully that during his lifetime no foreign or domestic tumults disturbed the peace of his realm. But two factors chiefly contributed to this: one was the peace he contracted with William II of England, the other was his gift of his sister Matilda in marriage to William's successor, Henry. As to the peace with William, [15] monkish writers of the period relate various tales clearly meant to demean Edgar's dignity. They record among other things that he negotiated with William that the whole of Scotland should in future be an English fiefdom and that he and his successors would recognize the kings of

1   The marriage of Malcolm and Margaret is described on 1, 127 as 'laying the first foundation of future British union'. Clerk's interest in Margaret is solely dynastic: he has nothing to say of her sainthood or her work and influence in Scotland, merely calling her 'the most excellent and eminent woman of her time' (2, 10).

2   A slight perversion of Paris's sense. He wrote (trans.): 'Three of Margaret's sons became kings, so that the nobility of the kings of England, driven from its own bounds by the Normans, devolved upon the kings of Scots' (*Historia Major* [London, 1684], 4).

3   Thomas Craig, *De Unione Regnorum Britanniae Tractatus*, ed. and trans. C.S. Terry (SHS, 1909), 162.

4   Ibid., 154.

England as their liege lords. One must marvel at the inventive industry of these men in their efforts to detract from the majesty of the Scottish crown: all the charters of Edgar they adduce have been proved to be spurious fabrications.[1] But since these are the same people whose ignorant notions of religion make wiser men laugh, one need not be surprised if their time-serving judgement as historians led them into error and sacrilege on topics such as nationhood and kingship. I shall say no more on this matter apart from noting that Edgar's subjection is not mentioned at all either by Florence of Worcester, who lived in his time, or by Simeon of Durham or Howden, who are elsewhere very hostile to the Scots. There is in any case no point in citing concessions which Scottish kings may have made on their own authority without consulting the estates. The law of Scotland invalidates such concessions. It would be a wretched people indeed who could be deprived of their freedom at the whim of some sovereign.

Observe, meantime, the diligence and zeal with which Anglo-Norman kings laboured to win even the bare title of king of all Britain. Failing to achieve it by force of arms, they or their ministers resorted to what they thought was the next best expedient: to make posterity believe it by suborning the monks - the only writers of those times—to substantiate their claim in forged charters or fictitious chronicles.

[26] In the reign of Malcolm IV the Scots, it would seem, degenerated amazingly from the virtue of their ancestors. It is hard to understand what induced them to allow this weak king to go cap in hand to Henry and prostitute the honour and glory of his kingdom for the sake of a few fields in England.

[27] Henry's plan of forcing William to accompany him on his expedition to France was intended to expose the Scots to the hatred of their French allies. But when it came to nothing he grew tired of William's continual pleas and acceded to his request for permission to return to his own country. All this greatly increased Scottish resentment against the English, and King William himself was held in such contempt that the Scottish people would have chosen another king if there had been one available in the royal family.

[29] Some writers, including Buchanan, give a rather different account of William's capture, alleging that he was kidnapped in peacetime. I think this hardly likely and prefer to follow other authorities....[2] [30] About the peace-terms that followed his capture I can find no certainty, though there is some agreement that William was detained until his longing to be free got the better

1   Clerk's marginal note (trans.): 'see James Anderson on Edgar's charters.'
2   Clerk's marginal note (trans.): 'see Matthew Paris and Polydore Virgil.'

of him and led him to pledge his whole kingdom in fee to England for all time to come and to swear not to enter into foreign alliances against Henry's wishes. This is what most historians relate. Another version of events states that William was released and returned to Scotland in exchange for fifteen hostages and four castles (Roxburgh, Berwick, Edinburgh and Stirling) and that later, after Henry's return to England when the war with France was over, he was summoned along with his nobles and bishops to York, where all swore solemn allegiance to Henry and entrusted their kingdom to his protection. But much the most reliable account is that of Matthew Paris, whose words are worth quoting on a matter of such importance.... [31] This makes clear that it was while he was a captive at Falaise that William swore allegiance. As to the bishops and nobles, however, I prefer to think that they swore their oath when summoned to York.

So, under a feeble and womanish prince, Scotland bred a race of weak-kneed bishops and degenerate, cowardly, slothful nobles. There are some who doubt or deny that their consent was ever given. Others, accepting the truth of the story, claim none the less that the Law of Nations allows for human weakness in that no promise wrung from a king in captivity can affect a free people. They further believe that the action of the bishops and nobles should be discounted, since in Scotland neither the king alone nor his lords have the right to give away their kingdom's independence if the people are not consulted, that is, if their delegates in parliament either oppose the transaction or know nothing about it.

I myself can hardly pronounce on what happened so long ago. The king's being captive certainly means that his action could prejudice no one. In support of that view many cases could be cited, but a similar one involving England may suffice. When Richard I of England was returning from the Holy Land, where he had crusaded after the fashion of the time against the foes of Christianity, he was captured in the realm of the duke of Austria and then sold to the German emperor, Henry VI. Seeing no other way of securing his freedom, he pledged his kingdom as tribute to the emperor and was 'invested' with it, as they say, by him. English historians pass this matter by because it so happened that the emperor renounced his superiority on his deathbed. [32] But had he not done so, by no manner of means would the people of England have felt bound by King Richard's deed. As to any other discreditable trans-actions between William and Henry II, these were put to rights under Henry's successor, as we shall soon see.

Church affairs in Scotland were equally perturbed at that time. Henry did everything he could to ensure that his own lordship over Scotland would be matched by that of English over Scottish bishops, or at least that the latter would recognize the archbishop of York as their metropolitan. Since the

Scottish bishops were upset by this idea, Henry found a novel means of getting his way. He craftily induced the weak King of Scots to petition the Pope by letter to confirm this subjection as highly advantageous to the whole church in Britain. The Pope could hardly fail to oblige two great monarchs. There is extant a bull of Pope Alexander III to his legate Roger, archbishop of York, which quotes King William's letter and sanctions not only the subjection of the Scottish church but also the English king's rule over Scotland.

I know how fierce has been the controversy over William's letter, with some calling it a forgery and others claiming it was written under duress, but the whole dispute will vanish if the following arguments are duly considered.

When Britain lay shrouded in the mists of false religion, it was first among the Scots (so many people think) that the light of Christianity began to shine, introduced by Roman soldiers who during their occupation were stationed principally in Scotland or on the Scottish border. However that may have been—and I have no wish to defraud any other part of Britain of due credit in the matter—everyone agrees that the first British bishop was Palladius, the apostle of the Scots. Later, as even English historians acknowledge, the Scottish church was so highly regarded internationally that almost no religious matters were decided in Europe without its advice. Then an argument arose over the date of Easter, one which racked Christendom for a great many years, while at the same time the claims of the Roman papacy became daily more extravagant. The Scottish clerics backed the Eastern church and opposed Rome. Easy to see, then, why the Scottish church lost its credit for sanctity with the Popes and was supplanted by that of England, which had sided with Rome throughout. Emboldened by the praises heaped on their church, the English bishops began to think about extending their jurisdiction, and had no difficulty in doing so, because the Scottish church was then in as shaky a condition as the Scottish state: it did not even have enough bishops to consecrate new ones.

This was the background to what I may call the 'ecclesiastical homage' exacted from the Scottish church by the English bishops. William and his predecessor were so weak in the exercise of their royal authority that the Scottish bishops were free to seek patronage elsewhere, and the result of this licence was that all ecclesiastical jurisdiction in Britain devolved on the archbishops of Canterbury and York.

[35] From a neighbouring monarch imbued with such virtues[1] King William and the whole Scottish people expected a great deal, and indeed the ensuing

---

1   Roger Howden's eulogy of Richard I has been quoted.

friendship between Scots and English clearly showed posterity what agreement between them could achieve.

Planning a crusade, Richard first aimed at a sacred observance of justice. He restored what his father had unjustly gained and to conciliate William revoked the harsh terms he had been compelled to accept. Hostages and castles were returned, William and his heirs absolved of undertakings forcibly or [36] fraudulently elicited. Above all, Richard freed the kingdom of Scotland from English dominion and fixed its boundaries as they had been under Malcolm Canmore.

All this, however, was not solely due to his sense of fair play: two further factors contributed. One was a payment by the Scots of 10,000 marks in English money, a vast sum for those days. The other was Richard's concern for the peace of his realm while he was absent, likely to be threatened by angry Scots. Whether the money was ever actually paid has been doubted, but it seems likely that Richard enforced his bargain, especially one made for a holy cause which the churchmen of that time would not have short-changed to please anyone.

But on the subject of the treaty between those British kings let us listen to Howden, who lived at the time and is considered a reliable historian....[1] [41] Such was the bond of friendship between those kings that England and Scotland have never stood closer together. Richard and William vied with one another in acts of kindness and good will, the former being wise enough to see that kingdoms are strengthened by good relations and that he had no more useful friend than the royal neighbour with whom he shared an island and its surrounding seas.

D. Limitation of royal authority in England under Henry III

[59] So, with unprecedented solemnity, numerous acts were passed or ratified in open parliament, not only acts which Henry's father, King John, had confirmed, as I have already mentioned, but also many others which in one way or another might seem to conduce to the freedom of the people and the good of the realm. All these the king sanctioned calmly and swiftly like a prince under the law and as though he were a prince who had always lived by the law....

---

1   After quoting Howden, Clerk transcribes from Rymer's *Foedera* Richard's charter assuring proper treatment of William when called to court to pay homage for his lands in England, and then transcribes William's acknowledgment of this from Anderson's *Historical Essay*. 'I choose to put in these charters that the Reader may have under his eye the real transactions of those times and not be sent to search for them in other Authors' (Clerk's marginal note in English, 39).

[60] Thus the English won their freedom and showed the successors of William the Conqueror that their support of monarchy owed nothing to deference to the specious titles of a hereditary lordship but rather that they chose such a system of rule as would best promote and safeguard the advantage and freedom of the people. Since then it has usually been accepted in England that the royal authority and the freedom of the people are indivisible, in that neither can exist without the other. Nor has the royal dignity suffered as a result, but has rather increased, since it is plain that those rulers of Britain who have won the most credit and achieved the best results both at home and abroad have been those most scrupulous in observing the law and protecting public freedom.

E. Edward I and the Scots

[67] With the conquest of Wales Britain was divided into two peoples: the Anglo-Normans and the successors of the old Scots and Picts. That this division lasted for many centuries shows how greatly man's power is surpassed by that of God, for until the time appointed by divine Providence no force or counsel could bring these peoples together.

Elated by his successes, Edward now set himself to win the *imperium Britannicum*. Fortune gave him two chances which only the Destiny of Britain kept him from turning to account. One was by marrying his son to Margaret, the heir to the Scottish throne, as a result of which he hoped that natural succession would lead both nations to own the same lord. The other was the death of the self-same Margaret which split her country into factions and made it a prey to the strongest power....[1]

[71] The Maid's untimely death brought incredible suffering to the whole of Britain, the entire island groaning under faction and carnage. England almost lost its new-found freedom to its overweening king, and Scotland experienced every sort of woe: Edward's lust for power was so frenzied and bloodthirsty that Scotsmen even today recall his time with pain.

So long as the marriage-plans were afoot, the English king somewhat restrained his ambition but, his hopes once frustrated, he broke all bounds and claimed for himself unprecedented honours, behaving as Scotland's feudal overlord and in all his letters styling himself ruler of all Britain (without, it would seem, any sanction from God).

---

1   Clerk proceeds [67-71] to describe the marriage negotiations and the treaty of Birgham, citing Prynne, 3, 195 (error for 395). The reference is to William Prynne, *The History of King John, King Henry III and ... King Edward I* (London, 1670). Prynne calls this his third volume.

[75] On the day appointed for the competitors to meet again, Edward signified through the mouth of Antony, bishop of Durham, that he was ready to give judgement by virtue of his right as overlord of Scotland. The speaker began with the fable of Brutus in which he greatly delighted, supposing that he placed his coming to Britain beyond all risk of controversy. Then the writings of Marianus Scotus, William of Malmesbury, Roger Howden, Henry of Huntingdon and Ralph de Diceto were ransacked, nor was anything forgotten from the screeds of holy fathers or the letters and charters of Roman pontiffs which might further the cause. All this in the order in which it was spoken is displayed by Prynne, quoting from archives in the Tower of London. But examination shows how truth was obscured by fables, evasions and tricks of speech, leaving one aghast at King Edward's malice and the bishop of Durham's effrontery or ignorance. The matter is a small one, but since that speech was the cause of all the troubles that followed I shall say something about it....[1]

[77] With more nonsense of this kind the bishop concluded, making no mention of much that was fresh in the minds of those present. It had plainly been his task to gloss over the fact that Edward had broken his word so soon, for in the matter of the marriage he had sworn a solemn oath that if no children were born of it he would restore Scotland's right to independence. And that was the situation that now obtained, since it was not the Scots' fault that the marriage had never taken place.

But the Scots did not dare to open their mouths, much less object, though none could fail to notice the bishop's disregard for the truth. Had they wished, they could have refuted Edward's claim to overlordship out of his own mouth, for previously in his letters and [78] embassies to the Scots he had always treated them as a free people. But the competitors and their backers would not risk his anger, caring less for freedom than for furthering their separate claims.

There can be no doubt at all that the competitors agreed among themselves to betray their country's honour.... Some seek to excuse their shame on the score that they did not dare reply when surrounded by troops. There are also writers who ascribe to Robert Bruce the spirited answer that 'he was not so eager for a throne as to detract from the freedom bequeathed by his ancestors'.[2] That reply, if he had made it, would have assured his future fame and been a credit to humanity, but the truth is far otherwise, for the same Robert Bruce, when asked with the others if he would submit their dispute to Edward as superior of Scotland, answered that he owned the king of England as his lord

---

1   Clerk instances the bishop's misrepresentations, drawing without acknowledgement on Anderson, *Historical Essay*, 172-3.
2   Buchanan, *Ruddiman*, I, 135.

[79] and was ready to accept his judgement.[1] Moreover, to preclude future denials, Edward had their replies recorded with their signatures and seals appended....[2]

So, with his absolute authority over Scotland confirmed as fully as could be, Edward began to rule entirely as he pleased and Scots learned for the first time the meaning of obedience to a king. Though they had lived under kings for many a century, the governance of their country had been shared between the king and his nobles in such a way that one could scarcely tell which had counted for more: the majesty of the throne, the power of the nobility, or even sometimes the good of the people as a whole.

[84] Was Edward's decision in favour of Balliol just? I shall not pick a quarrel with those who say it was, but anyone who chooses to investigate ancient Scottish practice or the customs of other nations will find that preference was most commonly given to the first male descendant of a younger daughter. Resorting to the fountainhead of feudal law itself, we find this was the view of Gerardus. It is true that Obertus, that other great feudalist, disagreed, but Gerardus is followed by most, including Baldus, Alvarottus, Hottomanus, Duarenus, Schonerus, Cujacius and our own Craig.

[85] After Balliol's inauguration and homage Edward became so puffed up with pride that he began to tyrannize his own people as much as the Scots and indeed so far forgot himself that he made all Britain suffer from the power that the Scots had allowed him. Vanity, the hardest of vices to conceal, was manifest in Edward. Worse still, it soon became clear that his primary aim in claiming lordship over the Scots was to lay siege to the freedom of the English; he would use a vanquished, subservient people to help him bring the victors to heel. When they saw his true nature, most Britons had cause for regret: the English that they had encouraged his ambition by subsidizing war, and the Scots that they had too easily allowed themselves to be handed a king.

[93] Prynne gives us a long catalogue of the Scots who swore allegiance to Edward [in 1296], but unmindful of the historian's duty breaks out into abuse against the whole race of Scots [94] for later rebelling against Edward and his heirs: I can understand a man spewing out his bile in this way, but wiser heads will make allowance for the times and the cause of freedom. Some would say with Brutus in Appian that 'Romans are bound by no oaths or promises to tyrants'[3] or with Cicero that 'pirates stand outside the law and no faith need

1   Clerk's marginal note (trans.): 'see Prynne, 3, 493, where Bruce's words are quoted at length.'
2   Clerk's marginal note (trans.): 'see the instrument in the French language reproduced by Prynne, 502, and Walsingham, 56.'
3   Appian, *Roman History: Civil Wars*, II, xix, 139. The Greek quotation has been badly mangled by the copyist.

be held with them'.[1] However that may be, one is bound to think that Prynne would have written more fairly if he had either omitted that passage of abuse or shown equal care to give the names of those Englishmen who (as we have seen) swore allegiance to Louis the Dauphin and then promptly crowned Henry III. To pass judgement on individuals is everyone's prerogative, but about entire peoples one should speak with more caution: their destiny is known to God alone.

[94] The Romans invariably admitted conquered peoples into fellowship with themselves and often admitted them to their senate itself and a share of their prosperity. In this way they set an example of prudence as well as humanity. If Edward had followed it, England and Scotland might now have been long united. But he followed a very different course, imposing cruel governors on Scotland, expelling the owners of the most fertile lands and giving full rein to the victors' rapacity. On the pretext of reinforcing his army he even raised troops, paid for by the Scots, [95] to satisfy his own lust for power and ensure himself the means, when occasion arose, to destroy England's freedom as well. Every town, every castle in Scotland was manned by English garrisons, and he appointed his own magistrates to make sure that Scotsmen would suffer in the flesh for their country's misfortune.... Finally, to hide from them every trace of their ancient freedom and dignity, he repealed their old laws and told his new subjects to get used to the laws of England. After settling all this to his liking, Edward returned to London in triumph and thenceforth so totally forgot himself as to behave as the conqueror not just of Scotland but of all Britain, subjecting the whole people to new burdens and taxes, with the proceeds of which he bribed a corrupt and subservient parliament to give legal sanction to a betrayal of popular rights.

[133] Here, then [in Edward's Ordinance for the government of Scotland, 1305], we see a union of the kingdoms of England and Scotland, but only such a union as exists between master and slave. Some will say that Scotland was allowed to keep her parliament. So indeed she was, a parliament of the sort we have seen in our own day, one tied to observing the king's supreme will and beholden to courtiers and parasites. Then, as recently, authority over Scotland was vested in a monarch who was enmeshed in English policies and a deputy whose task it was to carry them out. There was nothing for a Scottish parliament to do except waste time on details and give formal assent to levies and taxes and similar instruments of bondage. As for the laws imposed by

---

1   Clerk's marginal note (trans.): 'Cicero said that no perjury was involved if one does not pay ransom promised to pirates. But Grotius [De Jure Belli et Pacis] rightly repudiates his view, Book 2, ch. 13.' See Cicero, De Officiis, iii, 29.

Edward on Scotland, some of them were those of King David and his successors but the vast majority were taken over from English usage. That is why, if I mistake not, there is such a commixture of Scots and English law in the book which the Scots call *Regiam Majestatem*. The question of that book's authorship was not worth raising,[1] nor need we go on arguing about whether the Scots got their old laws from the English or the other way round, since I think I have traced the mixture to its source as a relic of Edward's domination.

[143] Even English writers say of Edward that he was more given to tyranny than the king of a free people should be, but he also had outstanding virtues which mark out a king from other men. Strong-willed and valorous, provident and wise, in spite of many vices he deserves to be ranked among leaders whose deeds have made their people great and famous in the eyes of posterity. And it seemed that England's fortunes were bound up in Edward alone, for along with him perished the *imperium Britannicum* he had built with so much blood and sweat.

F. Wallace and Bruce[2]

[96] When Scotland's freedom was at its last gasp it found its champion in Wallace, a man who had almost none of the qualities which the leader of a great enterprise needs beyond bravery and physical strength.

[104] All Scottish writers agree[3] that [after the battle of Falkirk] the two leaders exchanged words across the river, words that would soon bring about a great change in Scottish affairs. 'Wallace,' cried Bruce, 'will you never give up or make an end to this madness? This is no time to let your wild ambition bring death and destruction to the heedless mob. A leader should consider, not only why he is fighting a war, but also what outcome he can hope from it, measuring his strength against that of his enemy. Had you done that, you would hardly have challenged the all-powerful king of a battle-hardened race when your people are so poor, so divided, your army of irregulars so lacking in leaders, so

---

1   Clerk's marginal note (trans.): 'I do not think it was written by Glanville.'

2   Clerk's account of their exploits follows Buchanan closely. For minor changes of emphasis see Intro., pp. 14-15 above. The rhetorical passages translated here are exercises on conventional *topoi* of humanist historiography.

3   Whether or not based on fact, the story of the exchange between Wallace and Bruce after Falkirk was necessary to Scottish historians to provide a link between the two champions, neatly making the words of the former motivate the latter's change of heart. The gist, common to all versions and first found in Bower, is that Bruce asks, 'Why are you doing this?' and Wallace replies, 'Because you have failed to do it.' The story gained widest currency through Blind Harry, but the versions with which Clerk challenges comparison are those of the sixteenth-century humanists: John Mair, *Historia Majoris Britanniae*, IV, xiv; Hector Boece, *Scotorum Historia*, XIV, v; Buchanan, *Ruddiman*, I, 139.

short of provisions and arms. If desire to be a king has driven you to fight, take thought, I beg you, and ward off your ruin while you may, for the Scots will never be minded to reject the rightful heirs to their throne and give their crown to a commoner like you of no distinction whatever. So lay down your arms; make your soldiers see sense and revert to their loyalty and duty. Your only safety and protection lie in the friendship of King Edward, whom you will not find a harsh or unforgiving prince.'

Wallace replied with ungovernable anger: 'Who is this who accosts me so boldly and foolishly? Bruce you may appear, but I recognize no Bruce in what you say. No one with the blood of Scottish kings in his veins would have slandered and abused me, poor commoner as I am, for engaging to defend our country's freedom; rather he would have thanked me, favoured me, urged me to fight on to the end. Think of the shame and dishonour you have brought upon yourself. Was it not bad enough to be forced to give way to Edward's might and ambition without offering yourself to be his slave? Could England's king not have gone to England to find hirelings to legitimize his tyranny? Did he have to [105] find a Scot, and the true king of Scots at that, to work Scotland's ruin and his own? See the trophies the English have raised from yesterday's victory: they convict you more than any words of mine. Spears, pikes, shields, the bodies of Scotsmen piled around in heaps tell the story of your unfeeling heart. All Scotland hates you and calls you traitor, ravisher of its freedom and—basest name of all—Edward's lackey, the tyrant's tool. How many women have you widowed on a single day? How many parents bereaved? How many children orphaned? For all these woes it is you whom your countrymen blame, you and your father and grandfather, not Edward, who could never have ruled us without your cowardly, fawning assent. Little enough his armies could have done if you Bruces and the other great men of Scotland who follow your lead had loved their country properly and guarded its freedom. And why accuse me of wanting to be a king? Even in his absence I have constantly acknowledged Balliol. Faint-hearted as he is, and stripped of royal honours, I would have set Scotland free in his name. But I so love my country that I would not grudge the throne to any Scots leader whom the people thought worthy of that burdensome honour. So come then, Bruce, since you are so greedy for Scotland's crown that you would wear it by someone else's favour, take on the trappings of royalty if you will, and in splendid servitude pay court to Edward, the most proud and vain-glorious of mortals. For my part I yield without delay, crushed by malice and worn out by my people's divisions. I resign the high office which you rightly say I was rash to assume. [106] Better or luckier men than I may surpass me in leadership by far, but in love of my country and zeal for its freedom no man shall ever be my rival.'

[138] So died Wallace, the bravest leader of his age, whom Alexander the Great and Julius Caesar might not only have pardoned for his courage but honoured and numbered among their friends.

[152] While it still remained in doubt which side would first attack [at Bannockburn], Bruce is said to have addressed his soldiers as follows:[1]

'I would do you wrong to suspect your courage or check your ardour with an untimely speech. There across the river stands the foe that has so often stained these fields with your fathers' blood, slaughtered the helpless and the young, raped your womenfolk, pillaged your houses and burned them to the ground. Believe me, those English you see before you will prove cruel masters if you yield them a cowardly inch, for their looks are menacing and their one intent is to make slaves of you again. Like the poorest sort of slaves they mean to chastise you and are preparing their whips even now. So I bid you recapture the spirit of your forefathers who were worthy of their country's freedom, and when you go into battle remember that you carry in your hands your country's fame and glory; it is freedom you fight for, mankind's supreme good. All Britain awaits the outcome of this day, for no part of this island can be enslaved without damage to the whole, and the destinies of the British peoples are so intertwined that what happens to one affects all. Remember how bravely and firmly your ancestors checked the power of Rome, and how nobly they later defended their freedom against the mightiest of the Britons, these self-same English. Think too of what has happened in our own times. All the injuries England has done us through bloodshed and enslavement, do they not demand cure, do they not call for vengeance? [153] If this does not move you, lift up your eyes to the hills yonder, where a countless throng of your fellow-citizens, men and women both, shall witness your courage or cowardice. You are your country's sole hope. Lay on, then, with a bold and resolute spirit. That is what is needed to counter the enemy's proud thoughts and threatening looks. But if fortune deserts us, look for no safety in flight. In front lies the foe, on the left flank the stormy sea, with not a vessel to be seen. Behind us looms Stirling, the English fortress, well-armed and manned: pass that and Forth will drown you in its waters. Least of all can you escape to the right, where your countrymen will give you no quarter, seething with wrath and indignation at your shame, the women themselves more cruel than the men, more cruel than the enemy. Your choice is to conquer or die a wretched death amid taunts and jeers and well-deserved torments. Follow me, then, through wounds and

1   Clerk's marginal note (trans.): 'Bruce's speech. All historians have been allowed the right to invent speeches for their leaders, provided they are probable and in accord with historical facts.' Pre-Bannockburn speeches are assigned to Bruce, not only in Barbour and Bower, but also in Mair, V, 2 and Boece, XIV, xi; not, however, in Buchanan.

C

slaughter, through streams of blood and the souls of the dying to eternal glory and the sweets of victory.'

G. Asylum in France for David II

[195] In 1333 the Bruce faction shipped the entire royal family to France, having secured a trusty ally and friend in King Philip, who received them honourably and gave them safe asylum until their fortunes improved.

But we should note here in passing that the French king was not so much a trusty ally and friend to the Scottish royal house as a mortal enemy to the prosperity of Britain. The single, unchanging wish of French kings has always been to see the British peoples divided; they have abhorred all unions between Scotland and England and made it an invariable article of policy to cultivate the friendship of those who chiefly threatened Britain's welfare. They had recently backed the followers of Balliol and were now backing those of Bruce, but always with the sole aim of deploying them against the king of England when occasion arose. One sees the same policy still at work today when the French talk of restoring the house of Stuart.

H. Edward III's peace proposals, 1363

[230] These[1] show how earnestly, in his great wisdom, the English king sought union with the Scots. Following his grandfather's example, he had pursued the same goal, first by skilful policy and later by bloody force of arms. But on this occasion, as usual, the Scots held out firmly against all the English moves. When the proposals were brought before parliament by King David, almost the entire nation came out in open revolt. They were therefore rejected, and with so much indignation that a union of the British peoples would never again be negotiated by men but would be left to God alone to accomplish.[2] The terms offered to the Scots were such as would probably not have been spurned by any other people so crushed and hard-pressed, so beset with troubles and daily exposed to a powerful nation's hate. But patriotism prevailed, or more probably one should say that it was inveterate hatred of the English which led them to make light of their afflictions so long as they could be free of the English yoke.

---

1   The proposals have been summarized from Rymer's *Foedera*.
2   Clerk uses this formula habitually to describe the 'providential' union of 1603.

BOOK 3
1363 to 1603

A. Controversial successions in Scotland and England; the Scottish dislike of leisure

[17[1]] Robert II had been a cautious rather than warlike king and is memorable for nothing so much as that his clandestine marriage to Elizabeth Mure of Rowallan has caused some writers to question their descendants' right to the throne.

He was succeeded by his son John, earl of Carrick, who chose to change his name and be called Robert too. Since my theme is the relationship of the British peoples, I need hardly comment on this prince's birth which has been the subject of much learned discussion. Suffice it to say that the fable transmitted by Buchanan, Boece and others that he was born out of wedlock has been more than adequately refuted. The secrecy of his father's marriage did indeed give rise to rumour, but its legitimacy has been put beyond doubt now that so much documentation has been brought to light. Anyway, in my opinion,[2] there is no point in disputing the succession of kings who have ruled in Britain *de facto*, since it deserves to be an axiom in relation to monarchy that possession of the crown cancels any defects of birth [*vitia sanguinis*].

So now we see a son who in all respects resembled his father, for whether his weakness was of mind or body he let his kingdom be governed by courtiers and allowed lawlessness to prevail throughout the country. From the time of his coronation he was king in name only, his brother Robert continuing to wield supreme power.

Nor were things much different in England, where King Richard's reign was so disturbed that he was obliged to make an almost abject peace with his neighbours....

[18] The internal dissensions that then racked Scotland do not lie within the scope of my book, but anyone who cares to investigate history will find that

---

1   Reference to the folio numbering of SRO, GD18/3202/3B.

2   The remainder of this paragraph is a late addition to the MS in Clerk's hand (?1750). The blustering tone may cover up awareness that he could have been wrong about Robert's having been born in wedlock. See Intro., p. 16 above.

the Scots have always disliked leisure [*otium*], growing restless in peace and provoking wars either at home or abroad. It was a time of great cruelty in Scotland: some atrocities were carried out against the king's wishes, others by his order or permission. And yet the royal house stood firm, which was not the case in England, where Richard's misdeeds brought about his enforced abdication. His successor, Henry IV, was later to serve as an object-lesson to the English of the woes [19] that can result from a doubtful title to the throne and the importance to the state of maintaining the rights and prerogatives of monarchs (except where religion or the freedom of the people is threatened).

B. Scotland's choice between France and England; the 'ingratitude' of James I

[41] The leader of the English delegation,[1] Lord Scrope, bewailed the unhappy fate of Britain, formerly divided into many peoples, now into two only, English and Scots, but those more at enmity than all the others had been before. 'In your hands', he said, 'it lies to end this long disgraceful story of continual warfare, pillage and slaughter. The remedy is union between our peoples, [42] and there is no better means of bringing it about than intermarriage between our royal houses, in the hope that some day the right to rule over the whole island will devolve on a single individual. Such a marriage we offer you, letting Providence determine which of our peoples will give Britain a king by right of birth, not conquest. And this I must impress upon you all: do not allow any foreign king, strengthened by your alliance, to disturb Britain's peace and tranquillity. Experience shows us that neighbours quarrel readily, and that nothing is easier than to set the British peoples against each other.'

Here the ambassador turned to the French delegates and added: 'These men also have a wedding in mind. And why not? Let every nation pursue its own interest. But think, my lords, how a French and English marriage will differ. Charles VII is a king in name only who hopes to profit from your friendship by renewing treaties that you have found disastrous. It would be cruel to remind you of what Britain has suffered, and you most of all, but you cannot have forgotten what bloodshed these treaties have caused you. You say they enabled Scotland's young men to make a brave show in France with their riches and titles of honour. A brave show indeed, and nothing but a show, for which of you brought anything back home to Scotland but wounds and scars and

---

1   The supposed presence of French and English delegations at the meeting of the Scottish parliament at Perth in 1436, each seeking alliance through the marriage of James I's eldest daughter Margaret, gives Clerk a chance to invent speeches setting forth the rival claims of their countries for Scotland's friendship. The idea, but not the substance of the speeches, comes from Drummond's *The History of the ... Five James's*. See *The Works of William Drummond of Hawthornden* (Edinburgh, 1711), 10-12.

empty titles? Finally, is it prudent, whatever some may think, to marry your princess to a Dauphin who has nothing to offer worthy of this match, scarcely even the hope of a throne? If alliance with the king of France is what you want, you shall have it in the marriage I offer you, for [43] the only rightful king of France is my lord Henry.'

To this and much more in the same vein the French king's delegates responded: 'The English are revelling in their luck and forgetting the facts. Modesty would have suited their king's envoy better than pride and boasting. Had he recognized how changeful are human affairs, he would have recalled that it was France, or rather the least of its provinces, that gave England its kings, and that Henry himself and all his nobles of note are of French extraction. England to this day is ruled by the descendants of William of Normandy and by Norman law. But Fortune, he tells us, has turned against France and its royal house. True, and it has favoured the English, but we Frenchmen have not lost hope or courage or loyalty to our kings, and we have not lost our hatred of the kings of England who violated and betrayed our rights. All we need is this alliance, strengthened by a new bond of marriage, to be a shield that will not only let us rest in peace but also give us hope to avenge the wrongs England has done us. So you Scots should be wary of thinking that you will no longer need our friendship. Fortune can turn against anyone, and your peace can be threatened at any time if a more powerful nation like England should challenge your rights and privileges. Cast your eyes around: wherever you look you find shining reminders of our friendship—in your towns, your fields, your garrisons, and most of all in the breasts of your soldiers, for it need not shame you that the military training [44] in which you take pride derives from France, that training-ground of war. We could list many other benefits you have from us, and great ones too, but they are not of a kind that need our commendation, nor do you need to be reminded of them. So now consider the English request. They want an alliance that in the past they have often disdained, and they want it, not for Britain's good, as they claim, but to give them a title to rule the whole island at will. Believe us, the English care nothing for the life of your king or the peace of his realm. Give them their way and they will plot the downfall of your royal family, infiltrate the country and make you their slaves. It will happen as we say. If your king were to die without male children, Scotland would fall to Henry or his heirs through his wife. And where then would be Scotland's freedom and glory, its vaunted antiquity? Would it be a kingdom at all? Would it not become a province of England, stripped of its laws, its parliament, its trade? But speeches are needless when we already have your firm assurance on this treaty....'

[45] The English complained of King James's ingratitude.[1] Why did he prefer
the friendship of France when he owed his life, his kingdom and his fortunes
to the English? They even thought the princess should have been returned to
her birthplace. But these benefits had been erased by numerous injuries later
done to the Scots king. Moreover, one cannot judge the gratitude or faithful-
ness of kings as one might those of private persons. For it is almost always the
case that their highest obligation is to the welfare of their people, so that every
treaty they enter into is to be judged as it furthers the welfare and advantage
of those it should favour. Kings must, on the other hand, always take care not
to break, deceitfully or without just cause, agreements contracted in good faith,
because perfidy and deceit are vices all honest men hate.

[116] Whether to accept this offer of marriage[2] on the terms proposed now
became the subject of a debate in Scotland which I shall summarize briefly.
Plausible[3] arguments were widely advanced in its favour. It was the only way
to confirm lasting peace between the neighbouring kingdoms, and the only
sort of treaty whose terms could be cordially agreed to. Alliances framed by
human policy were unstable; only such as Nature seemed to have intended
would endure, and nothing seemed more contrary to Nature's laws than a
durable alliance between Scots and French, peoples so different in language
and culture, geographically so far apart. On the other hand, the peoples of
Britain were impelled to unite by sharing the same sea, sky and soil, by having
almost the same laws and customs, by speaking the same language, by looking
alike, by thinking alike [similitudo corporum animorumque]. [117] Frequent
intermarriage between Britain's royal houses would eventually ensure a natural, legitimate union of crowns and ultimately a union of the peoples' hearts
in permanent peace and friendship.

 The Francophile argument was that the English made promises easily but
were not to be trusted to keep them; their every gift was a Trojan horse.
Edward I had claimed the title of king of Scots when bound by solemn oath
not to do so, and his successors had made the same claim on devious grounds.
There had been numerous dynastic marriages but they had borne little fruit,
friendship rarely lasting longer than the wedding. The usual English practice
had been to woo Scotland only when they had wars to fight at home or abroad
or were laying claim to France; thus they wanted our friendship only when
they needed it. By contrast, the French connection had plainly been accom-

1   This sententious paragraph replaces a long passage in which Buchanan answers specific allegations of
     ingratitude levelled at James by Hall and Grafton.
2   Henry VIII's proposal for marriage of James V to his daughter Mary.
3   Speciosa. Clerk's choice of this ambivalent adjective, which he more often uses in its pejorative sense of
     'specious', illustrates his attempt to present this debate impartially.

panied by every kind of practical advantage, bringing more power and honour
to Scotland. Scots noblemen at the French court had never been treated *de
haut en bas*[1] or slighted as they were by the overweening English, but had always
been treated courteously and kindly like fellow-countrymen, or rather like
brothers who had been brought up alike since birth. Some Scots even went so
far as to assert that the difference between their relationship with France and
England was the difference between freedom and slavery, civilization and
barbarism, brotherly love and rabid hostility. 'Henry's offer adds up to two
things: that our king becomes a captive and we lose our friends—both of which
breach our independence.'

Fiercely-worded speeches of that kind so stirred up anti-English feeling that
all hopes of the marriage were abandoned.

C. The Reformation bond with England

[145] Henry's wars in France provided respite from military invasion, but
Scotland could not enjoy the pleasures of peace, as factions began to commit
cruel outrages and highland clans attacked each other savagely. The country's
political leaders took insufficient care to act in unison, and their rivalries and
disorders were fomented by Cardinal Beaton and his clerical inquisitors. For
religion in those days seemed less to be a matter of saving mankind than of
destroying it, and churchmen curried favour with the court by violently
suppressing conscientious dissent. Although Jews, Muslims and pagans were
allowed to live peaceably under the law, Reformers were punished with
torture and death.

So it gave immense pleasure to the inquisitors when that holiest of men,
George Wishart, was condemned and burned at the stake on the orders of the
hated cardinal. But they did not foresee [146] how the Reformation cause
would be strengthened by his death. That cruel act caused the whole population to turn away from Catholicism as though with one accord, and from that
moment onwards Scotland's nobles, who had cried down political union with
England, began to press eagerly for union in matters of religion.

[169] Mary Tudor was followed on the throne of England by Elizabeth, whom
the best of her successors could only hope to equal. It was under her rule that
British union first began to take root, starting, very properly, with religion.
Rome's authority was gradually rejected as both peoples sought [170] to
restore Christianity's original simplicity. But the divine Founder of that
religion decided first to use a woman's rule in both countries, and the example

---

1   *Grande supercilium expertos* (lit. 'having experienced the lofty eyebrow'), an allusion to Juvenal, VI, 169.

of the weaker sex, to temper Britons' minds, to purge them of their usual harshness or rather barbarity, and then to join them together in closer bonds.[1] For it is certain that the British peoples had never before been closer together than they were in Elizabeth's time.

D. Mary Stewart's return to Scotland[2]

[182] All who attended her felt equal admiration and pity, for as well as being endowed with surpassing beauty, fine qualities of mind, and many other gifts, she had also known Fortune's bitterest blasts. She had lost her father before she was seven days old and then been exposed to the dangers of sedition at home. She had been driven overseas more to exile than marriage and narrowly escaped shipwreck on her voyage to France. At the French court she had been taught nothing but Roman superstition and frivolous manners. An illustrious marriage had promised more joys than it brought, and finally, to complete the picture of suffering, the deaths of her husband, the great king his father, and her excellent mother, had thrown her into sorrow and bereavement. Yet these were but the prelude to greater misfortunes which would follow this poor woman to the end of her life, as we shall later see.

E. Elizabeth and James[3]

[207] Elizabeth ruled as much in Scotland as in England. She controlled the king not only in his childhood through Moray and successive regents but also in his adolescence and early manhood. She so managed him with the prospect

1   Clerk's reading of the divine plan seems strained at this point. He gives no other indication of regarding Mary's influence in Scotland as helping to promote union.

2   Here Clerk re-phrases, transposes and alters elements from the corresponding passage in Buchanan. Compare W.A. Gatherer (ed. and trans.), *The Tyrannous Reign of Mary Stewart: George Buchanan's account* (Edinburgh, 1958), 53-4: 'Born amid the bitter storms of war, she lost her father within six days. She was taught diligently, indeed, by her mother, an accomplished lady, but she was abandoned amid domestic rebellions and foreign wars, a prey to the strongest, and exposed to all the dangers of outrageous fortune, before she was of age to understand her evil case. She left her native land as if cast into exile, saved with great difficulty from the arms of enemies and the fury of the sea. There, it is true, fortune smiled upon her for a little time: she was exalted by an illustrious marriage. But it was an illusory rather than a real happiness, for by the death of her mother and her husband she was again thrown into sorrow and bereavement, her new throne lost, and her ancient one far from secure. But apart from the fascination of her varied and perilous history, she was graced with surpassing loveliness of form, the vigour of maturing youth, and fine qualities of mind, which a court education had increased, or at least made more attractive by a surface gloss of virtue. This, far from being genuine, was a mere shadowy representation of virtue; so that her natural goodness would be weakened by an earnest desire to please; and the seeds of virtue, wizened by the allurements of luxury, would be prevented from reaching ripeness and fruition.' On Clerk's Marian 'episode' see Intro., p. 17 above.

3   This passage encapsulates the nearest approach to a binding theme in the latter part of Book 3.

of succeeding to her throne that the present union of the British crowns can be called her achievement.

BOOK 4
1603 to 1706

A. Introductory

[1[1]] Would that I could now bid farewell to the dire madness of war, to battle and slaughter, fire and sword. Would that I could steer this little work of mine out of stormy seas into a quieter harbour. The union of crowns gave grounds for such a hope, but blessings do not ever come unmixed: it had harmful results which have vexed the two kingdoms almost to this day. The Scots with good reason lament that they have lost their seat of government to England, and the English bear a grudge that some of their privileges have been shared with the Scots. Among both peoples old hatreds still lurk which can only be dispelled by sound legislation and the force of long habit. So I ask my readers to take careful note that when I speak of the advantages of a united Britain I mean to be understood in a general sense only. Unions are strengthened by the sacrifices that their peoples are now and then called upon to make. Those who think otherwise should imagine an England split into regions, a return to the old Saxon Heptarchy, or suppose that the Caledonian kingdoms of the Scots and the Picts had won back their ancient jurisdictions. There would be some gains no doubt that individual peoples could boast of, but to Britain the loss would be immense, for any return to the primitive forms of human society means exposure to the dangers and distresses of a savage state of nature.

B. Proposals for union under James VI and I

[2] The delegates from England [who offered the English crown to James] made a great show of unrestrained joy, but were secretly upset to be transferring power to the king of their old enemies.... Nor were the Scots as pleased by this turn of events as is commonly thought. The more intelligent regretted what was happening to their country: that it was to forfeit the bounty of a resident monarch and lose the advantages and delights of a royal court. The only Scot whose joy knew no bounds on this occasion was King James himself,

---

1   Reference to the folio numbering of SRO, GD18/3202/4.

who, along with his needy courtiers, was gaping for a fortune more in keeping with his high sense of his own dignity....

He journeyed to London by easy stages, trying to win favour with the English public, and was entertained on his arrival with marvellous celebrations laid on in a spirit of generally feigned rejoicing. But he saw through the charade and entered into it, concealing his true perceptions, having learned from his cradle to be quite a proficient time-server.

Anxious not to seem to have forgotten his own people entirely, soon after his coronation he applied his mind [3] to ways of quenching the age-old hatred and rivalry between the two nations, and especially of lessening English hostility to the admission of Scots noblemen to places and privileges at court. His first idea was that poison lay concealed in the very names of England and Scotland, which he determined to abolish, substituting the old name of Britain to designate both. Some of his English counsellors thought this a tough proposition, which was therefore referred to parliament, that is to say the parliament of England. When this met in the following year, James made an admirable speech recommending a union of the kingdoms as well as the crowns as the surest safeguard for Britons and the only cure for old wounds which would enable all his subjects to enjoy the benefits of his rule....

I have no doubt at all that he would have had his way, if only he had acted at once on his accession, when his sycophantic court would have agreed to anything. But as experience has quite often shown us, English attitudes can change a great deal in the space of one year. Their country had been flooded with fortune-hunting Scots, who were already threatening to monopolize the royal favour. Accordingly, when the English parliament heard of the King's zeal for union, its response was to dissemble: it humoured James by naming commissioners to treat with the Scots, but without the least intention of achieving such a worthwhile goal. The Scottish estates debated the matter a little later, but added conditions which later ruined the whole project: that the authority of the estates was not to be diminished, and that there was to be no alteration to the laws of Scotland or infringement of the ancient rights of the kingdom. So it seems that the Scots wanted confederation rather than union, for it was plain to all that the British could never become one people unless a single British parliament had supreme authority to legislate for all.

James could have seen an omen in the attitude of the Scots of the hopelessness of uniting his subjects, but he continued to show enthusiasm for it ...

[6] When the commissioners met at Westminster in October 1604, two points of controversy came chiefly to the fore: whether the old name of Great Britain should supersede those of England and Scotland, and whether English public offices should be open to Scots and vice versa. On the first point, some English delegates were against changing names unnecessarily, unless major

benefits were to accrue, which they could not foresee. They also pointed out that the founding of a new kingdom was always an arduous undertaking, especially when it involved uniting diverse peoples. It ran into obstacles with respect to privileges and ancient titles of honour. Often, too, and not least in this case, it could result in a weakening of the royal prerogative. But the contrary view was that ancient rights and privileges were in no way affected by a change of name. The Trojans who had journeyed to Italy with Aeneas retained their original honours when they united with the Latins. And if the English and their king enjoyed greater prestige than the Scots in the eyes of the world, [7] that prestige would be enhanced, not lessened, by union with a country which also had much to be proud of. With regard to the second point, the King's ministers declared that it was natural justice that the subjects of the same king should share the same privileges, and they adduced many instances from Livy and Polybius to show how the Greeks and Romans had communicated the right to hold public office to peoples, sometimes con-quered, with whom they had united.

These disputes released so much ill-will and long-felt hatred that it was found necessary to bring them to an end. Accordingly, the King admonished the delegates not to meddle with matters that came under his prerogative. It was for him, he declared, to name his joint kingdoms and to appoint officials exactly as he pleased.

The delegates then turned their attention to the remaining matters of common concern and eventually reached agreement on the following....[1]

I have done no more than summarize these terms of union, not wishing my readers to waste their time on such a ludicrous transaction. (They can find the exact wording of the terms in Spottiswoode's History.) The King saw clearly that they contained not even the shadow of a union but only such things as either commonly obtain in international relations or that he could have decreed through his prerogative....

[11] Flawed and useless as it was, the King referred this outline of a union to his parliaments, but in vain, for old hostilities broke out so violently that he had enough to do to safeguard his own authority and keep peace between his kingdoms. There was indeed no limit to the abuse hurled by pamphleteers against the King and his compatriots. The court was astounded, but James himself determined to be tolerant, waiting for his kingdoms to be reconciled by habit and mutual dependence. The most striking account of all these attitudes can be found in the pages of the learned Craig, who wrote works on succession, on homage, and on union full of bitter comments on English

1   Articles of union summarized from John Spottiswoode, *History of the Church of Scotland* (London, 1654), 481-6.

writers of his day. I do however find that his long-suppressed writings[1] show excellent judgement. They also show that, from that time onward, the King acted in all respects like a true Englishman, and, while continuing to favour his acolytes, totally abandoned the cause of Scotland.

It remains to consider [12] the views on union held by intelligent men of that time, so that later transactions can be seen in a comparative light. As I have already shown, English and Scots agreed in wanting the kingdoms to be joined, but few were willing to sacrifice any of their rights. We know that since Roman times all families of peoples have delegated a great deal of power to a [common] head of state, an emperor or king. The British, however, considered this a threat to their freedom, having delegated too much authority to kings who were incapable of carrying the burden. If only they had followed the call of freedom by vesting power in a [common] parliament as well as a king, they would have found a system of government ideally suited to their genius. But at the start of James's reign both Scots and English were so far from doing this that they endeavoured by all means to retain their own privileges and their own separate councils. The English denied the Scots access to their public offices, and the Scots grudged the English their increase of power. Neither would countenance any lessening of their parliament's authority. So new rivalries arose which brought about a crisis in relations between the two peoples.

But the most serious impediment to union at that time was disparity of wealth and population. It struck the English as outrageous that such a small and poor nation as Scotland should be allowed equal suffrage in a British parliament, which was indeed what the Scottish commissioners aimed at, inasmuch as they wanted [13] the entire membership of the Scottish parliament added to that of the English.

To get round this difficulty, England's Lord Chancellor, the great Francis Bacon, devised a model of a supreme governing body in which Scots would be admitted, but his proposal, though published, did not make clear how many votes the Scots were to have. He thought it essential in the case of union that the number of delegates from each country should be fixed, but said only that wealth and population should be the determining factors. The other leading English dignitaries appear to have held the same view. But the Scots thought otherwise, if we may judge by Craig, who in his outline of a British parliament clearly lays down the following limitations as a firm and indissoluble guarantee of friendly relations for all time: that each country's parliament should retain

---

1   Thomas Craig's treatises on succession and homage had finally appeared as *The Right of Succession to the Kingdom of England ... translated by J.G.* (London, 1703) and *Scotland's Sovereignty Asserted, being a Dispute concerning Homage ... translated by George Ridpath* (London, 1695). His *De Unione Regnorum Britanniae Tractatus* remained unpublished and was the only MS certainly consulted by Clerk in writing his *History*.

its separate jurisdiction and authority; that each nation's laws should be subject to change only by the parliament that passed them; that no new levies or taxes should be raised, or wars declared, without the approval of both parliaments; and that criminals should be tried by the laws of the country where the crime was committed.

All this is more than enough to show that no union closer than that of the crowns could have been hoped for at a time when the thinking of the two sides was so far apart. Necessity alone could have brought them closer.

I have been unable to discover what form of union the King himself favoured, but [14] have no doubt that separate parliaments suited his ambition. He could hope that each would curb the other's excesses, while he could rule more freely by keeping them apart. Yet he did sincerely try to find a means of bringing his peoples closer together, for he was always well-disposed toward his fellow-Scots, whose loyalty he knew he could always rely on. So he approached his goal by a different route. Abandoning conferences, he introduced legislation to confirm and increase his authority. By this means he thought it would be easy to control both peoples and dispose of their rights and fortunes at his own discretion.

Since the English had tasted a high degree of freedom under Elizabeth, James was daunted by the task of getting them to accept the yoke of slavery. He therefore began with the Scots....

[15] Thus through his prerogative, legitimate or not, he pursued almost the same objective that he had hoped to achieve by uniting the kingdoms.

C. From James to Charles: ecclesiastical union

[15] The other events of James's reign are foreign to my purpose. To the end of his life, both at home and abroad, he fostered peace by means not entirely laudable, and the peace he achieved was worse than any war in that it bred a corruption of manners that threatened ruin to flourishing peoples. He was called the Solomon of his age, and to say truth he was not without mental endowments, but such as would have adorned a private man better than a prince. No one was ever more flattered in his life, almost no one more abused after his death. For some captious critics it was enough that he was born in Scotland, an alien; others complained that by uniting the crowns he had thwarted constitutional change.[1] But all would have preferred him to be the servant of peace, not its slave. He was a lesson to princes not to shrink too cautiously from war or encourage his enemies by appeasement....

---

1   *Spem rerum novarum sustulisset* (lit. 'he had removed the hope of new things').

Charles I succeeded his father with every good augury for a prosperous reign, and the hopes of Britons would not have been dashed if they had taken advantage of what Providence gave. Peace abroad, quiet and enviable prosperity at home—they lacked nothing but recognition of their own good fortune. But, [16] as often happens, they grew dissolute through the abuse of leisure and yielded to various passions. The natural fickleness of the British peoples never showed more clearly than in this unhappy reign. Among the many forms of madness that abounded the worst was religious fanaticism,[1] which has always done more harm to humanity than the sword itself.

This habit of mind first began to flourish in Scotland, for the presbyterians raged against James's restoration of episcopacy as though he had introduced the plague or some dangerous disease. The court's encouragement of episcopacy created a longing for presbytery among the people, who thought the road to heaven totally blocked so long as bishops were directing the traffic. But these irrational attitudes are not to be attributed only to the superstitious spirit of the age. They also reflected political considerations in certain quarters. Nobles, barons and others who had been over-generously enriched by previous monarchs were especially fearful of being made to hand back to the bishops church property long in their possession. And their fears were better grounded than the court would have it, for the bishops began to assert their rights strongly and seemed to regard external pomp as essential to the Christian religion. They behaved with all the arrogance we commonly find among Roman ecclesiastics, and made no allowance for the customs of the time or the tender consciences of the weak-minded mob.

It was under these circumstances that King Charles, reversing natural priorities, began to undertake a religious and ecclesiastical union between England and Scotland in place of the civil union that had eluded his father. In 1637 he tried to introduce the liturgy in Scotland and threatened even sterner measures, [17] thus making all his subsequent actions suspect to the people. From this source alone descended the torrent of future miseries that was to involve all Britain in slaughter. I have no mind to chart its course in detail, being worn out already by British disputes, but my task requires me to trace them briefly in this turbulent and disgraceful period.

D. 1638–1649

[17] The episcopal party in England did much to defame and discredit the Scots, calling them factious rebels and a shame to Christianity. Every trick was

---

1   *Dira superstitio*. Both in classical Latin and eighteenth-century English the primary sense of the word was religion carried to irrational extremes.

used to incense the King and his ministers against this unhappy people, until its public freedom in which it took such pride was totally enchained. So the Scots were obliged, first to send begging letters to the King to excuse their conduct, and then to send emissaries to the English to solicit support for what they called the tottering cause of British liberty and to prevent a road to universal slavery from being opened up through their flanks. But when these tactics failed, they took up arms against the King around the year 1638.

[21] When negotiations for peace were restarted at London [in 1640], new problems arose. Cunningly the Scots crept into favour with the English by insinuating that their common freedom was in jeopardy and could only be assured by a show of armed force; that they were not to be regarded as enemies, as before, but rather as guardian angels who had taken up the cause of God and men. What can the mask of religion not hide? There is not the least doubt that these moves by the Scots were inspired by Cardinal Richelieu and the court of France, which was supplying the rebel leaders with money, arms and provisions, encouraging the break-up of English unity, and hatching other plots to drive Britain into civil war.

But a worse sign of the times was that the leading party in the English House of Commons was totally under the influence of the Scots, doing nothing without their advice.... They were loaded with honours, called brothers, and solemnly voted £340,000 sterling. Finally, in 1641, having meddled too officiously in other people's business, they agreed terms of peace with the King. [22] The sum of these was that the Scottish parliament, meeting at Edinburgh, was to establish a constitution closer to a republic than a monarchy. The retreat from Newcastle was sounded, and the northern English counties were never so glad as to be rid of their armed guests.

Anxious to retain some vestige of authority in the Scottish parliament, the King rode post-haste to Edinburgh, inspected the army on its return home, and with remarkable generosity received the troublemakers into his favour. His demeanour in parliament won over many, but his opponents stood firm by their principles. Though he made every effort to tame their ferocity with a prodigal scattering of honours and rewards and assurances, he was finally forced to accept the situation and agree to the following terms.... [23] Thus Charles was left king in name only, but continued to bestow titles on his enemies.... It was as if the order of Nature was reversed. Contempt for the throne began to be rewarded as loyalty had been before....

Then the English followed the Scottish example in attacking the King, [24] using every means to weaken his majesty. Their rebel leaders, avid for supremacy, stopped at nothing to turn the fair face of the kingdom into infamous anarchy. So houses collapse when too much stress is laid on one pillar or beam. For as weight is carried evenly by every part of a well-designed building, so every magistrate in a well-ordered kingdom must bear his equal share of the burden. But in Britain in those days the King was a mere shadow and his former advisers and partners in empire sought absolute power for themselves....

[25] It was the King's weakness that he would yield to any terms sooner than give up one jot of his beloved system of church government, which was the principal cause of contention. He forgot that an essential part of personal freedom is the right of choice in matters of religion. If only he had recognized that it was characteristic of the British to keep changing their preference for forms of church government, he might have overlooked their mischief for a while and waited until they gradually recovered their senses. But Providence, it would seem, had already ordained their punishment, for the parties rushed to arms with such haste that one could hardly tell which were the aggressors.

At this crisis the Scots, who had sown the first seeds of the mischief, tried to intervene as mediators....

[31] This treaty [the Solemn League], which lawyers of that time were accustomed to refer to as a declaration contrary to fact, was approved in Scotland, first by the General Assembly of the church and then by the estates, in 1643. Even among the King's friends there were many who were blind enough to approve it. But wiser heads throughout Europe thought otherwise and endeavoured to mock the whole affair. Foreign observers found it astonishing that the Scots, under a treaty which they were required by law to uphold, should be bound to defend a king against whom they had taken up arms; also that the English, abandoning their own rites, should convert so easily to the worship and discipline of the Church of Scotland. Henceforth the entire administration of Scotland was in the hands of its clergy. Though the terms of the League lay outwith the sphere of civil government, it was the ministers who were allowed to send a delegation to plead for its ratification by the English parliament....

[37] After this [Marston Moor], the King's cause began daily to decline. Many whose loyalty had wavered before now openly adhered to the fanatics, thinking that nothing could be done against the joint force of England and Scotland. But at the same time the Scots began to lose respect from those who had recently worshipped them as England's divine saviours. Although the earl of Loudoun and other Scots leaders [38] had been admitted to the councils of the English fanatics, the credit for the campaign in northern England went entirely to the English generals and troops. For example, the victory at Marston Moor was sometimes attributed to the earl of Manchester and sometimes to Cromwell, hardly at all to Leslie whose troops formed by far the largest part

of the confederate army. Manchester's generalship is not in dispute but conflicting reports of Cromwell's came from different quarters. Many hailed his conduct in the battle as outstanding, while others kept insisting that he was nowhere to be seen in it, having watched the struggle from a point of vantage. So providential fates may have saved him to scourge Britain. But credit was certainly due to the Scots for their attack on Newcastle. This restored the coal-supply to Londoners at a time when almost all of them would otherwise have died of cold. Not gratitude, however, but resentment followed, which later gave way to open hostility.

But the ingratitude of their English brothers was the penalty which the Scots deservedly paid for rebellion. God, growing angrier, proceeded to afflict them with terrible disasters on all hands. The earl of Montrose, in arms for the King, filled northern Scotland with bloodshed and slaughter, pillage and lamentation, while Edinburgh and most of southern Scotland were consumed by a dreadful plague. So the whole nation languished and would have come close to total destruction but for two great men—the earls of Argyll and Loudoun—who sustained it more by policy than force of arms.

[54] The English and Scots disagreed on what do with the King [in 1646]. The former said it was the business of the English parliament. The King was on English soil. The Scots were not allies in a common cause but mercenaries hired at the outset of war. Having come for English money, they had no right to leave with any of the spoils of victory. Highly indignant, the Scots argued back that the King was theirs as well, the father and lord of both nations. He was free, not captive, having freely entrusted himself to their care; it was for him to choose where he wanted to stay. But if captive he were, the Scots had a duty under the Law of Nations to protect him, and could not hand him over to the English without taint to the honour of Scotland. As for their help, it was the height of impudence to call them mercenaries. They had succoured England in terms of the Solemn League; their country was exhausted by the cost of the war; English soil was still wet [55] with blood they had shed in the common cause of freedom. But if mercenaries they were, they should be given their due—not a tenth had yet been paid—and the King should be allowed to live wherever in Britain he felt safest.

The English found it hard that the Scots should want to benefit twice over, from their rights as allies and their pay as mercenaries, but ... decided to calculate what was due to them in order to get them out of England....

These terms agreed, the question of the King arose again, but when the English saw how difficult the problem might be, their parliament intervened with a solemn declaration that the Scots, while in England, had no competence in law to deal with the King. The point of this judgement was to give the Scots a hint of what they might expect if they failed to hand the King over: their money would be withheld to compensate the English for damage and loss.

[56] The Scots thought it necessary to refer this matter to the estates in November, and the King was encouraged by the delay. Relying on many friends in parliament, he believed that legislation would check the army's greed and offer him safe lodging in his ancestral realm. But his hopes were soon dashed. The rebel leaders used various tactics to win over a majority, with threats to some and promises to others, even inducing some to believe that the King would be best off if he trusted himself to the English. So envoys were sent to the army with orders to hand him over on the understanding that no harm would befall his majesty or his person. This action of the estates displeased the Scottish people as a whole, but how it could be remedied none could agree.... This was the unhappy end of the Scottish expedition into England. Half of their money was paid, the rest is still owing to this day. No nation was ever so praised for undertaking the defence of another or so rewarded with loathing and indignity. The English took the glory and the victors' prizes. The Scots, in thrall to the doctors of their kirk, [57] brought home nothing but stripes, humiliation and fasting.

[57] The policies of the Independents were controlled by Cromwell, a scoundrel of exceptional ability [*ingeniosissime nequam*], ready of speech and decisive in action, an outstanding artist in hypocrisy. Casting up his eyes and invoking God's name, he would weep and pray, swear and protest, until his hearers were caught in the nets he spread for them....

[59] Summoning Argyll and the church leaders to Edinburgh, he acted a part to perfection, and with amazing skill so far outdid them in deceit and sanctimony as to have Hamilton's expedition publicly condemned as a violation of the Solemn League.... Some say he concerted with the Scottish leaders his plans to punish the King, but the evidence points otherwise, for all the public statements of the principal churchmen make clear that they stayed true to God and their religion by honouring the King very highly. They were republicans in church matters but monarchists otherwise, and they later deplored the unnatural parricide committed on Charles. One must therefore conclude that Cromwell's sole aim on this visit to Scotland was to cultivate the ministers' friendship and lay the groundwork for the future greatness he already had in mind for himself. The Scots, that is to say, missed a perfect opportunity to emerge from the shadows of error. Had they carried out their obligations under the Solemn League and fought for the King with a proper unanimity not even the whole riff-raff of schisms and factions in England could have hindered the peace of the realm. It is all too certain that the future happiness of Britain will depend on the causes of that civil war being thor-

oughly examined, and on the rejection of principles which could, once again, lead a giddy people to make similar mischief. The same results or worse are bound to ensue unless king and [60] parliament are accorded in all respects their separate rights and privileges. And further to that, if a nation is to be free, clergy and laity must attend to their own functions without meddling in those of the other. Any kind of tyranny is grievous to Britons, but infinitely the most damaging is that of the clergy.

[61] It was as though a band of highwaymen or thieves in the night had sat in judgement on some innocent wayfarer or father of a family and condemned him to death because he had not handed over his clothes and his money immediately on demand but had defended himself and killed one or two of his assailants in the struggle. So it was with the King. His judges, exalting themselves over the people whom they claimed to represent, disregarded all laws human and divine and laid murderous hands on their sovereign, solely because he had defended his rights and refused to abdicate his rule to faction. This was the end of Charles I, an excellent prince, worthy of a much kinder fate. He is blamed by most for his over-commitment to episcopacy, but I see this rather as reflecting a vice of the times, for the whole of Britain then suffered from a disease of the mind whereby everyone would sacrifice his life and his country for whatever religious opinions he had formed through education or prejudice. Love of one's neighbour was unknown; [62] partisan zeal ruled in place of law and order. Britain suffered a fate which history shows has befallen other nations with similar vices: a fine system of government was cast aside and replaced by hideous tyranny.

E. 1649-1658

[64] Scotland, which had been first to undermine the late King's authority and had led the rest of Britain into civil war, was now the first to show long-delayed penitence and revert to its duty by declaring Charles II king.

[69] Montrose, so far from complaining of the severity of his sentence, gallantly wished that he had flesh enough to be hung up in every town in the land to commemorate his undying loyalty to the King. So he perished in the flower of his manhood, a man without equal in those days for magnanimity and variety of talents.[1] The supreme penalty was also paid by about forty of his friends and supporters. A few years later these instances of cruelty were of great

---

1   Although several times praised for his brave generalship, Montrose has also been criticized, implicitly for licensing atrocities in the north as a 'scourge of God' (see extract above, fo. 38) and explicitly for undertaking his last expedition 'more for his own glory than to help the King' (fo. 65).

service to courtiers and episcopalians by justifying their similar treatment of presbyterians.

[81] The ministers[1] were hoping for a bloodless victory, not wishing (as they claimed) to have the blood of their English brothers on their hands, but Cromwell in the meantime was constantly on watch to bring the Scots to destruction. One of his tricks was to let the Scots hear that his army was short of supplies and intent on making its escape. To give credence to this rumour he moved camp and withdrew to near the town of Dunbar. Some say his plan was to embark his troops and take safe passage to England, and many have believed he was in genuine trouble and not tricking the Scots at all, but nobody who considers the outcome of his move will believe it was made under duress. Like Hannibal, Cromwell was a man of habitual cunning and duplicity, qualities which governed all his actions both in peace and in war. The Scots followed up his withdrawal by seizing the camp he had vacated, pressing hard on his rear as though victory was already in their grasp. In so doing they had every opportunity to achieve it, but the soldiers were held back by the tender-hearted clergy who thought the hour had come for their bloodless triumph. It would be more to the honour of Scotland, they declared, to make the English yield and send them home safe than to punish their errors by the sword. With such vain notions on their lips, they occupied the hills overlooking Dunbar and surrounded Cromwell whom they took to be on the point of surrender. The troops chafed [82] at their leaders' delay. Earnestly they begged permission to descend and meet the enemy in fair fight, which they said was a safer and more glorious tactic than to hang around the camp while the English escaped in the ships that lay anchored off-shore. Their grumbling increased when the next day showed vessels coming in to land and English baggage ranged on the shore, as though Cromwell had decided to embark it. He planned, having readied his own men for battle, to entice the Scots down from the heights or tempt them into making careless mistakes through over-confidence. Nor was he disappointed, for the Scottish troops and their leaders behaved as though Cromwell were already a prisoner in their camp. Their negligence did not escape his attention, but to make his victory easier he held them at bay until nightfall, hoping that a surprise attack under cover of darkness would catch them off-guard or asleep. His chance soon came. Rain during the night led the Scots to discard every vestige of military precaution. Then,

---

1   The pages preceding this account of the battle of Dunbar contain scathing comments on 'ecclesiastical tyranny' in Scotland: the ministers' bullying of the young king, and 'the grotesque and ridiculous folly, which no sane man would credit' of their purges of the army. Clerk's antiquarian interests did not extend to the reconstruction of battles, his accounts of which tend to be flat-footed. He is more animated than usual on Dunbar.

at early dawn, Cromwell led out his troops, attacked the Scottish outworks, and so terrified [83] his opponents that first the Scottish soldiers and then their leaders took flight.... This was that celebrated battle of Dunbar, fought on 3 September 1650. I am aware that others give a different account of it, saying that the Scots came down from the heights against the advice of some of their leaders, and that they were attacked and routed by Cromwell before they had time to form ranks, but I think my account is more probable. For many years after the battle a story persisted among the Scottish rank and file that their army had been betrayed to the enemy by Leslie and his commanders. Why else, it was asked, had they been told to dowse their tinder-fires, neglect the watch, and stop taking care of their weaponry? Why had the King's best friends and supporters been kept from the field? Why such disparagement of the enemy, such sure expectation of a bloodless triumph? But soldiers who fail in the exercise of their duty always find others to blame. I myself ascribe everything to the will of God, some degree of chance, and Cromwell's shewdness. The Scots deserved a beating, and deservedly punished they were.... [84] Cromwell, who well knew how to profit from his victory, set out directly for Edinburgh to lay the foundations of the slavery under which, deservedly, Scotland groaned for the next ten years.

[84] It gave the King secret pleasure to find so many of his enemies exposed to public anger by the bad tactics and humiliating flight [at Dunbar]. He hoped, moreover, that the country's leaders and especially the ministers might thereby be induced to treat him in a more mannerly fashion. And in this he was right, for at that juncture all Scotland seemed to incline towards him as the only remedy for its woes.

Cromwell's victory would indeed have been no bad thing for the Scots if that mood had persisted. They lacked neither courage nor resources. But the chance was thrown away by the ministers and the factious nobility. All those who exercised any authority in the running of the country had become so infected with a hunger for power that nothing could induce them to hand back any to the King. Supreme authority was claimed by the earl of Argyll. Though his austere behaviour had earned the King's dislike and the malice of the lords, he so controlled the civil and religious administration [85] that Charles had to follow his instructions. And he it was who cooled the people's ardour for their king, knowing that if he yielded to popular demand and restored the ancient form of Scottish monarchy, all the ministers would have decamped to Cromwell.

In response to the country's wretched condition Argyll arranged for the estates to meet at Stirling.... [86] Most of the measures they proposed had the same end in view. Religion being regarded as the mainstay of government, religion took pride of place in their concerns. Apart from the appeal it had for the people it had got so entwined with civil affairs that there was no disentangling it from them. Now whether this religion they cared so much about was truly religion or anything more substantial than words and delusions[1] the reader must decide for himself, but it is a fact that the estates toiled hard to give the ministers satisfaction—witness this grotesque decree[2] in which I read that all who had aided the King's father some years back under the duke of Hamilton were to do public penance in church, as though they had violated women's chastity or committed some crime which was commonly in Scotland subject to censure by the kirk.

After enacting that ludicrous measure they gave serious thought to crowning the King. One might perhaps have thought that the ministers would have considered this ceremony useless, especially in turbulent times with a purposeful enemy breathing down their necks. But the proposal was greeted with general applause, no doubt so that they might not seem frightened of Cromwell, and also to let the rest of Britain know under what conditions they would accept a king.

[99] After capturing Dundee, Monk campaigned throughout the north of Scotland, conquering as much of the country as his victorious army could reach. And in line with Cromwell's aim to subdue Scotland permanently he placed garrisons in every strategic location.

But the most significant aspect of Cromwell's rule is that he followed the example of the Romans, who gave citizenship to those they defeated and shared all the privileges of the conquerors with the conquered. Nowhere else did he think this policy so essential as in dealing with a people accustomed to freedom and their own laws. He knew that the Scots had been overcome more through their own internal divisions than by force of arms, and that as soon as they agreed among themselves and collected their strength they would shake off his yoke. Accordingly, he devised some form of British union and allowed the Scots to send thirty delegates to consult with the English parliament about the new Commonwealth of Britain. These were elected by the shires with equal representation of nobles, barons and burgesses, but I do not know of any who attended the discussions apart from the earl of Argyll and the laird of Swinton. Otherwise the constitution of the British Commonwealth parliament was drawn up by Englishmen. It did not last long, however, for

---

1   *An vox tantum et umbra inanis* (lit. 'or only a voice and empty shadow').

2   *APS* records no such decree by the Stirling parliament of 1651. Under the Act of Classes, 1649, supporters of Hamilton's expedition had to 'satisfy judicatories of the kirk' to be eligible for public office (*APS*, vi, II, 146-7).

Cromwell, seeing all roads open to his ambition ... [100] dissolved parliament in 1653.

[104] Cromwell's rejection of the name of king enabled him more plausibly to strengthen his authority as Protector. He arranged for himself to be installed once again with wide and absolute dictatorial powers, as if Britons had been born into slavery and had never known the taste of freedom.

Later, in the exercise of his tyranny, in making mock of the whole British people, and in fulfilling his immoderate ambitions, he went far beyond what any king before him would have dared to attempt. The miracle is that in 1658 he died peacefully at home among his friends, and indeed on 3 September, a day he was accustomed to celebrate. Some see a judgement in the fact that he died on the anniversary of two of his victories over royalists. Certainly we may say that, if he had not died then, he would have experienced the British people's vengeance on his tyranny one way or another. And yet, notwithstanding his vices, one can see that he possessed a vast and vigorous will. His was the first real union of Britain. Many other leaders of military and political distinction have attempted it, [105] as we have seen, but found that supremacy over Britain as a whole was easier to win than to keep. Cromwell gave a shining example to posterity of what a united Britain could achieve, for if we leave out of account his usurpation and tyranny, we find that he made the name of Britain more famous throughout the world than it had ever been before.[1]

F. 1660–1688

[115] The two parliaments resumed their ancient forms, but unfortunately Cromwell's coalition of the three kingdoms totally vanished.

[117] The King's council then debated the question of what to do about Scotland. Much as they all hated Cromwell's acts, most of the English seem to have approved of his subjection of Scotland as a sort of adjunct to the kingdom of England, and wanted to keep it that way. The taming of Scotland had cost English kings so much blood over the centuries that it hardly seemed sensible to set it free again. But the King's view prevailed that the Scots should be given back their nation as before.... He well knew that they had been the authors of all his previous misfortunes, but in fairness was willing that these should be ascribed to the bad advice of certain individuals rather than the nation as a whole. He was mindful, too, of the blood shed by Scots on his behalf and that he had been the cause of their enslavement by Cromwell. But

---

1   For qualified recognition of good effects of Cromwell's rule in Scotland, see extract below from fo. 118.

Scotland's manumission also owed much to the earl of Lauderdale, who assiduously encouraged the King's love of his ancestral kingdom and obtained its freedom as a reward for all that he had suffered on the King's behalf.

So by royal command Cromwell's castles were razed and their English garrisons removed along with every trace of Cromwellian rule. To the degree that the Scots knew no greater shame than to be beaten in fair fight and overpowered by the English they were able to share in the joy of the King's restoration. [118] But there are many to this day who swallow their pride and praise Cromwell's rule, saying that under it Scotland prospered as at no other time, with trade flourishing and justice firmly upheld. This view results from comparison with the next regime. For although divine Providence seemed to have granted Britain freedom and happiness, Scotland enjoyed these least, being totally subjected to government by wicked, rapacious and cruel courtiers.[1] No justice was ever done if it conflicted with their mercenary interests, while the sum of their policy was to exalt the King above the law and keep the people captive in gilded chains. As for Scotland's trade, not only was it sacrificed to English greed but almost all the shared privileges the Scots had enjoyed were cancelled, as though they were foreigners or inveterate enemies, thus ending such advantages as they had had since the union of crowns in trading with England's American colonies.

In church matters they were no less afflicted. Either to follow the English example or out of hatred of presbytery, bishops were restored against the wishes of most. This could have been a matter of very little account if tender Christian consciences [119] had been treated gently, but presbyterians were persecuted worse than Catholics. Twice forced into rebellion, they were punished accordingly, put to death or tortured or variously proscribed. I would not say their harsh treatment was entirely undeserved—they had done much amiss under Charles I and behaved much too obstinately under his son—but nothing they did can justify the cruelty of that administration in the eyes of good men. And here I cannot omit to mention that, soon after Britain's freedom was recovered, it was proposed to the King that in all consideration of Scottish business he should admit English as well as Scottish advisers to his council. Indignantly rejected at first by the King, this proposal later became practice, with the result that England's chief ministers of state were consulted on all Scottish matters.

---

1   Compare Clerk's 'Testamentary Memorial' on 'necessitous, rapacious and mercenary court-favourites' (Appendix C. p. 184 below). As he moves into territory that he associated with Fletcher's parliamentary speeches, these triple adjectival constructions seem to echo Fletcher's 'greedy, ambitious and for the most part necessitous men': *Political Works* (London, 1737), 274.

[119] The Scots' proposal ... that he should complete the great work of union begun by his grandfather was less welcome to the King than was believed, for he secretly chose to keep his loyal and loving Scottish subjects hostile to England in case, through the natural fickleness of the British peoples or as a result of earlier troubles, a situation should arise where he would need their help to put down disturbances in England. [120] But since this was a motive he could not safely reveal, and since the wiser of his courtiers recommended union, he allowed Lauderdale and other Scottish nobles to take soundings on the matter in the Scottish parliament.

[124] Finally the whole contrivance[1] went up in smoke. Some would have it that the King's aim in starting these talks was to promote not union but division and to emphasize obstacles that would dash hopes of union for all time to come. Such a policy could only be traced to the advice he received daily from Lauderdale, namely that his best means of strengthening his rule was to keep English dissidents in order through terror of the Scots. Lauderdale well knew that the history of Scottish invasions of England had been far from happy, but he thought the time might come when England would be weakened by faction and the King or his successor might need Scottish aid. He therefore kept whispering in the King's ear the well-worn axiom, divide and rule. Thus he showed his true colours as an instrument of the throne. If he had considered what was best for the people, he would have given just the contrary advice.

[124] The remaining history of the government of Britain under Charles II I leave to others, noting only that a happy relationship between English and Scots would have been possible if only they had wanted it. But due to the fickleness of the people and the licence and ambition of courtiers one may doubt if, even in that reign, Britain was more often at peace than at war. Conspiracies, rebellions, massacres, proscriptions, perjuries—the noise of these things filled every corner of the island. The religious and civic life of the whole nation was thrown into confusion[2] [125] to satisfy the unbridled passions of some courtiers and their mistresses.[3]

The King's untimely death is attributed by many to papist intrigue and by others, with more probability, to his voluptuary excesses. But however he died and in spite of the ministers of state he employed, he deserves to be ranked

---

1   In fos. 120-4 Clerk has recounted the failure of the Scots to win exemption from restrictions under
     England's Navigation Act and their subsequent agreement to hold talks on union in 1667, postponed by
     England until 1670. His summary of the Somerset House negotiations derives entirely from the Minute,
     as printed in Defoe, *History*, 'General History of Unions', 21-30.

2   *Divina & humana omnia miscebantur.* An alternative translation is 'religion and politics became totally
     confused.'

3   'And their mistresses' (*scortorumque*) is a late addition to the MS in Clerk's hand (?1746).

among Britain's better kings. He had many vices, but also great intellectual gifts which in a less decadent time would have assured his future fame.

He was succeeded by his brother, James II and VII, whose actions I would rather conceal than bring to light. His bad administration brought one comfort to Britons, that it opened the door to liberty and taught their future monarchs how to reign. In Anglo-Scottish relations his major concern was to bring both national churches under papal control; as for political union, he unquestionably undermined it, like his brother before him and for the same reason. His strenuous pursuit of his religious policy provoked popular rebellion and he was finally forced to cede Britain and its colonies to William of Orange.

G. 1689–1706

[125] The start of William's reign gave Scotland its best chance ever for an agreed union with England. Fearing the vengeful return of the king they had deposed, the English were reduced to such desperate straits [126] that they would have consented to almost any terms that would bring the Scots under the same rule as themselves. William, who recognized the force of united councils from his experience of the Dutch confederation, had raised the matter with the Scottish magnates, and accordingly in May the estates of Scotland proposed union with England and nominated commissioners to negotiate it ... and wrote to William as follows....[1]

[127] This alacrity of the estates would have done no harm if they had merely told William of the people's wish for union, but they went further, sending three delegates to offer him Scotland's crown. Thus the act of one moment shattered the link they had been trying to forge. The crown once offered and accepted, all thoughts of union were set aside. The Scots made prisoners of themselves to the English and later duly paid for their lack of forethought. If they had restrained their revolutionary ardour for a few days only, kept the crown in their hands and put first things first instead of shamefully doing what was expected of them, surely they would have won fair terms from the English and brought prosperity to their country long ago. Nor would William, their god, have regretted such a delay, for he was to learn that nothing better could have happened in his reign than a union which would have united the councils of his kingdoms and quelled the seeds of discord that were to torment him wretchedly throughout his life.

So ... Scotland was left with nothing but its name and ruled like a province of England. Tokens of freedom [128] kept people quiet for a while: the

---

1   This letter, which envisaged an incorporating union under a single parliament, is twice quoted in Book 6 (see below, pp. 108 and 131 below).

restoration of presbytery was welcome to most, while regular meetings of parliament blinded the mob with deceptive reminders of the past. But trade declined daily as a result of the war against France, which the Scots, with nothing to gain from it, were called upon by England to join. Their merchant ships were seized by the enemy and pillaged, their young men pressed into the army overseas to the detriment of industry. All of which could have been borne if the Scots had been allowed some credit or advantage when peace came, but, to the contrary, they were treated by the English and the confederate leaders not as allies but mercenaries. The treaty of Ryswick ignored Scotland, did not even mention it, made no attempt even indirectly to offer reparation for its losses. But Scotland had come to expect such rewards for serving the English cause. Furthermore, Scotsmen had no part whatever in the numerous embassies sent to foreign nations at that time by the King of Britain. It was as if they themselves were foreigners, and that the fellowship of the British peoples gave them no rights except to be killed by the French. Scotland, I have said, enjoyed a token freedom under William, but a shadowy token at best, for it was governed entirely by Englishmen and England was the workshop where all Scottish policies were framed, [129] church and state matters alike being determined by a few English courtiers. The King's choice of High Commissioners to the Scottish parliament, the mandates he gave them, the giving or withholding of the royal assent—all these were entirely directed by English ministers, who even in the King's council had to be consulted when Scottish business was transacted.

Reduced to wretchedness and almost despair by these practices, the estates of Scotland determined to assert themselves and began with measures to restore their trade....

[129-131[1]] A brief factual account of these measures and England's counter-measures, from which William is exonerated. Clerk concedes that Darien would in any case have failed because of the organizers' inexperience, incompetence and profiteering.

[131] It was now true indeed [132] that the Scots had become England's slaves, since they were denied not only their rights as fellow-Britons but their rights under the Law of Nations. They could not live without trade, yet were hindered from practising it by English embargoes and their own poverty. Moreover, in the years since the union of crowns, they had conducted their own affairs in such a way that now they could neither live in fellowship with the English nor secure their freedom by breaking away.

1   Much of the rest of Book 4 can be summarized. Relevant political issues and events of 1690-1706 are sketched hastily by Clerk with very little comment. Several speeches in Book 6 cover this ground retrospectively.

So throughout William's reign one heard nothing in Scotland but curses and complaints. As one calamity followed another,[1] there were always some to stir up public feeling in secret and blame the rule of a good and brave king as the cause of every trouble. Anti-English feeling was so fierce and indignant that even chance occurrences were laid at their door.

But the time was approaching when union would at last remove or alleviate these hatreds and rivalries. So, to explain this great event properly, we must turn first to some remote causes....

[132-6] English and Scottish responses to the succession issue. William recognizes that the future peace of Britain depends on the Scottish parliament.

[136-49] Anne's initiation of the conference on union, 1702-3. Clerk's long account of the negotiations is entirely translated from the Minutes (Defoe, *History*, Appendix, 112-31). From these he infers [148] that the English broke off negotiations because of Scottish intransigence over the future of the Company of Scotland.

[149] The Scots went home angry, few of them trusting the English commissioners' assurances that dealings would be resumed and completed. They believed that only under the gravest compulsion would the English ever concede anything to please the Scots.

So mutual hostility increased daily. England's prosperity and Scotland's wretchedness were so incompatible that armed insurrection would have caused less surprise than the fact that the two nations had been at peace for so long.

[149-56] The Act of Security 'shows the Queen's advisers that substantial measures, not words alone, were needed to pacify the Scots' [150]. Her assent to it in 1704 forestalls rebellion and leads to her being hailed as 'mother of the nation'. She hopes that the Act anent Peace and War (1703) will 'persuade the English to share with the Scots the *imperium Britannicum* that they had usurped' [151]. William Atwood's book 'revives ancient and obsolete fables of England's dominion over Scotland' [152]. England's Alien Act [152-3]. James Anderson answers Atwood [153]. The affair of the *Worcester*: anti-English feeling causes a miscarriage of justice [153-5].

To remedy the situation the Queen dismisses ministers less inclined to union and appoints Godolphin as Lord Treasurer, 'a man of great conciliatory powers'. The Scottish estates agree to re-open talks on union, debating only whether commissioners should be nominated by parliament or the Queen. Hamilton stands out for nomination by

1   Glencoe receives no specific mention (see Intro., n. 5, p. 22).

parliament but yields 'in the expectation that the Queen would nomi-
nate him'. The parliament of England responds to Scotland's offer of
friendship, repeals the Alien Act and nominates commissioners [156].

BOOK 5
Negotiation of the Treaty of Union, 1706

The 'conference' on Scottish representation in the parliament of Great Britain

[50[1]] Predictably, this proposal[2] did not much please the English commissioners, who feared from it what they were always from the start most wary of, namely, that speeches from both sides would lead to quarrels reflecting the strong convictions, anger and impatience of both nations, and that these would disrupt negotiation and perhaps nullify attempts to bring about union. Disturbed by such considerations, they withdrew into private session, [51] but not knowing how to refuse the requested discussion they soon returned, and the Lord Keeper on their behalf informed the Scots that on the next evening at six o'clock they would be willing to discuss the proposals now on the table. The Scots in the meantime offered the English soothing assurances in private[3] that they would not be so inflexible as to frustrate the Queen's hopes and the wishes of the whole British people. And both sides undertook to bring to the discussion, not flourishes of eloquence, but relevant arguments and above all patience and calm.

At the appointed time the commissioners all assembled, and at first sat in total silence.[4] This was soon broken by England's Lord President of the

1   Reference to the folio numbering of SRO, GD18/3202/5.
2   The initial English offer of thirty-eight seats in the House of Commons had been received by the Scots commissioners 'with the utmost dismay and indignation' (49). They then proposed a 'conference' on the matter, a departure from the normal practice of negotiating through exchange of written papers.
3   This is Clerk's only reference to 'private' negotiations between Scots and English commissioners outside the formal sessions.
4   Compare the corresponding passage in Clerk's 'A journall of the proceedings of the Scots & English Commissioners...' (SRO, GD18/3132, 77-8): 'Our Lord Chancellor in a speech gave the reasons why we insisted on a greater number, but it was a long time after he had done before any of the English offered to speak, so that the conference at the beginning resembled a quaker meeting, but at last the E of Pembrook spoke a little in answer to him, he again was answered by the E of Marr, afterwards Secretar Harley made a very foolish speech wherein he told us that he did not doubt but we came there to give down some of the 38, for that we certainly thought them too many, he was answered by Sir David Dalrymple, therafter the Lord Treasurer spoke and was answered by my Lord Stair, then the Lord Keeper spoke & was answered by the Chancellor. The Duke of Devonshire also spoke a little, but being a very indifferent man, he made such a speech as resembled him self. The Laird of Pitmedden likeways spoke

Council who discoursed with his usual eloquence and politeness on their proposal that the Scots should send thirty-eight delegates to the British House of Commons. The Lord Chancellor of Scotland replied to him, explaining what was sought by the Scots. Then Lord Treasurer Godolphin, that shrewd and good man, made a long speech which was answered by the earl of Stair, second to none in his time as a natural and forceful speaker. Next came a speech from Mr Secretary Harley, a law unto himself for effrontery.[1] Further speeches on the English side came from the duke of Devonshire, Lord Wharton, the Attorney General Sir Edward Northey, and finally the Solicitor General Sir Simon Harcourt, a speaker of quite exceptional fluency. Others who spoke for Scotland were the duke of Queensberry (easy, felicitous and brief), the earl of Mar (not so much an orator as a bold man of action), [52] and the earl of Loudoun, who in a vigorous, manly style displayed no mean knowledge of his country's laws and customs. These were followed by the two brothers Sir Hew Dalrymple (Lord President of the Court of Session) and Sir David Dalrymple (Lord Advocate), whose merits can be inferred from the offices they held. The last Scottish speaker was William Seton, younger, of Pitmedden. He was a man more conspicuous for probity than eloquence, but on this occasion, as later in the Scottish parliament, he gave no ordinary testimony of his zeal for union.

It would shame me to attempt to match the style of each speaker's contribution to the discussion, so I shall place before my readers a summary of the arguments.

The Scots asserted that in the best models of national unions the make-up of the common council or parliament had been determined partly by population and partly by the dignity of the participating nations. Accordingly, in ancient times, when cities or peoples united, it had been quite proper for some to have at least twice or thrice the votes of others. The same thing could be found in modern constitutions, like England's or Scotland's, where some shires were allowed to return a disproportionate number of members to parliament. It would be fruitless to enquire now how such a distribution of suffrage had come about, but in founding this new kingdom of Britain nothing stopped us from correcting such anomalies as might exist. In designing this new parliament we had two alternatives: either [53] to abolish the existing parliamentary structures in both countries and create a new one for Britain as a whole, distributing seats on a basis of population and national dignity, or to combine

a little being persuaded that there was a necessity for him to open, but had better said nothing.'
There is some discrepancy on the order of speakers between the journal and Book 5 and between both and Defoe, *History*, 'Of the Last Treaty', 12-13.

1   *Qui neque dicendi neque audendi ullum nisi quem vellet modum noscebat* (lit. 'who used to recognize no limit of speaking or daring other than he might wish'). The reference is presumably to Harley's sarcasm, recorded in the previous note.

into one the entire memberships of the two parliaments as constituted at present. That is to say that the Scottish nobility would join with the English to form the upper house, while the lower would be composed of the Scottish barons and burgesses added to the English members. Scotland's national dignity, indeed justice itself, demanded this concession from England. To proceed on any other basis would, they feared, frustrate everyone's hopes for union.

The English replied as follows:

'What you say about unions is quite true in theory, yet we find that in fact, when parliaments have united, their membership has been determined not so much by considerations of national dignity and population as by revenues: the amount that each nation contributes to the common good through taxation and so forth. We admit, of course, that our English parliament allocates its seats very differently. Some counties return more members than others without any regard to population or revenue. But a parliamentary model bequeathed by our ancestors cannot be approached like the framing of a new one. It does not permit considerations of justice or equality; to alter it at all would be to put our whole society at risk. [54] And parliamentary reform is harder to achieve the more people it affects. Roughly seven hundred members comprise our two houses. You can therefore well imagine how union would be obstructed if the ancient constitution of the parliament of England were to be changed in any way.

'That is our dilemma. It leaves us no choice but to preserve in its entirety a parliamentary structure that has stood the test of so many centuries, and to meet the case of union by adding to our ranks a certain number of Scots to form the parliament of Britain.

'You say it is a slight to the dignity of Scotland that we should retain our full complement of members and be willing to admit only a fraction of yours. But what a revolution we are bringing on ourselves by this arrangement! Consider how your votes may affect the balance of parties in the house. And that is only one of many inconveniences that we are forced to disregard to promote this island's welfare. As for your dignity, so far from being lessened by joining with us, it will surely be increased through mutual exchange of honours and privileges.'

The English advanced many other arguments, all to the same purpose, all making clear to the Scottish commissioners that it would be labour in vain to try to have all their members included in the parliament of Britain. But even among the Scots [55] many foresaw problems if the bodies were to be joined in that way; Scotland, they feared, would soon become a wasteland if so many men travelled south. They did indeed recognize a possible impediment in those Scottish acts which threatened dire penalties on anyone attempting to

D

injure or diminish the honour and dignity of the estates, but since they had been given freedom to negotiate, and since there was no way that harm could come to Scotland unless the treaty were ratified by parliament, most of the commissioners agreed to concentrate on obtaining fuller representation than the English had so far proposed. They therefore urged that, in accord with universal custom, Scotland's suffrage should be determined, not by revenue, but by considerations of national dignity and population. There were approximately eight million people in Britain, of whom at least a sixth or a seventh were Scots; therefore Scotland should be allowed a sixth or seventh of the Lords and Commons in the British parliament, more or less a hundred representatives in all, to look after Scottish affairs. Scotland's wealth, they kept saying, was not to be measured by taxes or revenues but by its people. Revenues would increase in the course of time, but at present, before Scotland felt the benefits of union, it was impossible to say by how much, for there was no limit to the prosperity that both peoples could hope for from union. 'Let us therefore institute a population census for the whole of Britain, and we undertake to accept [56] the proportion of seats that is our due. Meantime we beg you to lay aside suspicion and any rooted prejudices you may retain. Let offences and injuries, however they arose, be utterly forgotten. Be fully persuaded that we are as sacredly dedicated to the peace and welfare and prosperity of Britain as you are yourselves. And that being so, the number of delegates we send to parliament need matter to you little, for the more they are, the more Britain will find its most ardent devotees among the Scots.'

Then the English replied:

'It is natural justice that those who have money should have the spending of it. Therefore, in a common parliament, the proportion of votes should be determined by wealth; otherwise you have greedy and spendthrift people claiming rights in more than belongs to them. It is true that Scottish revenue will grow after union, no one knows how much; but to that objection we have a ready answer. There are levies and taxes now in force in England which are temporary only and will end when our debts are repaid. None of these can increase the revenue from Scotland because we have already agreed to compensate you for them. It is therefore quite clear that Britain's revenue will derive much more from land taxes than from duties on trade or liquors, and our transactions of recent days have also made it clear that scarcely a fortieth part of the land tax is to be raised in Scotland. [57] Judge, then, how eagerly we seek your fellowship from the fact that we are assigning you thirty-eight members, when a just estimate of wealth in terms of public revenue would entitle you to scarcely thirteen.

'But, you will say, the land tax in Scotland could in future be raised. So indeed it could, and so it would be in England, always in the same proportion.

'Another point not to be overlooked is this. You have recently been pleading Scotland's widespread poverty in order to beg off our taxes, and we have very readily accepted your excuses in the matter of the land tax and others. How amazing, then, to find you now clamouring for a burden more heavy than any tax or duty! Could any burden fall more heavily on Scotland than a multitude of members of parliament? It is natural to expect that taxes raised in Scotland will be spent in Scotland—that would at least be good British policy, to ensure that money needed for your public expenses would seem voluntarily contributed rather than exacted. But one cannot say the same about the cost of your multitude of delegates. They will be making regular journeys to England, [58] and on every occasion Scotland's resources will journey with them.

'If our aim had been to trap you under guise of doing you a kindness, there we had a perfect opportunity. But it is your fellowship, your welfare, your prosperity we seek, not your ruin, destitution and misery. We do not want to deal with a dejected and exhausted people, shorn of all its worldly goods. We want strong, active, thriving partners with whom we can do business. We want something like a union of equals, not a union where one party buries the other with pretended favours and concessions. And while on the subject of your representation, we advise you to take note that there are counties in England which can yield more to Britain's exchequer than the whole of Scotland. Think how invidious this union would be if Scotland were to be given more weight than those counties in the common council of the kingdoms.'[1]

Much more was said on both sides of the question, but nothing to give the Scots any comfort. Their perseverance was later rewarded, however, by a small concession on the part of the English, which will be reported in due course.[2]

1   By describing parliament here as 'the common council of the kingdoms' (*commune Regnorum concilium*), in which one of the kingdoms must not be allowed to carry more weight than an English county, Clerk seems to comment ironically on English deafness to the Scots' argument *ex dignitate Regni*.
2   The English next day raised their offer to forty-five.

PART TWO

From Book 6

BOOK 6: The Debate on Union
in the Scottish Parliament, 1706-7

[1¹] The Queen's first concern was to summon the English and Scottish parliaments to ratify the treaty which the commissioners of both nations had drawn up at London.

Accordingly, thinking it essential to begin with those who had most at stake, she directed the estates of Scotland to convene at Edinburgh on 3 October, 1706.

Meantime the duke of Queensberry, who (as we have said) had been appointed her deputy in Scotland, made his preparations to set out for that kingdom. Armed with the royal commission and authority, he was enthusiastically received with shouts of good wishes by the mob that poured out to greet him, and was conducted to the palace of Holyrood at Edinburgh.

There let us leave him, contemplating the momentous task committed to him, while we briefly examine the condition of Scotland at that time.

This kingdom was labouring, as before, under numerous distresses and various factions. There were many who had so fervently longed for a union or association of the British kingdoms that they were ready to accept one on terms good or bad, believing that the welfare of all Britain and of the Protestant religion in particular depended on it. [2] Others greatly wanted union for a quite different reason. They hoped that resentment over English oppression would quickly and easily induce all sectors of the population to shake off the English yoke, including even the rule and authority of the Queen herself—goals which they saw as more likely to be achieved the worse the terms of union were. There were also a great number of Jacobites who disliked the notion of all kinds of union equally, since they saw that any Anglo-Scottish accord would be based on designating a successor to the British throne other than the one whose hereditary title they favoured. (The supreme good of

---

1   Reference to the folio numbering of SRO, GD18/3202/6/2, the second of two surviving MS copies of Book 6. The first has been heavily corrected by Clerk and is often barely legible. The second has incorporated Clerk's corrections and is easy to consult (apart from the first twenty sheets which are in Clerk's difficult hand) but the copyist has introduced errors of his own. Where I have translated the reading of MS 1, or departed from the reading of both MSS, this has been stated in the notes.

4 Britain lay, they judged, in restoring James Stuart.) A further group of cautious
and fearful souls dreaded all change, all innovation. Happy so long as they
5 thought themselves free, they could rejoice in Scotland's poverty and other
distresses by preferring them to the uncertainties that union would bring.
Some such, including numerous churchmen, fell victim to terrifying dreams
and delusions and prophesied woe of all sorts for themselves and their posterity
from the threats they imagined that union would pose to the Church of
Scotland. Episcopalians feared just the opposite: that the establishment of
presbytery under union would ruin their hopes of restoring bishops. [3] And
there were also presbyterians ready to affirm that union, meaning the domi-
nance of the weak by the strong, would finally force bishops upon them, since
those 'spiritual lords' would have legislative power in a British parliament.

In listing these factions I say nothing of individuals—the malevolent, the
ambitious, the time-servers, and some envious men who thought nothing well
done that was done without them. So it did not take long, in the midst of such
divisions, to recognize the extent of the problem that lay ahead and the
passionate hostility that union would arouse.

These initial reactions amazingly distressed the duke of Queensberry and all
supporters of union who had hitherto supposed that they had earned the glory
of a successful outcome and that the merits of this treaty would assure their
everlasting fame. They would therefore have been reduced to utter despair,
had not perhaps the Destiny of Britain, the firmness of the Queen, and the
unshakeable courage of the Commissioner prevented it.

It was decided that the best way to start was by summoning the Ministers
of State and the Scottish Privy Council to determine how the factional
condition of the country might as far as possible be cured. But on this they
failed to agree. Many took fright at the rumour of an expected defection,[1] and
began to waver. Eventually, after various proposals had been made, they
determined to follow the practice agreed on by the commissioners in England
and to suppress publication of the Articles of Union until parliament met. [4]

Their reasons for this decision were the same that had influenced the
commissioners and were justified by the event. Since opponents of the union
could not point to its terms, there was a temporary abatement of calumny and
abuse. A breathing-space was given for calm reflection which helped the
passage of the treaty a good deal.

Now the eyes and minds of all Britons, and indeed of all neighbouring
peoples, were turned on the parliament of Scotland. Never in the whole
history of Britain had any event so stirred expectation. Everyone knew that

---

1   There was doubt about the voting intentions of the marquis of Annandale, recently replaced as Secretary
of State (HMC, *Mar and Kellie*, i, 296, 302).

on that parliament depended the destiny of the island, the Queen's authority, and the religion, prosperity, welfare, peace and security of the entire British people.

At last, eagerly awaited by all, the day came for parliament to assemble.

I need hardly waste the reader's time by describing the pageantry which traditionally marked these occasions in Scotland. Enough to record that when the estates had gathered in Parliament Hall, the royal commission establishing the Commissioner's authority and jurisdiction was produced and read, and then the Lord Clerk Register read out the Queen's letter as follows:

[4-11] Here Clerk translates the Queen's Letter (*APS*, xi, 305-6) and the formal speeches of Queensberry as Commissioner and Seafield as Chancellor (ibid., Appendix, 98-9). Parliament orders the speeches to be printed. The Articles of Union are read for the first time.

[11] Discussion followed about the minutes of the commissioners for union. Many saw no point in making them public, but publication was ordered to satisfy public curiosity with a full disclosure of the facts and to ensure that the estates had everything put before them.

Now, as though entering on civil war, men of opposite parties prepared to do battle to the death. An assembly which at other times recalled the Roman senate in its prudent deliberation and dignified manners now began to look like a wrestling-ring where members came forward like prize-fighters ready to exchange blows rather than thoughts. Straight away there was a considerable dispute over the admission of certain members who had been elected to fill vacancies caused by death.

Heated disputes on such matters were normal. A member's rank, or the party he was likely to favour, often determined his admission or rejection. On this occasion candidates may have solicited votes more zealously than usual, perhaps because each one supposed that his hearth and home were at stake.

These cases settled, a motion was put for the Articles of Union to be read again on the ground that they contained many points which might be obscure on first hearing and require explanation. This was opposed by those hostile to union who wanted to reject the treaty out of hand rather than have the articles re-read and separately considered. They argued as follows:

'In a matter of such weight, where not only our system of government and our established constitution [12] but also our kingdom itself and its parliament must be utterly abolished, where moreover we are expected to convert our allegiance to something like other gods, it will be fruitless for parliament to institute debate without first consulting the people. Parliament alone has the responsibility to serve and protect the people—its welfare, its peace, and its interests—but not to the extent of enacting its own death, which the Articles of Union clearly prescribe.'

AGAINST
UNION

In reply it was said that the aim of such harshly-worded speeches was all too easy to detect. They were a delaying-tactic, to give time for the opposition to prejudice and inflame public opinion by falsely interpreting terms of union which had hardly been read, much less understood. 'Scotland is not to be destroyed and abolished, as you claim. Rather a nation already destroyed is to be restored to life and growth. Under union the British peoples will retain their separate names, their places and titles of honour; their rights and privileges will not be reduced or enfeebled but increased and embellished. And if the views of learned men on this matter are relevant, consider the opinion of the learned author of *De Jure Belli et Pacis*, who states that

> when two nations are united they do not lose their separate rights but communicate them to each other, as the rights of the Sabines and those of the Albans were transferred to the Romans, thus making (as Livy says) a single republic. And so it is of kingdoms, when they are not linked merely by treaty or by having a king in common but are truly joined into one.[1]

As for the consent of the people, the tribunal to which the estates appear to be appealing, remember that this meeting of ours was appointed by the Queen, not so very long ago, [12A[2]] in order to consider union with the English. As the royal proclamation summoning parliament confirms, it was primarily to do so that the people delegated its authority to the members elected. And even if it had been otherwise, one could well argue that parliament's authority is pre-eminent. But what point would there be in consulting a people which for almost a century has been demanding this union as what Britain most needs? This parliament will not be breaking new ground or claiming a jurisdiction unprecedented or unheard of by the people. Did it not, a few years back, and without consulting the people, alter our country's and its own constitution by transferring the crown from James Stuart to William of Orange and his wife Mary, and since to Queen Anne? Did it not abolish the episcopate, which then formed its third estate? On its own initiative it increased the membership of this august assembly, indeed without adequately considering fair representation of the shires. There may be some here who secretly deplore all those steps. They should none the less remember that the assembly which took them not only gave the Queen herself her right to our throne but also established the nature of the authority which this parliament has.'

1   Clerk's marginal note (trans.): 'see Grotius, Book 2, Ch. 9, 9.' The passage was cited by William Seton younger of Pitmedden in his speech on Article 3 (Defoe, *History*, 'Abstract of Proceedings', 78) and by Clerk in 'A Letter to a Friend', 10, but had been familiar to supporters of an incorporating union at least as early as 1702. See J. Robertson, 'Andrew Fletcher's vision of union', in R.A. Mason (ed.), *Scotland and England, 1286-1815* (Edinburgh, 1987), 222.

2   Two sheets are numbered 12 in MS 2.

The opposition was silenced by these arguments, and having failed in their aim of deferring this business altogether, they tried to slow it down by degrees. So they began to ask for a few days' grace to collect their thoughts and [13] make enquiries. Their tactic was seen through, however. When the question of allowing a short adjournment was put to the vote, the majority determined to proceed at once to a further reading of the articles. Next they objected to the taking of votes: the purpose of the reading should be to clarify issues and allow general criticisms of the treaty to be raised. Here the objectors were allowed to have their way. It seemed fair that the whole banquet of terms should be laid out to view, each seen in the context of the others. The more palatable terms would perhaps make others less difficult to swallow.

Thinking that this decision had won them a victory, the opposition redoubled their efforts to stir up the mob, while parliament was kept busy in debate and the minutes of the commissioners' transactions in London were being scrutinized. Accordingly they sent messages to every shire in the kingdom, imploring the populace to provide whatever instant aid it could in the present crisis. 'Religion and the state are in peril; your native land lies dying; there is no one in parliament but ourselves to defend or protect it. You must hasten to help us. Delay will be fatal for us all.'

And so, from all parts of the kingdom, a crowd of turbulent troublemakers flocked to Edinburgh to the aid of these self-proclaimed defenders and protectors of their country. [14] Many who lived far away sent petitions to deflect the estates from the course they had embarked on and ward off this union which would be fatal to Scotland and harmful to Britain as a whole. The city had never seen such crowds. The buildings and streets around Parliament Hall were thronged, and there was every prospect of violence. Soon after these auxiliaries arrived a somewhat rash report circulated that parliament was getting stuck over the second reading of certain articles and was thinking of either abandoning its business or postponing it. It was then that the enemies of union first showed their presumption, exulting in extravagant and premature glee as though the treaty had been totally rejected. But when they learned their mistake they became so enraged that they could hardly refrain from using force. The Commissioner was their first victim as he made his way home from Parliament Hall. They savaged him with insults and threats, showing no human feeling, let alone respect for his royal status. Then they turned their impotent fury on parliament itself, loading it with abuse. Those they regarded as the champions of their cause they led home in triumph.

These leaders included the dukes of Hamilton and Atholl, the Earl Marischal, Lord Belhaven, George Lockhart, Andrew Fletcher, and other representatives of the barons: all either Jacobites or enemies of the court party. They were treated as heroes and indiscriminately praised by their supporters.

While parliament and the city were in turmoil, the Commission of the General Assembly of the Church of Scotland, then sitting, began to consider [15] how best in this emergency to look after their own interests and those of the church committed to their charge.[1] After considering various proposals they decided by a large majority to start by instituting a period of prayer and fasting, to be observed publicly as well as in private, asking God to guide the deliberations of parliament and people for the good of the church and the nation. Their right to do this was later questioned, since customarily prayer and fasting could only be ordered by parliament or the monarch. Many, however, claimed this jurisdiction for the church by Divine Right.

Attempts to endorse these religious proposals were made by several members of parliament, chiefly opponents of union who were far from being wholeheartedly concerned to uphold the church's authority. They jumped eagerly at the chance of espousing the fast, primarily in the hope of winning ministers and people to their side. But most members were outraged by this jesting with religion. 'In the case of plague,' some said, 'or war, or famine, it is right for us to fast and to pray to God sincerely to prevent or remove such calamities. But such is not the case now. The effect of this fast will be to aggravate anger and conflict, to excite the populace to violence and disorder by making them afraid of some impending catastrophe. [16] History shows us that fasts have very often been instituted for trivial, indeed thoroughly discreditable reasons, enabling ambitious or revolutionary leaders to win popular favour and get away with their crimes: waging war in a doubtful cause, attacking or besieging a city for no good reason, making treaties that might not be advantageous. Prayer and fasting has been a common trick of unscrupulous politicians. You know how commonly in war, when things have gone badly, chagrin is covered up with a great show of self-congratulation, and thanks given to God as though for some remarkable victory. That sort of impiety should have no place here in this house. If prayers are to be offered, let us ask that God will favour this long-sought union of the British kingdoms and bless us by granting our wishes.'

This view was taken not only by laymen in parliament but also by certain churchmen in their General Assembly. The more intelligent among them, such as William Carstares, the wise, learned and eloquent Principal of Edinburgh University, went even further, weighing the present against the past:[2]

'Our church did not fare too well in the old days', he said, 'when ministers were overmuch involved in politics. Civil administration is best carried on by the king and his parliaments. [17] We churchmen should leave the job to them

1   Clerk's father was a lay member of this commission.
2   Reading *praesentia cum praeteritis librantes*. MSS *liberantes*.

and get on with our own—religion and the cure of souls entrusted to us—and we should practise those with a diligence and zeal worthy of our Heavenly Maker.'

But the ministers fought pretty resolutely in the matter of prayer and fasting, for the spirit of faction had got into them too. They finally decided to send a letter exhorting ministers to institute fasts in their separate congregations and parishes. These were as solemnly observed as those normally ordained by parliament or the monarch, which was all the more gratifying to the clerics because they saw it as a mark of that absolute authority vested in the church which they had long sought and claimed.

Their next undertaking was to outline an act to be referred to parliament, that would protect the government of their church under union. They decided to submit to parliament the main heads of this act in the form of a supplicatory address, which ran as follows:

[17-19] Here Clerk translates the Address by the Commission of the General Assembly to the Parliament, 11 October 1706 (SRO, CH1/3/8, fos. 230-32).

When this communication was read in parliament, [20] some members moved that these religious questions should be debated forthwith, as the churchmen wished, since it had always been customary in parliament to give priority to matters concerning the church. Men of all parties took this occasion to vie with one another in appearing as champions of the kirk, and especially those who had consistently opposed or made trouble for its ministers, *i.e.* the Jacobites and episcopalians. Their ruse was sufficiently transparent. Their interest in the state of the church in Scotland was only to serve their own ends, since the establishment of presbytery was as little to their liking as the union of the kingdoms. But they thought it politic to adopt this and similar time-wasting tactics while gathering forces to combat the militia or force a dissolution of parliament. The ministers were later satisfied by parliament's resolution that the guarantee they sought would be added to the treaty before it was approved, and that their form of church government now by law established would be a basic and inviolable link in the chain binding Britain together. With this business out of the way, the estates proceeded to the reading of the articles, with much dragging of feet and cries of protest from the opposition.

Varied, random remarks were made on individual articles as the parties joined battle and displayed their true colours. Some sought clarification; some carped; most tried to discredit the whole treaty by interpreting it amiss, heaping abuse on the negotiators. In their envy or ill-will they forgot that their delegates had been given a free hand to negotiate by the Queen and the estates themselves and were now referring everything to parliament.

On the first article various preferences were expressed for different kinds of union, as will be related below. On Article 2, with regard to limitations to be imposed on future rulers of Britain, a wide range of visionary political schemes was put forward and the opinions of every writer [21] about forms of monarchy rehearsed. On the third to eighth articles members invented the strangest chimeras to inflame the mob and keep it firmly on their side: that Scotland was to be surrendered to the English, that its laws were to be entirely subjected to theirs, that its trade was to be subjected to intolerable tax-burdens, that its people were to be wiped out by poverty and starvation or forced to emigrate.

All these notions were industriously spread abroad and swallowed by the mob with amazing avidity, but what chiefly upset it was a rumour that the honours of Scotland—its crown, sceptre, and sword of state—were to be handed over to the English. No lie was too absurd to be used in the attempt to plant seditious thoughts in weak and wayward minds. It is hardly surprising that the mob broke all bounds and continually threatened to resort to violence to avert such a national disgrace.

On the following days the remaining articles were read as far as the fifteenth, dealing with the so-called 'equivalent', or compensation due by England to Scotland. This was long and fiercely fought over. Some bemoaned the impoverished and debt-ridden state of the kingdom. Others declared that a nation which could not pay its own debts was hardly in a position to pay those of others; they thought the outcome would be that Scotland would be overwhelmed by the debts of England. Others again thought the Scottish commissioners had miscalculated. [22] These disputes so prolonged debate that it was decided to clarify the whole matter by appointing a select committee of parliament to investigate every provision of this article and report back. Union supporters hoped that this inquiry would either lead to an adjustment of the equivalent to Scotland's advantage, if she was found to have been short-changed, or else remove the grounds for complaint. Three members were appointed from each estate: from the nobility, the marquis of Montrose, President of the Privy Council, the duke of Argyll, and the marquis of Tweeddale; from the barons, Sir Alexander Campbell, son of the earl of Marchmont, George Baillie and John Haldane;[1] and from the burgesses, Robert Inglis, John Erskine and Hugh Montgomery. To these were added James Gregory and Thomas Bower,[2] professors of mathematics at Edinburgh and Aberdeen respectively, learned men expert in figures.

1   MSS *Hadinus.*
2   MSS *Bonerus.*

After the sixteenth and seventeenth articles a longer pause was made at the eighteenth, dealing with tax-laws relating to both the public and private spheres of law. Here again opposition members saw an excellent opportunity for delay. They united in moving[1] (and many of the other side agreed with them) that all English acts dealing with excise on trade and liquors should be published, since it was incongruous for a people to be subjected to laws or conditions of which it had no knowledge. Due process, and the majesty and dignity of parliament, demanded that everything be laid open to view, while the peace and welfare of Britain depended on union being negotiated [23] with the utmost wisdom and care, lest the whole nation regret too late what it had embarked on. They said it was absolutely incumbent on the estates to lay aside party disputes and undertake this hard task, since nations, once united, could not be disjoined without all kinds of danger to religion and society. Overwhelmed by these arguments, the unionists were forced to give way, although they could see that this delay put their cause in jeopardy. It was therefore decreed that the select committee mentioned above should enquire into all facets of British trade, and in particular, by comparing the duties charged by England and Scotland, should investigate what additional tax-burdens Scotland might experience under union. As for the English tax-laws, the book that summarized them, though somewhat prolix and knotty, was ordered to be published, but with the proviso that meantime debate should begin on the other articles of union. It was evident to most members where all this would lead, but fools as well as wise men had to be gratified, and the trifling advantage they foresaw from the manoeuvre was made clear by the unfortunate outcome. For after the English tax-laws had been published, inaccurate accounts of them based on misunderstandings were widely circulated, so that things went from bad to worse. There was an outburst of anger and hatred, contention and abuse. 'Our people will be ruined', was the cry. [24] 'We are bled white already, and as poor as can be; these taxes are the last things we need.' This kind of talk was accompanied by threats, and neither the majesty of parliament nor the dignity of the Commissioner was sufficient to safeguard supporters of union from the rage of the mob.

The agitation reached parliament itself on October 20th,[2] a memorable day which seemed likely to put an end not only to discussion of any form of union for all time to come but also to the authority of parliament and the lives of the delegates who had treated with the English. For when debate had continued until nightfall, and darkness had emboldened those lurking outside, the Commissioner was surrounded as he unsuspectingly left the house to go home.

1   Reading *proposuerunt*. MSS *praeposuerunt*.
2   Clerk's mistake. The riot was on 23 Oct.

He was shouted at, almost knocked down by stones, and would surely have been killed if his guards had not hurried him off to the palace. This seemed like the beginning of a long-planned outrage, yet I can scarcely affirm that this was the night when all the conspirators had decided to come out in open insurrection, for many people seemed unsure of what plans were afoot; they milled about in the streets in a state of confusion, and confined themselves to scattering taunts and threats. What the conspiracy lacked above all was a leader: the assemblies and riots were poorly co-ordinated. Though many had secretly fomented insurrection, no one was bold enough to lead it openly. The duke of Hamilton led the anti-union faction in parliament, [25] and the rioters called on him to lead them too; his popularity was such that they thought he would deny them nothing. As he left Parliament Hall they greeted him as their chief and begged him to take charge of the kingdom in its hour of peril. Promising to do whatever he told them, they accompanied him to the home of his brother-in-law, the duke of Atholl. One can hardly suppose that these great men were displeased by such ardour, but I find no evidence that they made any reply to the people's demands. Both had determined to wreck the union in any way they could, but not at the cost of civil strife and bloodshed.

While the mob stood waiting for orders outside the duke of Atholl's door, their anger boiled over in a dastardly attack on the Lord Provost of Edinburgh, Patrick Johnston, who lived in the vicinity.[1] Johnston, who was also a member of parliament and had been one of the commissioners for union, was a defenceless, harmless man, well-deserving in all other respects. But the crowd decided to do away with him. They rushed straight to his house and set about trying to break down the door with beams and any instruments they could lay their hands on. Alarmed by the noise, his wife ran to the window in desperation; her loud cries for help roused the city guard who came to the rescue. Dispersing as best they could, six of the trouble-makers were taken and imprisoned. [26] Thus the provost's family was saved, but the rising was by no means put down. The crowds in the streets grew noisier. All the lights in the city were extinguished so that the ring-leaders could not be identified. There was much stone-throwing, much breaking of windows and doors. Even the guard, heavily outnumbered, was challenged and attacked. It was a long and dangerous night for everyone, but especially for those who favoured union: no one was safe in his own home.

Among various projects of the disorderly rabble was one to seize the lower gate of the city and prevent the Queen's militia from coming to the aid of the guard. In this way they thought to bring the unionist majority in parliament

---

1   This account of the attack on Johnston draws on Defoe, *History*, 'Carrying on of the treaty in Scotland', 28-9.

under their control. But by the grace of God and the Destiny of Britain, help came in time to prevent these disasters. The Commissioner got wind of the plan. He reckoned that it was safer to infringe some of the city's laws and privileges than to allow it to be taken over by the frenzy of criminals. Delay on his part would encourage the mob; a long-smouldering fire would erupt into a great conflagration. He recalled that outbreaks of civil war almost always stemmed from the negligence and sloth of magistrates. They were easily prevented, but once blood had been shed soon got out of control, so that harsher measures had to be applied. So, after obtaining the approval of some members of the Town Council, [27] the Commissioner instructed the militia to restore order in the city and keep watch over the safety of parliament and the populace. As well as bringing peace, the army's entry into the city put a brake on similar disturbances in future. The plotters began to recognize the gravity of their actions, and that slighting the Queen's majesty and the authority of her Commissioner and parliament would not go unpunished.

In societies torn apart by faction it is sadly often the case that what magistrates do to preserve the peace is interpreted amiss. Those who can agree on nothing will unite in rejecting what should heal their divisions. So the Commissioner's action which brought peace to the city was maliciously criticized, and the leave given to the army to enter the gates was loudly and bitterly condemned. Some said it was unthinkable for a free parliament in a free kingdom to be surrounded by troops. Parliament seemed under attack, as though members were being forced to alter their votes to suit a handful of courtiers. Others blamed the provost and his council for letting mercenaries into a town which had always relied on its own citizens for protection, and for entrusting to mercenaries its rights and privileges, indeed the freedom and welfare of the whole nation. The Commissioner's friends did their best to excuse what he had done on grounds of necessity. But the real cause of anger soon became clear: the opposition's hope of provoking riots and forcing the dissolution of parliament had been frustrated. Trusting in the mildness of a woman's rule [28] and the gentleness of her deputy, they had thought they could get away with anything. After-wards, all they could do was to try to win over the militia to their side, which they did with all manner of flattering speeches and bribes, appealing to them to abandon[1] the cause of union and go against the Queen's wishes. Finally, having found the troops more dutiful than they expected, their last recourse was to accuse them of disloyalty for blocking their efforts to act (as they claimed) 'in the public interest'. By taunting the army with weakness and cowardice they emboldened their own supporters.

---

1   Reading *deserere*. MSS *disserere*.

On the day after the disturbance the Commissioner summoned the Privy Council and explained to them what had happened the previous night. They expressed various views on how to check the risings that had started in the city and were spreading throughout the kingdom, but they first thanked the Commissioner for the timely help he had provided. They begged him to persevere in his task of protecting the commonwealth against the threat of rioting and upholding the Queen's sacred majesty and the authority of parliament. An edict was also proclaimed enjoining all magistrates of the shires and burghs to take all steps to prohibit and prevent seditious gatherings. The Edinburgh council was to hold masters responsible for keeping their servants out of broils, and university professors were to ensure that their students remained within bounds on pain of death. In case of rioting anywhere in the kingdom officers of the militia [29] were to be allowed to use force to maintain the peace, and granted indemnity if rioters were killed or wounded.

On 25th October, when tempers had cooled a little, parliament reassembled. By direction of the Privy Council the Lord Chancellor reported on the dangerous public disorders and revealed the whole course of events: how some of their number had been threatened, others attacked; how no corner of the city had been unaffected by the tumult; how the outcome of these threatening events would have remained in doubt but for the army's entry into the city and the Commissioner's care for the peace of the realm, the Queen's majesty and the authority of parliament. He went on to refer to the Privy Council's edict prohibiting seditious gatherings, as sanctioned by various acts of parliament. His speech occasioned a huge parliamentary battle, many members becoming so enraged about the troops in the city that one was led to suspect that the riots had had their roots in Parliament Hall. It was certainly clear that those hostile to union had no great aversion to the rising. None of course dared to sponsor it, but many wanted to excuse the populace, and predicted the most awesome tumult and bloodshed that would ensue when Scotland's rights and privileges were placed at risk in the surrender to England known as union. After much argument along these lines, the High Constable, the earl of Errol, protested against the army's continued presence in the city, claiming that he alone had the privilege of protecting parliament with guards who were on duty in the streets day and night. [30] The Earl Marischal added that his traditional right was to set guards within Parliament Hall, but that the recent action had infringed not only the rights of the High Constable and himself but also those of parliament and the city of Edinburgh. Adhering to these protestations were the dukes of Hamilton and Atholl, the marquis of Annandale, the earls of Wigtown, Strathmore, Selkirk and Kincardine, Viscounts Stormont and Kilsyth, Lords Sempill, Oliphant, Balmerino, Blantyre, Bargany, Belhaven and Colville, and from the barons Sir James Foulis of Colinton, George

Lockhart of Carnwath, Andrew Fletcher of Saltoun, John Brisbane, William Cochrane, and many others who need not be named.[1]

Next, in the name of the whole house, a motion was made to thank the High Commissioner for his action in restoring order and to urge the Privy Council to persevere in guarding the kingdom against popular disturbances. This roused the opposition, and especially the protesters, because they feared it would lead the Commissioner to abuse his authority in a dictatorial manner. But when they saw that a majority was in favour of the vote of thanks, they proposed to divide the motion, dropping their objection to the thanks but expressing outrage that the care of the kingdom should be entrusted to the Privy Council while parliament was in session. These trivial, time-wasting disputes resulted in the motion being passed [31] as put—both thanking the Commissioner and investing the Council with responsibility for the safety of the realm—but with a rider reaffirming Edinburgh's charters against allowing the army into the city. Many, however, wanted the troops moved out, objecting that the estates appeared to be meeting more in prison than in parliament. There were bitter exchanges on the subject, with the marquis of Annandale particularly outspoken in his criticisms:

'Shall we (he asked), who live in a free kingdom, put up with this barbarous restriction even before we have agreed to join our kingdom to another? This union spells death to our nation's liberty, but not until it is passed into law should we be ringing our parliament with troops. See what has become of the freedom of the estates of the realm of Scotland! Should their representatives sit mute? Should their mouths be sealed by a soldier's sword? We have all heard the story of the dumb man who thought to kill his father until love for his father taught him to cry out.[2] Let that example teach us not to sit here in silence while our fatherland is destroyed. But in this free kingdom our tongues must be bridled by the army! What use are these soldiers who stand with drawn swords at the doors of this venerable building? Are we not safe enough within the walls of this city, long famous for its loyalty to this and all earlier parliaments? Are we not safe enough relying on our fellow-citizens, whose oldest instinct has always been to guard the well-being, peace and prosperity of the kingdom? Let guilty men fear, let traitors tremble, and honour be to those who protect our freedom and our rights. We within these walls have nothing to fear. They call us the fathers of our fatherland, and rightly; so let us care for our fatherland and serve its interests before our own, [32] its needs

1   Lists such as this derive from the parliamentary record. Here Clerk gives up less than half-way through the list of adherents (*APS*, xi, 309).

2   Cf. Lord Belhaven's speech on Article 1: 'Shall the Hazard of a Father unbind the Ligaments of a Dumb Son's Tongue; and shall we hold our Peace, when our *Patria* is in Danger?' (Defoe, *History*, 'Abstract of Proceedings', 36).

before our private advantage. If any think otherwise—but I accuse none, I hope none can be so shameless—let them come to their senses; and since the fortune of Scotland has given us this chance, let us seize it in a manner worthy of our ancestors, worthy of the name of Scotland. The soldiers should go;[1] they should go fight our enemies and win glory abroad; but if they stay here, let them act for the good of the people who provide their daily rations. They are here, some say, to keep peace in the city. Not so! Rather to strike fear into faint hearts and restrict our freedom of expression. Free-born men must be free to debate the state of their country. And if there is to be a treaty, it will not be valid unless entered into by free peoples, acting not under duress or in fear or for promised rewards but with national interests at heart.'

This sort of talk quite failed to persuade parliament to shed its defences, but a good effect of the marquis's speech was that the troops remained quietly at their post, neither giving or taking provocation. So ended the Edinburgh riot. But the opposition did not totally lose hope. They laboured tirelessly to confuse public opinion and inflame it by stigmatizing unionists as traitors.

From October 25th to November 1st the house read the remaining articles. Then it moved on to more particular consideration of each. [33] How to relate its proceedings I scarcely know, for what I now seem to hear is not the sound of voices but the din of battle. Feelings ran so high, divisions so deep, that my story seems more of a civil war than a parliamentary debate. But not to keep my readers waiting longer on the threshold, I shall tell it as best I can.

There was first of all much confusion and disagreement over voting: whether votes should be taken after the second reading and discussion of each article. The opposition wanted to defer decisions until the views of the English parliament were known. They argued that since the present proposal for union had originated in England, it was proper for the English to declare their reaction to it first. It would be humiliating for Scotland to agree to proposals after earnest consideration, only to find them scornfully rejected by England, as had happened rather often before. Since the union of crowns the Scots had many times proposed a union of the kingdoms. Even under James VI, articles of union had been agreed on by delegates of both countries, approved by our parliament, and thrown out by the English in an insulting manner. Experience should warn us not to keep on doing what we had so often regretted.

The answer given to this specious reasoning was that it was the prerogative of British rulers to summon either parliament at will and give it matter to debate. The main reason why this session [34] had been called was to give us a chance to settle union on our own terms. It was a tribute to our honour and

---

1   *Discedant, effugiant, abscondantque se* (lit. 'let them depart, let them flee, let them hide themselves'). An example of pseudo-Ciceronian rhetoric which defies plausible translation.

dignity that we would be in a position to offer eternal friendship to the English
and propose terms on which the whole British people might unite. If the terms
had been offered by them to us, we might well have seen them as imposed by
lords and masters on slaves and vassals. 'Conquerors know that it is better to
give laws than receive them. The laws we frame now the English can accept
or reject. We offer peace or war; let them choose which they prefer.'

This was a devious argument, craftily voiced by some union sympathizers
in fiercely contemptuous, anti-English tones. The opposition fell for it. They
thought that anti-English feeling would induce anti-union feeling and give
them a majority in the end. So now, as though the object of the exercise were
to dictate terms to England, they wanted this changed and that added, asserting
parliament's authority to alter the treaty for Scotland's advantage. Delaying-
tactics were a thing of the past: every article was to be scrutinized by everyone.
But the brains of factious men are infinitely fertile. Either they could not bear
to give quick assent to anything, or they did not want union on any terms at
all. So a new obstacle was thought up. Many members stated that they had
been elected by their shires and burghs with a mandate to oppose union
strenuously, and that [35] various shires and royal burghs had sent addresses to
parliament to the same effect, subscribed by vast numbers of signatories.
Edinburgh had been among the first to deprecate union as ruinous to the
monarchy, the dignity of parliament, the people's freedom, and its own rights
and privileges. The shires of Perth and Linlithgow had written along the same
lines. But although these addresses had been read in the house, they had no
impact, because the will of parliament, strengthened by mature deliberation,
was considered of more account than the voice of the people led astray by one
faction or another.

The next disputed question was where to begin. Some wanted to start at
the beginning, while others declared that they could hardly approve Article 1
if they had objections to the rest. When confusion seemed imminent, a vote
was taken, and it was decided to debate the first article first. The opposition
then tried to raise another obstacle, arguing that the religious issue of providing
for the security of the kirk should be given priority over every other article.
The good of the kirk has always, through the ages, been a favourite argument
among Scots of all parties claiming to be its most loyal supporters, usually for
reasons unconnected with piety. On this occasion the majority saw no reason
[36] to debate such a measure before union in some form had been approved.
But after much time spent on these disputes it was unanimously conceded that
approval of Article 1 would not be binding if later articles were rejected, and
would be followed immediately by provision for the security of the church.

Then Article 1 was read, 'that the two kingdoms of Scotland and England
should be united into one kingdom by the name of Great Britain.' Against this

was cited immediately the declaration of the rights and privileges of the Scots which had been sanctioned by parliament just after the arrival of King William III in Britain in 1688.[1] This had subsequently been confirmed by several acts of parliament and was by many regarded, not undeservedly, as the fundamental guarantee of Scottish sovereignty.

This move surprised union supporters, who insisted that nowhere in the Claim of Right or any subsequent act was union said to violate our rights and privileges. On the contrary, the Claim favoured union, since it was primarily with union in view that parliament had approved it. This was borne out by reading from the parliamentary record. The 'Letter of the Estates to King William' contained the words: 'we want nothing more than that the two kingdoms should join together in a single body politic under one head and sovereign and become one nation with [37] a single parliament'. It added: 'and as proof of our will we have nominated commissioners to treat for an entire and perpetual union, and if difficulty shall arise we refer it to your royal judgement'.[2] A notable feature of this letter was that it had been signed by many who were now furious opponents of union.[3] But this line of argument merely angered them more. They said wise men sometimes changed their minds, and mistakes of the past now had to be corrected. Some disliked the Revolution settlement, others disliked the present government; the only thing they agreed on was to condemn the proposals before them in speeches of great bitterness and diversity. The article actually under discussion was not equally obnoxious to them all, but their criticisms were directed, now at the commissioners, now at the proposed form of union, now at other articles in particular, and most often at the whole lot together. To relate them all would be superfluous, and confusing for the reader, so it will be enough if I subjoin to each article a summary of what was said on each side.

On this occasion the most memorable speeches were those of Lord Belhaven from the nobility and William Seton from the barons. The first made a strenuous and (as we shall see) ineffectual attempt not only to attack union but also positively to ridicule it, employing all the ornaments of rhetoric, as he supposed, and a variety of visions produced by an overheated imagination. [38] The other, who had himself been a commissioner, endeavoured to defend union with arguments culled from treaties of different kinds between different peoples. But I shall not take up time repeating their speeches, since the design of my work requires me only to summarize, without fear or hope of favour,

---

1   *APS*, ix, 37-41 (11 Apr. 1689). A rehearsal for this debate took place on 28 Oct. after preliminary reading of Article 18. On that occasion Annandale cited the Claim of Right and was answered, along the lines reported here, by the earl of Stair (HMC, *Mar and Kellie*, i, 304; Hume, *Diary*, 177).

2   Ibid., 60-1 (24 Apr. 1689).

3   The 3rd duke of Hamilton is the only signatory recorded by *APS*.

what they and other speakers had to say. The following arguments against Article 1 were voiced by the duke of Hamilton, the duke of Atholl, the marquis of Annandale, the Earl Marischal, the earl of Buchan, and Lords Balmerino and Belhaven; also by George Lockhart, Andrew Fletcher and William Cochrane from the barons, and by the advocates Dougald Steuart, Sir David Cunningham and Robert Fraser from the burghs:

'For many ages past, our estates have met and debated with the single goal of leaving Scotland in a better state than they found it. They have legislated for the honour, glory and majesty of the kings of Scotland, and for the welfare, peace, prosperity and rights of the Scottish people. Why then is our single aim now to surrender disgracefully everything cherished by our ancestors and all free men, spurning and ignoring the wishes of those who put the kingdom in our care? Union is a great and hazardous matter; it is equally a great and unprecedented crime to broach fundamental change in our constitution without consulting the people. We have no jurisdiction or authority to do so. Our authorization is to promote Scotland, not to destroy it; to defend and augment our liberties, not throw them away. [39] This crucial article shows a clear surrender of the name of Scotland, one of the oldest kingdoms of Europe. We are now voluntarily to accept the yoke that England has threatened us with for centuries. Our liberty, that dear Scottish liberty born in blood and sweat, gloriously maintained by our fathers for our benefit, must perish in an instant. Our church, dignified and made famous by the blood of martyrs, must be utterly destroyed, shipwrecked in an ocean of Anglican ritual on the rocks of priesthood and vanity.[1] Our towns and cities must be left defenceless and betrayed to our English rivals, their ruins an example to posterity of a nation shamefully betrayed and despoiled of its honour and dignity. We have nothing to look forward to but utter devastation, famine and poverty, and, worst of all, perpetual servitude to cruel overlords. Remember your ancestors (so said the duke of Hamilton),[2] for who, at the mention of their venerable names, would not take heart to be worthy of them? Call to mind the brave deeds of the Bruces, the Douglases, and such, and you will burn with the same patriotic flame and not be idle spectators of calamities to come. But they say the English offer us trading opportunities, privileges, wealth. As for trade, the whole world

---

1   *Ecclesiam ... in Oceano ceremoniarum Anglicanarum interque scopulos sacerdotalium ineptiarum naufragium facturam.* An unusually elaborate metaphor, probably not Clerk's invention.

2   This sentence and the next resemble but do not exactly translate part of Lockhart's quotation from Hamilton's 'pathetical Remonstrance'. Clerk's note on that passage (Lockhart, *Memoirs*, 252-3) reads: 'This speech indeed of the D of Hamiltone was very handsomely expressed & a great many more to the same purpose yet in all this he play'd the Montebank extreamely, for at the same time that he was caballing as the head of the Tory side he was in secret with the D of Queensberry every night or at least 2 or 3 times in a week.'

is as open to our merchants as to other brave men, and prosperity comes through enterprise and daring. What are [40] those English privileges we want so badly? We need no one else's to smooth our way. And if their wealth is the attraction, let us not earn it as the reward of this wicked betrayal. Our countrymen crowd around and beg us with tears not to set this brand of shame on ourselves and our children. Our country commends to us the lives of its citizens, the dignity of its parliament, the majesty of its throne, the sanctity of its church, and the care of its rights and privileges and commerce, for today's decision affects the fate of this assembly, our sovereignty and freedom, all that is dearest to us, the welfare of our people and their children. Scotland cannot fail to assure our happiness: take care it is not we who are seen to fail her.'

Such populist harangues were answered as follows:

'The country should be thankful that we can debate its future freely, thinking not of war against our English neighbours but of a peace to be strengthened, not of separating kingdoms already joined together by nature and their crowns and various common interests but of improving the union that exists. We on our side can also congratulate ourselves that our speeches are not directed to catching the wind of popular favour but to investigating our country's real needs. As befits good citizens, our task is to set aside personal resentments [41] and partisan loyalties and consider how Scotland's strength can be restored, its security confirmed, its royal house placed on a firm foundation and assured for all time, its people's welfare promoted and protected. As for the ancient honour and glory of our kingdom, the best way to show that we care for these things is by working hard to preserve them. But an opportunity is at hand which, as far as human wisdom can foresee, will ensure that the sovereignty so gloriously guarded by our forefathers will be passed on intact to posterity. We all here profess the same goal; we all say the good of our country is what we wish for, strive for, even scheme for. Yet we seem to approach that goal in quite opposite ways. The union which you say will ruin us totally we shall present as the base on which to build a more prosperous and altogether greater future.

'There is no dispute about the union of crowns. To uproot it after one hundred years would mean destroying Britain. James VI's accession by right of birth to the throne of England had at least one good result: a peaceful subjection to his rule of a people long hated [42] but never conquered by his own. So our royal house now rules Britain. James's descendant, our great Queen Anne, now rules over English and Scots, who are united[1] in the need to preserve the joined crowns not only as a thing advantageous in itself but as the basis of closer union involving a full communication of privileges.

1   Reading *uniti*. MSS *nati*.

'This the English offer us on certain conditions, and our dispute is over whether to accept them. Disputants should always begin by segregating points of general agreement from those that are trickier, and if we follow that method we shall find that our whole controversy hinges on the point contained in Article 3, that in the United Kingdom of Britain there should be one and the same parliament. The other concessions we must make are either adjustments to the needs of a united Britain or else trifles compared with the advantages union will bring. Some may dislike the naming of a successor to the present queen, the passing over of the son of James VII whom they see as the rightful inheritor of the British throne. We urge these people [43] to look facts in the face and recognise that, union or no union, a majority inside and outside this house will support the Hanoverian succession. The people want it; Britain needs it; it will happen whatever we do here. Many have trouble with the English duties to be levied on our trade and liquors, but these will be shown to be less heavy than is thought and easily offset by what we gain from the treaty as a whole. There will be objections from some of the nobility that Articles 22 and 23 impair their honours and dignities, but others among them will take the contrary view, and in any case one must wonder whether the private prerogatives and fancied dignities of one or two families should outweigh the public good and the honour and glory of all Britain. The only difficulty remaining is the one just mentioned about parliamentary union, which can either be discussed now or set aside until we come to Article 3.

'It has long been remarked that the kingdoms should have been joined at the same time as the crowns, for a hundred years' experience has taught us that the one union without the other is bad for Britain. Even the English, who are happier than we in enjoying the royal presence every day, [44] find that happiness precarious in so far as we envy it. And as for us, we have suffered so much from the union of crowns that we must either regret it entirely or wish the bond had been more firmly tied. But Destiny decreed that Scotland should be an object-lesson to all kingdoms never to join their crowns without a full communication of privileges. No one here would wish "to revive that unutterable pain,"[1] to recall all we suffered in detail. But a few points in passing are worth drawing to your notice.

'Since 1603, our monarchs have abandoned their ancestral homes and gone abroad, taking with them the pride of our race. We were left with nothing but the bare name of a kingdom, and to make matters worse, our trade, our wealth and a great number of our people emigrated also and followed the court. Of this it is enough to remind you of what was said[2] in this house by a

---

1   *Infandum dolorem quis renovare … vellet?* An allusion to Virgil, *Aeneid*, II, 3.
2   Here Clerk's marginal note, *Vid. Fletcheri Orationes*, has been put into the text by the copyist of MS 2.

distinguished member, whose speeches have showed us our state as in a mirror. This is how he painted our kingdom's servitude: "Our queen and all her predecessors since the union of crowns have been like captives in England, rendered incapable of giving the least help to their ancient subjects in this part of Britain. Whatever concerns our profit and advantage is settled by English councils and English decrees. Our parliament itself is subject to their will, its acts [45] approved or otherwise according as they please. While our commerce is poor or non-existent, and the ruinous state of our towns and cities shows our country's destitution and depopulation, the royal commissioners in parliament have bartered away our freedom, betrayed our laws, and sacrificed much else that is dear to a free people, being either corrupted by English bribes or moved by an obsequious love of dependence. Our noblemen at court, in possession of lucrative places and pensions, have left their country stripped of its people, its wealth, its trade and navigation, so that all that remains for us is poverty and starvation and one other thing, a thing hard to credit, worse than slavery itself, which we as well as the English (to our shame be it spoken) have brought upon ourselves as ministers to their cruelty—that our blood must be shed and our bodies torn in the service of their glory."[1] If then it is true, as these speeches suggest, that the English must be served, let us serve them not as masters but as friends tied to us by a total community of interest.'

At that Andrew Fletcher, the author of those speeches and a most learned and eloquent man, flashed out in anger and impatience: 'Many times, indeed, I have said such things here about the ruinous state of our kingdom, but it is iniquitous to use them as arguments for this hateful and execrable union. Let me show you, if union you must have, that the federal kind alone can be a cure for our ills.' And in support of that view he advanced many points which will be related under Article 3.

Fletcher was followed by a shrewd and able speaker, the earl of Stair:

'When our bodies are sick we resort to medicine [46] and in times of crisis must try every means of restoring them to health. So it is with these national misfortunes which we see growing worse every day. We feel sickness buried deep within the veins and entrails of our kingdom. But alas, how fruitless have been all our efforts to cure it.

'Long ago, when our forefathers had been crippled, exhausted, and almost wiped out by countless bloody wars against England, they placed their hopes for a better future on a union of crowns, and pressed for it eagerly. But they quickly regretted their mistake, finding out too late that the English had not

---

1   Clerk's marginal note (trans.): 'Fletcher's speeches on the state of the kingdom, delivered in the Scottish parliament, have been published and are in everyone's hands.' The foregoing sentences convey the gist of Fletcher's criticisms but are not *verbatim* translation.

granted them community of privileges. What were they to do? They proposed a closer union, but this was rejected with derision. So they contrived a new kind of union, a shameful one of communal servitude. They passed laws which brought Scotland so totally under the heel of King James as to leave it with almost nothing of its ancient freedom, hoping that the English would follow their lead and enslave themselves too, so that both nations might fall under the absolute rule of their monarchs. But the English saw their peril and took steps to protect the freedom they had earned with their blood. They saw themselves trapped between the king's all-too-servile Scottish subjects and his burning ambition to rule. Here was the root of the troubles that later brought the fortunes of both kingdoms to crisis-point under James's son, Charles. For our forefathers grew restless in bondage and tried to regain their old freedom, an undertaking so vast that it led to civil war [47] (which later they glorified by calling a war of religion). Joining with the English, our countrymen stripped King Charles of his authority and transferred it to committees of the realm. Thus in shunning what was bad in the former administration we plunged into worse, a condition of anarchy (which they dignified by calling a republic).

'This price our ancestors paid for their rebellion and hoped it was sufficient to expiate their crime. But God was not placated; they were destined to suffer more, passing from anarchy into slavery again under Oliver Cromwell, a commoner and a criminal. When Cromwell died they had recourse to Charles II, whom they had earlier forced to leave the country, all of them trusting to his restoration for the peace and prosperity of Britain. Once again, as our constitution permitted, we thought nothing of surrendering Scotland's freedom to propitiate an angry king. But to give Charles his due, he was graciously pleased to respect the authority of our estates, for he was a good-natured king, open to persuasion when he took good advice, as he sometimes did. So then, under him, and later under James VII, what attempts did we not make to patch up the wreckage that the union of crowns had brought about? We planned, we legislated to revive our manufactures, commerce and fisheries, to restore our ruined kingdom to health. But our efforts and ingenuity came to nothing. Soon poverty and misery of all kinds began to spread like a plague, threatening our very survival as a nation.

'What was next to be tried? We decided to resort to our original pattern of a mixed monarchy. [48] Under James, mismanagement of civil as well as religious affairs had alienated public opinion. So, when he abdicated, under the terms of our ancient constitution we transferred our crown to William of Orange and Mary. What riches we promised ourselves from a prince born among a people so zealous for freedom, so flourishing in trade and navigation and manufactures! And this must be said, that it was not his fault that things turned out badly. He allowed us to hold frequent parliaments and encouraged

us to experiment with new legislation, but all to no avail, for anything to
Scotland's advantage was suspected and opposed by the English. Among our
experiments, as though Europe were too small a market for our trade, we
followed the example of other nations and formed a company to trade with
the Indies. We built ships and planted a colony on the isthmus of Darien. What
we lacked were not men, or arms, or courage, but the one thing most needful:
the friendly co-operation of England. The pitiful outcome of that enterprise
is too sad a story to be told again. Suffice it to say that the English did not treat
us as partners or friends or fellow-subjects of a British king but as pirates and
enemy aliens. The union of crowns gave us no security; we were exposed to
the hostile rivalry of Spain; our colony was sacked; we suffered every cruelty
an enemy can inflict. Then, with our enterprising policies crippled and our
condition desperate, two options only remained to us: [48A[1]] either to
supplement the union of crowns with full union with England, or to change
our constitution and make it more answerable to our needs. At that time the
latter remedy seemed more to our advantage, and accordingly we set ourselves
to bring before parliament laws that were thought more serviceable and sane.
We pinned all our hopes on limitations we would impose before recognizing
successors to Queen Anne. This was that memorable act, passed not long ago,
whose provisions assured among other things a strong likelihood of war and
national disruption, with Scots and English ready to run each other through.
Does any wise man not shudder at that image? Think of a war between the
limbs of one body, the arms and the feet—war between the peoples of Britain
would end the same way: the ruin of one would be the death of both.

'Some of you will ask what prevents us from reverting to our old separation
from England on the death of the Queen (whom may God long preserve).
What stops us from recognizing a different monarch from theirs? Nothing, I
suppose, if our kingdom could be restored to its former glory and splendour,
but that is an objective shrouded with problems, hopeless to think about let
alone pursue. For any successor we appoint would surely be from our ancient
royal house of Stuart, and moreover from the reformed branch of that house,
one who would therefore have a claim on England too, which he would try
to enforce. [49] Anyone we designate from that branch of that house would
expect to be placed on the throne of Britain, the throne of his ancestors, at the
cost of our lives and fortunes. And if that were to happen, as happen it would,
where would it leave us? Exactly in the position we have suffered from for
long, with Scottish kings ruling us from England again. On the other hand, if
we separate our crowns and choose some foreigner as king, who shall we find
strong enough to shield us from the ill-will and ambition of the kings of

1   Two sheets are numbered 48 in MS 2.

England? For whoever the king of England might be, he would claim our
crown either by right of birth or on other pretexts which rulers never lack.
And in that case there will be no end to our woes, as we return to the old state
of war perpetual, settling every issue in blood and slaughter.

'You see, then, that all proposals for disjoining the kingdoms will end the
same way. We should dismiss them as the delusions of disordered minds and
pass on to other objections to this union.

'This union, you say, is a shameful surrender of the name of Scotland. Has
Scotland, I would ask, had any name since the union of crowns? Since then,
in great affairs of state at home and abroad, what mention has been made of
the Scots and their kingdom? Examine the treaties struck with foreign nations
since 1603: you will find not a single agreement or provision relating to our
offices of state, to our commerce, fisheries or shipping, or to any of those acts
or prerogatives of ours of which we boast so highly. Scotland figures in those
treaties only in the list of the king of England's titles and possessions. We are
a nation utterly unknown to the rest of Europe, we who once took pride of
place among its oldest kingdoms. Our army has no more renown than a paltry
travelling-circus. It is the English who appropriate all our glory, [50] who reap
the benefit of all our efforts, and in their triumphs wreathe their brows with
our laurels. After great victories won with much Scottish bloodshed, our only
role is to join the troop of mercenaries behind England's triumphal chariot.
Theirs are the rewards of war and the promises of prosperity; ours is the lot of
the broken-down stipendiary: wounds, scars, hunger, poverty.

'This being the state we find ourselves in now, what kind of surrender does
this union involve? Is it not rather the English who seem to be surrendering
their name, since in order to join with us they have determined on a change
of title, to be known in future not as Englishmen but Britons? Does it seem a
small thing to us that they agree to this, and let England cease to be a kingdom
and become a province of Britain? They used to take pride in the name of that
old race that subdued the Britones in the south of this island, but now, for the
sake of union with us, they ask to adopt the name their ancestors hated and
drop their own. The name of the English, so detested by us and the rest of
Europe, will cease to exist after union.[1] And in the whole world what name
has been more distinguished? It subdued France long ago and Ireland, gave
Holland its freedom, and colonized other parts of the globe for our British
monarchs; it is a name that almost rivals the greatest empire of old. And the
English must also take most of the credit for the terrible campaigns waged

[1]   Clerk's marginal note added to MS 1 in ?1746 (trans.): 'Most of them still call themselves English, but
       the name is less honoured.'

recently in Germany and Spain and Belgium, [51] though we too may boast some share in that glory, a share unacknowledged abroad.

'The English by this union, by letting us participate in all their fortunes, are surrendering to us their privileges, their trade, their overseas possessions. The way lies open to us now to share in their honour and glory and dignity. And this union alone can protect and guarantee our freedom, since in the guardianship of freedom no nation is or ever will be as zealous as the nation with which we are to join. With outstretched hands they invite us to join them. More than that, Nature herself appeals to us, for as Nature has divided this island from the rest of the world, linking indissolubly the seagirt lands that we cherish, so it is her will that we be linked together in fellowship and friendship. I beseech you not to spurn that fellowship and friendship which it has long been in your interest to seek and promote, for if you do you must make enemies of the English for ever.'

When Stair sat down, other speakers urged further advantages of union. With regard to the security of the church, it was pointed out that the genuine anxiety of some on the subject was as baseless as the pretended concern of others; it scarcely merited a reply, much less words of comfort. None the less, to reassure[1] the first group and frustrate the second, an act would be brought forward to safeguard the church against changes of mind on the part of court or people. Nor was there any need to fear that union would impair the dignity of any noble families, since our ancestors' great actions [52] are the birthright of their posterity: we inherit them, as we do their virtues and vices. Comparison could be made with the oldest of all unions, between the Trojans and the Latins. The dignity of neither people was impaired by it; on the contrary, the increase in their wealth and power enabled them to transmit a glorious name to their Roman descendants. And the Romans too, though they had little Trojan blood, boasted of descent from those Trojan exiles. 'So we can still take pride in our forefathers even if the kingdoms are joined, though it is to be hoped that between us and Englishmen in future the only rivalry will be in virtuous action, which alone should give us cause for pride. There is no need to look to the past for the fame we are entitled to ourselves. And as for the matter of popular consent, which you say this union requires, we have already pointed out that the proclamation summoning this parliament told the people to choose the representatives they thought fit to negotiate this very issue.'

A full day was taken up with speeches of this kind and various altercations. When parliament reassembled on November 4th, humble petitions opposing the treaty were read from the shires of Stirling and Dunbarton and the burghs of Linlithgow, Dysart and others, but they had no effect at all, and debate on

---

1   Reading in *solatium* MS 1. MS 2 *insolatum*.

the first article was resumed. The opposition had now changed their tactics. Foreseeing an unequal contest in the event of a vote, and that as well as being outnumbered they would have against them those whose rank and wealth gave them greater influence, they tried to propose another sort of union on what they regarded as fairer terms. This was presented to parliament as follows:

[53-4] Here, without identifying the mover, Clerk translates Annandale's alternative resolutions: to support union with England in respect of the succession, wars, alliances and trade, but reserving the independence of crown, church and parliament, or to support a settlement of the succession issue only, with similar reservations (*APS*, xi, 312-13).

[54] The opposition regarded these terms as conciliatory, but parliament was unimpressed, perceiving that their sole purpose was to divide union supporters and deflect them from the terms they had proposed. Nor was the opposition entirely united behind the federal option. Letters had come from France advising the Jacobites to accept the Hanoverian succession rather than agree to union on any terms at all, for the French and the British court exiled in France had shrewdly noted that a united Britain would have a single policy in constitutional matters, whereas a disunited Britain would (as so often before) suit the interests of its neighbours and of France above all. Even if the succession were temporarily settled to suit England, they could always hope to alter it later, so long as the Scottish parliament remained independent.

Whether this French advice was made known to all the opposition or only to a few of its leaders I cannot affirm, but sure it is that some of them would never have agreed to settle the succession unless under compulsion and reluctantly. Further delaying-tactics were tried by the Hamiltonians [55] but they were poorly thought out and failed to get the backing of the whole party. Finally a vote was called to put an end to the disputes. Before it was taken the duke of Atholl, foreseeing the outcome, made the following protestation on behalf of himself and his adherents:

Here Clerk translates Atholl's protestation that an incorporating union is contrary to Scotland's constitution and the Claim of Right (*APS*, xi, 313).[1]

Many of the nobility and the barons and burgesses adhered, but when Article 1 was finally put to the vote it was approved. The Hamiltonians moved that the names of those voting on each side be published, a motion that was universally acceptable, since some sought popularity and others the favour of

---

1   Clerk's marginal note in English: '*Vindiciis jurium* is put here to signify the Claim of Right, that is the claim of the Subjects against the Crown, a Word much in use in 1689.'

the court, while all looked for credit in the eyes of posterity. Not to defraud them of this expectation, I append their names and titles:

[55-61] **Lists of voters (*APS*, xi, 313-15).**

[61] A few words in passing about the voting as a whole. Of the 115 votes cast for union, 44 were from the nobility. The opposition mustered only 83 votes, 21 from the nobility. To compare the lists in terms of the wealth, public office, or titles of the voters would be labour in vain. Experts on Scottish affairs will have no trouble in recognizing who were the more distinguished. For the benefit of others, it is enough to say that this great transaction between the British peoples was not mainly the work of the low-born or the dispossessed, the needy or the recipients of court patronage. I am aware that the successful passage of union has been attributed by some to the bounty of the royal purse, but that report (as I shall later show) was based more on guesswork than on facts that ever came to light.

The next business before parliament was a vast number of petitions from various shires and towns. Notable was one from the Commissioners to the General Convention of the Royal Burghs against a so-called incorporating union, and others to the same purpose from the shires of Fife and Renfrew and the towns of Hamilton and Falkland. The reading of all these was a mere formality now that members had made up their minds. Sad examples appeared every day of how widely parliament and people had diverged, for not even one per cent approved what the former was doing. It was therefore thought essential [62] to calm popular discontent by legislating a settlement of the religious question. Unionists were sure that, if the ministers' minds could once be set at rest, their whole flock would be rendered more docile. With such legislation in view, a select committee of the General Assembly of the church had asked parliament to consider the following points:[1]

1. That the so-called Sacramental Test in England, which disqualified from public office those who did not belong to the Church of England, would be injurious to our church, even if it were not to apply in Scotland;

2. That for the security of the church provision should be made that its ministers not be subjected to oaths inconsistent with their known religious principles;

3. That the security of the church further required that future British monarchs swear a coronation oath to uphold its doctrine, worship, discipline and government as now by law established;

4. That a permanent commission should be established to look after the church's interests in such matters as supplying vacancies and valuing and

---

1   Clerk paraphrases and abbreviates the six 'observations' recorded in SRO, CH1/3/8, 274-5, and transcribed by Lockhart, *Memoirs*, 240-2.

apportioning teinds, and judges appointed to deal with church matters that formerly came before the Privy Council, such as preventing the growth of Popery;

5. That since the Abjuration Oath introduced in England to protect the succession contained words of doubtful meaning which Scotsmen did not fully understand, such should be changed [63] so that the oath could be taken with a clear conscience; likewise certain conditions to be placed on our future monarchs which might seem repugnant to the beliefs of Scottish churchmen should be altered;

6. That since it appeared from the terms of the proposed union that 26 bishops were to sit in the British parliament with the right to vote and legislate on civil affairs, the Scottish clergy, fearing that their silence on the matter might be taken for consent, declared to parliament their opposition to the involvement of churchmen in secular politics.

Certain lay elders on the select committee dissented from the above and submitted to parliament a summary of their reasons:[1]

1. That since the ministers had already won parliament's assurance that any union treaty would confirm the church's established status and legislate for its future security, they had little to gain by bringing these specific concerns to parliament's attention, and could be suspected of disaffection and mistrust;

2. That although parliament had been graciously pleased to discuss their first address, they were hardly entitled to present another, which would inevitably raise further points of contention and hold up consideration of the church's welfare; [64]

3. That the select committee's sixth concern expressed a criticism of the English parliament not authorized by the General Assembly;

4. That the constitution of the English and British parliaments was not their concern, which was rather to safeguard the interests of their church against malice and misfortune;

5. That now that parliament had approved the first article of the treaty, it was tactless and rash to bring before it resolutions which clearly ran counter to its will.

This protestation was signed by the earls of Rothes and Marchmont, Lord Polwarth, George Baillie of Jerviswood, Sir Alexander Ogilvie, James Campbell of Auchinbreck, and other elders who were also members of parliament.

The ministers had the excuse of favouring the opposition, but these disputes in the select committee are best forgotten. The churchmen could agree on one thing only: that the church should be perpetually secured under union.

---

1   Their reasons are fully stated in SRO, CH1/3/9, 27-35.

E

An act to that effect was accordingly drafted and well received by parliament on its first reading, but since three readings were customarily required for its passage, debate[1] was adjourned until the second.

To save time meanwhile, now that the funds voted by parliament the previous year for public expenditures had been used up, an Act of Supply was introduced [65] as the Queen had recommended in her letter. This was an almost annual exercise, and so far the court party had been reluctant to burden the people in this way, lest parliament should seem to have been summoned for that purpose alone. But it has long been a matter of satisfaction to Scotsmen that such taxes require the approval of the estates; and the British peoples are fortunate indeed never to be taxed without consent. To challenge such impositions has always been opposition policy, since the government's strength depends on obtaining subsidies for the defence of the realm. So it would not have been surprising if opponents of union had tried to delay matters. But although no issue could normally arouse fiercer animosity, the outcome of this debate favoured the unionists, consent being given unanimously for the supply of an eight-month cess. For the quick passage of this act two reasons can be found. The first was the opposition's tactic of not wishing to be seen to obstruct a royal command. The other was their hope that parliament would be dissolved once supply had been granted, especially in view of the persistent crying-down of union by the people. They could never believe that union supporters would hold firm to the end. [66]

At the next sederunt, debate was held up by the reading of petitions from some western parishes, mainly seeing union as a threat to the kirk that spelled spiritual death for the nation. It became all the more necessary to settle the church question quickly. Second reading of the Act for Security of Religion produced from some quarters the proposal of additional safeguards and from others the raising of captious questions and difficulties designed to sink union under a great show of care for the kirk. Amongst these was a stipulation that Scots be exempted from the English law requiring holders of public office in England to be Anglican communicants. Justice (it was said) demanded the insertion of a clause to that effect, since it would be an absurd anomaly for Scotsmen to be barred from holding offices in England under a union that offered full communication of privileges along with recognition of their church. Our churchmen attached much weight to this motion, which was, however, rejected by a majority vote, partly from a sense that only dire necessity would induce the English to consider repealing that law, and partly in the hope that a fairer deal could be negotiated in a British parliament. [67] Next came a plea that all public office-holders in Scotland should be required

---

1   Reading *consultationes* MS 1. MS 2 *consociationes*.

to swear that they sincerely regarded presbyterian church-government as truly apostolic and that they would never try to alter it. This also failed, some thinking it useless and superfluous, others objecting on theological grounds. Finally, when a number of further amendments had been passed or rejected, the act was sanctioned by parliament as a basic condition of union. Against it, Lord Belhaven entered a protestation that the act could not guarantee the security of the Church of Scotland, nor could any such security exist under an incorporating union that abolished the Claim of Right, the parliament of Scotland, and the sovereign majesty of the crown. To this protestation the dukes of Hamilton and Atholl and all opponents of union adhered.

The Act for Security of the Church of Scotland ran as follows:

[67-9] Translation of the Act (*APS*, xi, 413-14).

[69] The passing of this act did something to calm the outcries of the mob and the fears of the clergy; in the churches, by and large, the trumpets of sedition began to fall silent. Ministers who had formerly meddled over-zealously in politics now learned to leave the direction of government to parliament. This greatly upset the Hamiltonians who saw themselves abandoned by those they most relied on to stir up anti-union sentiment. [70]

A few days later, Lord Belhaven's recent speech in parliament was published and amazingly gratified the anti-unionists. It contained all the arguments the speaker could think of to support his case, some of them forceful but many so childish that little power of mind was required to see through them. What especially shocked intelligent people was the man's inconsistency, for not long before—in the parliament of 1701, to be precise—he had plainly pointed to the prosperity that union would bring to the British peoples. In that speech, which he also published, he showed how carefully that wise monarch Henry IV of France had undermined the Anglo-Scottish coalition at the time of the union of crowns under James I and VI. Foreseeing how the wealth and commerce of Britain would increase under union, Henry sent an ambassador to England with instructions to plot with his Spanish counterpart to keep England and Scotland distinct nations as before. To these foreign machinations Belhaven attributed the failure of James to bring his peoples together, since James's devotion to peace at any price made him shun any move that would anger or upset France and Spain. Presumably Belhaven had forgotten that speech or he would at least have acknowledged his changed view of union. It was now clear to all [71] that the Franco-Spanish policy of keeping England and Scotland perpetually under separate jurisdictions had become the strongest of all arguments for bringing them together.

Parliament next considered the second article of union which specified that on the death of the Queen, in default of her progeny, the throne of Britain would pass to Sophia, widow of the Elector of Hanover, or the heirs of her body, as had already been established by English law with respect to the kingdom of England, Ireland and its other dominions.

Since this was the hardest article for the Jacobites to swallow, they redoubled their efforts to wreck union altogether. Hitherto they had employed delaying tactics without much effect. Now their tactics varied, as they failed to agree on what to try next. Some wished it stated in the minutes of parliament that approval of this article would be conditional on approval of the rest. Others were for setting the article aside until the rest had been considered, since a settlement of the succession would be pointless if the rest of the treaty were thrown out. After fierce debate, a vote on these alternatives was taken and the first course of action was approved as the more prudent, with the stipulation as before that voters' names be recorded and made public. This took place on November 14th and debate on the article resumed at the next sederunt.

The opposition made further diversionary moves [72] in the hope of splitting the unionist camp. The marquis of Annandale led a move to set aside the articles of union and proceed directly to settle the succession on the reformed house of Hanover. The Queen should be petitioned to take note that the whole Scottish people were averse to full union with England but were unanimous and enthusiastic in supporting the Hanoverian settlement, subject only to certain limitations. He also urged that the house should adjourn while the Queen took counsel on the matter. There were varied reactions to his proposal. Some members were so sure that the welfare of church and state depended entirely on Article 2 that for the sake of it they were willing to embrace all the others, even if they did not like many of them. Others, notably Lord Belhaven, argued as follows. Parliament had already enacted that the throne of Scotland was not to go to the successor recently designated by England unless under conditions that would guarantee the sovereignty of the crown, the independence of the kingdom, the authority and frequency of its parliaments, the religion and freedom of its people, and their right to trade, especially with the West Indies. It would therefore be wrong, Belhaven declared, to legislate the succession without prior assurance that these conditions would be met.[1] 'Consult every kind of treaty since the beginning of time, and you will find no precedent for this. I shall instance only the first and worst treaty of all, that which the Devil made with mankind, though there was [73] more wit and honesty in it than in this now before us. For the serpent proposed to Eve the advantages of his treaty. "Take and eat (he said) this forbidden but lovely fruit, for God knows that if you eat it your eyes will be opened and you will be like gods, knowing good and evil."

---

1   Clerk translates selectively from Belhaven's speech on Article 2 (Defoe, *History*, 'Abstract of Proceedings',
     63-7).

'When first we heard that a treaty of union had been arranged by the commissioners of both kingdoms, nobody doubted that its terms would be such as would remove all rivalry, anger and hatred between the two countries and bring about a lasting friendship. But when it was published, people's minds were amazingly changed. Its fruit was so far from lovely that the whole people shuddered at the sight of it. To overcome such reactions it would have made sense to begin by pointing out the treaty's advantages for Scotland. You who support it might well have said, "Examine it closely, for although it looks dirty and horrid to the eye, you will find that its terms answer Scotland's needs; you will find it solid food to restore your lost strength; you will see great advantages to come from it, and as your fortunes improve you will come forth rich and flourish like the English, the richest nation on earth." But instead you mainly used arguments like this: "Eat, swallow down this morsel of a union, for although it pleases neither the eye nor the ear nor the taste, yet it must go down. Trust in the experience of your doctors, and ask your questions afterwards." I hope that our losses from this treaty may not be the same as our first parents suffered. From eating the forbidden [74] fruit they expected union with the gods, but they paid for their credulity by being thrust out of paradise and forced to bear the lot of mortals.'

He ended by supporting the marquis of Annandale's motion on the succession—that is to say, on the need for a settlement tied to a number of essential conditions—and added a good deal more to the same purpose, but his remarks gave more proof of resentment and ill-will than of good sense or eloquence. They drew a terse response from the unionists. There was no question of being asked to 'swallow down' union until its advantages were agreed on; nor did approval of one article mean approving the others. The proper procedure was for parliament to scrutinize each article in turn and determine which to throw out or accept and what amendments or substitutions to make. We had freedom of choice, but could best deserve that freedom by using it soberly and avoiding wild talk.

As for the notion of imposing limitations on the successor designated by England, many argued that nothing could be less to Scotland's advantage, however strongly the idea might appeal to most. It was a temptation to be resisted, like an appetite for things that were good in themselves but unseasonable. We had to accept that this settlement of the succession was the price of union with England. It was solely to secure it that the English had entered into negotiations with us and offered us their friendship and community of [75] privileges and trade. The proposal they had made us was indeed momentous for the whole island, for as soon as the Scottish succession was determined their interest in union would evaporate; they would tire of our company quickly enough once they saw us committed to the same future monarch as themselves.

'They see this land of ours as Britain's back door, open as long as our succession is unfixed, and a threat to their security. Nor are they wrong, for plotters against England's peace and prosperity come and go here in safety. But with that door once closed they think Britain will be firmly protected against her enemies. That is their objective, and the more intently they pursue it, the greater our chance of entering union on the best possible terms. What these terms are can be read in the articles before us. They may not all be to everyone's liking, but they will (we hope) satisfy all those agreeable to union. They are certainly the best our commissioners could negotiate. But we must guard against flattering ourselves with these vain dreams of imposing limitations on the successor. The English would laugh at us for doing so[1] [since, in the first place,] there is no legislation[2] of ours that a British parliament can be prevented from revising at its pleasure, undoing all restrictions on monarchical government; [secondly,] whatever limitations we might impose, no successor would be so faint-hearted as to decline the crown because of them, there being no check on his power that he could not easily break through;[3] [and finally because] we defeat our own interests by denying anything to a good ruler.

'A quick glance at precedents may clarify matters.[4] Remember [76] how earnestly the English wooed us at the start of King William's reign. In the first days after he came to power[5] in England they would have given us anything to persuade us to transfer our allegiance to him, so that they could hold us in a tighter embrace. But we could not stomach a moment's delay on such a great occasion. Here in this house we so vied with one another to show our loyalty and devotion that we crowned William and Mary before transferring the royal power to them. The result of our haste we all know: a rapid cooling of England's suit toward us, which even now they cannot bear to be reminded of. Britain's back door was shut on King James, an impregnable outpost was handed to William, and for the rest of his life we were not the equal subjects of the ruler of two kingdoms but the slaves and property of the English. The other lesson which our history teaches is that limiting the power of our kings does us no good at all. We cannot have forgotten how badly our ancestors fared as a result of imposing limitations on Charles I, when we arrogated to parliament the right to declare war and enter into alliances, and when later, after more or less cashiering the king, we also claimed the right to dispose of

---

1   The style of the following passage is unusually cryptic, as though Clerk were translating from notes, and has bewildered the copyist of MS 2. Connecting links are provided within square brackets in an attempt to clarify the sense.
2   Reading *nullis legibus* MS 1. MS 2 *multis legibus.*
3   Reading *quippe virtutibus suis nihil occlusum nihil arduum aut impervium inveniet* MS 1. MS 2 *aut imperium.*
4   Reading *Ut ea tamen ... elucescant* MS 1. MS 2 *Uter tamen.*
5   Reading *potitus* MS 1. MS 2 *politus.*

the major public offices.[1] Britain still bewails the outcome of these actions. Lessening the royal prerogative, slackening [77] the reins of monarchical rule led to total confusion, to subjects' hands stained with the blood of a king and the ravishing of our independence. Our perils and disasters would have been endless, had not parliament, conscious of its sins and mistakes, annulled those iniquitous, shackling limitations and rushed into penance (as is often the case) by actually increasing the prerogatives it granted to Charles II. These precedents should warn us not to repeat errors which have damaged our kingdom but to try the remedies which this union alone can offer, since the only remaining hope for Britain is to become one people under a single head.'

These arguments won the assent of the majority, and at this time the duke of Hamilton, not without some loss of credit, supported the marquis of Annandale's motion to settle the succession on the house of Hanover while rejecting the other terms of union. 'I see no better course at this time', he said, 'than to avoid future uncertainty by designating forthwith the same successor as the English on the best terms we can get, thinking more of Scotland's needs than of what this concession gives to others. Let it never be a reproach to me that in earlier parliaments I opposed a successor for the sake of a treaty with England, and that now I would reject this treaty on account of the succession.'[2] Doubts were widely felt about Hamilton's sincerity here: it was thought that the whole purpose of his speech was either [78] to sow discord among the unionists or to avert the suspicion that his descent from the royal house of Scotland gave him hopes of the succession himself. Whatever he meant, it soon became clear that he had spoken unadvisedly. He split, not his opponents, but his own side, to such a degree that, from then on, his friends and adherents became suspicious of everything he said or did. The Jacobites were violently inflamed, pointing out to him that they had hitherto opposed union to avoid a foreign successor, that only their King James had the right to rule Scotland, and that if his right and that of the royal house of Stuart were to be passed over, no concessions by England and none of the limitations wanted by some would have any worth at all. It was Article 2 which made them hate all the others and the concept of union itself. The sole aim of their policy had been to pose as nationalists in order to sink this alliance with England, since only an alliance under James would content them. (This, however, they were obliged to keep to themselves; it was illegal to talk so in parliament.) In an effort to conciliate them, the duke is said to have told them privately that he had spoken in the

1   Clerk's marginal note (trans.): 'See Acts of Parliament 16 September, 1641.' (*APS*, v, 354-5, c. 21.)
2   Hamilton refers to his 'resolve' of 13 July 1704 (*APS*, xi, 127) 'that this Parliament will not proceed to the nomination of a Successor, untill we have had a previous treaty with England in relation to our Commerce...'. Clerk here draws on Belhaven's report of Hamilton's speech (Defoe, *History*, 'Abstract of Proceedings', 65-6), esp. 'it was not to be supposed he would make use only of a Treaty, to throw out the Succession one time; and of the Succession, to throw off the Treaty another time.'

belief that it would be better to ratify the succession temporarily than to let union go through on the terms proposed. 'While our parliament retains its authority,' he told them, 'acts can be repealed and better ones passed, but [79] when parliaments and peoples have been merged it will be too late to alter the succession.' And in support of this he quoted the letters from his French friends already referred to.[1] Some of his arguments carried conviction; others appeared to cast doubt on his constancy.

After further debate on the succession it seemed proper to read out the acts of the English parliament governing it together with the conditions under which the crown would be offered, since these expressed fundamental principles of British freedom which would later apply in Scotland too. They deserve to be included here:

[79-80] Here Clerk translates seven clauses taken from the two acts of William and Mary referred to in Article 2.

[80] A great dispute next broke out over the need for more time to debate the second article. This was opposed by the unionists and the vote took place in a crowded house, the Hamiltonians grumbling that justice was being quelled by weight of numbers. The Earl Marischal entered a protestation in more or less the following words to which all the Hamiltonians adhered:

Here Clerk translates his protestation against designating the same successor as England before enactment of legislation securing Scotland's crown, parliament, religion and trade from English or any foreign influence (*APS*, xi, 325).

When this had been entered in the record and the names of adherents ordered to be published, as they wished, the article was approved by a majority.

Everyone's attention then turned to Article 3 which stipulated [81] that there should be one parliament in the united kingdom under the name of the Parliament of Great Britain. Those who had opposed the first two articles were especially hostile to this, but they first decided to revive the delaying tactics which had failed them so often before, in the hope of gaining support while their adversaries' cause weakened. They accordingly moved to defer consideration of this article until arriving at Article 22, which dealt with the constitution and make-up of the British parliament. That, they argued, should properly be discussed before they thought about abolishing their own. It would be more useful and relevant now to proceed to the articles governing trade and other privileges, in order to examine those advantages of union which its supporters had so eagerly promoted and lavishly praised. Many hours were devoted to various disputes on this issue before a vote was taken and the decision reached to debate the articles in numerical order, with the proviso again that approval of one would not be binding until the rest were approved.

1   Fo. 54.

Article 3 was read again. Speeches against it were made by the dukes of Hamilton and Atholl, the marquis of Annandale, and Lord Balmerino, but especially by Andrew Fletcher of Saltoun, along the following lines:[1]

'It is a hard thing when men are constrained to bring harm on themselves; harder still to give the finishing blow to this parliament of ours, with whose welfare the lives and fortunes of so many have been intertwined; [82] that we should hack to pieces this body, already grievously wounded, whose unworthy members we are. What can account for such barbarity? Perhaps that by approving Article 1 we became a sort of patricides, and now think to offer retribution by condemning ourselves to a painful death. But self-mutilation is the vilest of actions: humanity forbids it; free men should scorn it. Is it thus that we show our love for our country, and avenge the wrongs England has done us, by delivering ourselves in chains to our ancient enemy? Nations should be led to come together[2] by equitable treaties, not in ignominious surrender, not tricked or frightened or in any way forced into union. The English, you say, have called for our friendship. That is true. But ours is not the friendship of a mean-minded people, born to be slaves; it is the pure and uncontaminated friendship of free men, whom free men should be proud to own as their fellows. This fellowship they ask for cannot come about unless the honour and dignity of our kingdom and parliament are preserved, and except on that foundation no British union will last. For when the rights and privileges of our parliament are once signed away, our glory will be departed, our bulwark destroyed. There will no longer be a place for grievances to be uttered or the oppressed to find refuge. Without help or consolation we shall shed tears in vain, the English themselves will laugh at our distress, and the moral will be pointed that we brought it on ourselves.

'The worst disasters [83] encroach on the unwary disguised as acts of friendship and good will. That is how we should rate the good will and generosity of the English, who are making us the doubtful offer of a share in their privileges in exchange for ours, which we must kiss away when we surrender our parliament. There are many clear proofs of our own good intentions toward them. A fair alliance with England that would safeguard the honour and dignity of this kingdom has been among the oldest aims of our national policy which we have never lost a chance to pursue. But what they are after is not an alliance but dominion, and they will not succeed, for it is scarcely to be credited that we could endure any league with England other

---

1   ... *sed prae caeteris Andreas Fletcherus de Salton, in hunc modum.* The wording leaves it ambiguous whether the following speech is meant to be Fletcher's or a composite of opposition speeches. See n. 3, p. 128 below, and Intro., p. 23 above. Clerk has promised (fo. 45) to relate Fletcher's views on federal union under Article 3.

2   Reading *conciliandos.* MSS *consiliandos.*

than a community of the British peoples in which the rights of sovereign and kingdom, of church and parliament remained intact.

'Let us therefore take it upon ourselves[1] to offer the kind of union best suited to the needs and capacities of both peoples, and let the English choose to accept it or not. What we are proposing is nothing extraordinary or unheard of but in accord with the practice of many kingdoms joined in this way. We need not look back to the Greeks or Romans; there are many examples in Europe today of federal unions that have taken root and flourished, the finest being that of the Dutch and other peoples comprising the republic of Holland. Who is not struck by that model of polity and grandeur,[2] with its cities, its agriculture, its wealth, its army, its fleet, its commerce? All these might spur us to follow its example in many respects if not all. [84] For in my judgement[3] there is no tie of fellowship with England that needs to be resisted except this that would extinguish the rights and privileges of our parliament.'

All this and more was loftily spoken about the need for a federal union with England, but what never appeared in those speeches or in the pamphlets spread around at that time was any willingness to define how such a union could be adapted to the British situation. So great were the difficulties surrounding it that it was clear that in the end public opinion would detect the fraud and uphold the more sensible view that no form of federal union could be devised which would give Britain a lasting peace. The Hamiltonians therefore courted popularity by confining themselves to generalities and stuffing out their speeches with the imaginary benefits of their federal scheme.

Replies were made by the earls of Cromartie, Marchmont and Stair, Sir Hew and Sir David Dalrymple, Adam Cockburn (Lord Justice-Clerk Ormiston), James Murray of Philiphaugh, the Lord Clerk Register, and other supporters of union, much as follows:

'To resort to calumny when reasoning fails is no uncommon practice, nor is it new for patriots to be accused of patricide. But our adversaries ought to be aware that no abuse can deter us from taking up the cause of our languishing country and offering cures for its sickness. Furthermore, had they listened to

1   Reading *ultro*. MSS *ultra*.

2   *Quis enim istius formam polititiam magnificentiam ... non emirabitur?* Translation doubtful. *Forma* could mean simply 'beauty' rather than 'design' or model'. *Polititia* is probably a mistake for *politia* (system of civil administration) but might be Clerk's coinage meaning 'politeness' or 'refinement'.

3   *Nostro judicio*, 'in our judgement', appropriate if the speech represents the viewpoint of more than one opposition speaker. But Clerk's individual speakers often use the rhetorical plural (Fletcher himself does so at the start of his interruption, fo. 45 above). This particular judgement seems uniquely Fletcherian in that it drops the more conventional insistence, earlier in the speech, on preserving the rights of sovereign, kingdom and church as well as parliament. The words 'if not all' in the previous sentence also suggest Fletcher by hinting at the republican aspect of the Dutch model. By expressing what he takes to have been Fletcher's position here Clerk is preparing for Stair's attack, which argues the inexpediency of the Dutch republic as a constitutional model for Britain.

what was said under Article 1, and respected the fact that this house had approved it, they would have done well to hold their peace instead of reopening that question. For if it is the view of the majority [85] that Scotland and England should form one kingdom, then modesty at least should have bridled their tongues until parliament's will on the remainder of the articles was known. From Article 1 the others, and especially this third, depend as on a chain. One kingdom logically requires one parliament. Different parliaments, with different and separate jurisdictions, would pose the greatest imaginable problems. As a single kingdom needs a single king, so it also needs a single supreme authority, which in Britain's case means a single parliament. It is true that in France and some other foreign nations a number of assemblies or so-called parliaments[1] co-exist in one kingdom, but their example does not touch us, for in our case, under a mixed monarchy, the assemblies we are concerned with share legislative power with the king and are responsible for the whole sphere of public and private law. Our constitution prevents us from detracting in any way from the rights of our parliaments, and also indeed from the rights of individuals, but that does not at all interfere with our capacity to pass, amend or repeal laws as we choose in response to the needs of the people, as at present. And if we examine our constitution more closely, we find that nothing prevents the two parliaments of Scotland and England from being called together by royal command to discuss the common welfare of the whole island. This we find confirmed by the embassy we sent at the direction of King Charles II to negotiate an alliance with England, and especially by that learned [86] expert in our law, Sir John Nisbet, who was then Lord Advocate. It therefore appears that this article in no way infringes our constitution, since a joining together of the parliaments of both realms is implied by the condition of a single parliament in a united kingdom.'

At this the opposition became excited and began to shout, 'What sort of union of parliaments is this, which according to Article 22 would join sixteen of our nobles and forty-five of our elected deputies to the undiminished ranks of the English? Is this a united parliament of Britain in which barely a quarter of our members would vote?' Again the unionists kept insisting that it was pointless at this stage to discuss how many Scottish members would sit in the parliament of Britain; that question should be deferred to Article 22. For the present it was enough to decide if a parliamentary union was acceptable. If so, the only matter to be settled later would be whether all our members were to

---

1   *Comitia seu Parliamenta quemadmodum vocantur.* Clerk here uses the non-classical *parliamentum* to denote
     what he regards as a pseudo-parliament, a talking-shop with limited powers under an absolute monarch.
     Elsewhere his invariable term for parliament is *conventus ordinum*, 'meeting' or 'convention of the estates'.
     Consequently he can make no distinction in his *History* between a parliament and a convention of estates.

be admitted or merely a proportion determined by population, land-values, or the burden of public taxation.

As for a federal union, to clarify the matter for everyone's benefit, the earl of Stair said we must recognize that it was impracticable for peoples of different kingdoms and states to join together and still remain subject to the supreme authority of their separate councils and jurisdictions. That was why, in all such unions, the first thing found necessary was to institute a general assembly [87] with legislative authority over all matters affecting the common interest and security of the whole—a parliament, that is to say, or general council under some other name (the name hardly mattered) to decide peace and war, to form alliances, to regulate trade, taxation and all matters coming within the sphere of public law. 'Consider the United Provinces of Holland, where the head of the body politic is an assembly of the States General. Under that form of government those provinces have advanced to such a peak of prosperity that this Belgic lion might almost challenge the eagle of Rome. But beware of constituting the kingdom of Britain on a republican model. With us, to take a single example, the right of making war and peace is a royal prerogative, and although, not long ago, this parliament saw fit to decide that it would arrogate that right to itself after the death of our present queen (whom God long preserve), yet the English have no such arrangement, and if we want union with them on any terms at all the rights of the crown must be restored in their entirety. Think of the confusion that would result in Britain if we deprived our crown of supreme authority, as the Dutch federation has done, and then vested it in two parliaments with separate and conflicting jurisdictions. Endless problems—make no doubt of it—endless troubles would soon wear us down and make us rue that system of government. What we need above all is a basis, a bond that will secure the peace of Britain. You may ask what prevents us from establishing an assembly of the united kingdoms like that of the Dutch, with the same powers and privileges. [88] Nothing, indeed, nothing prevents us if we are willing to become a republic. But does not the mention of such a prospect horrify all right-thinking men? It goes against our destiny, against our natures, against the way the British peoples have ordered their affairs from earliest times. And leaving that aside, what would Scotland be left with under a federal union? With the transfer of authority in all public matters to a general assembly, this parliament must either quite cease to exist or survive in a lamed and mutilated condition, shorn of its majesty, its functions, its rights. Is it such a parliament we insist on preserving? A mere name, a shadow of that ancient body that counselled and sometimes controlled our kings, and now to be subjected to a general parliament of Britain!

'But to examine the disadvantages of federal union more closely, let us suppose it were practicable for each kingdom's parliament to retain its authority. Who in that case is to arbitrate when differences of opinion and policy arise? What if the English, in their usual manner, wish to assign supreme power without regard to our wishes, to designate again the heir to both kingdoms? What if they enter into wars or alliances, and perhaps come at last, as is not unlikely, to legislate for Scotland itself or to harm us directly? Back we must go to the old state of warfare, nationwide tumult, pillage and slaughter. You see then how crude, how poorly thought out is the whole case put forward for a federal union. If union is to be negotiated at all, it must be under a single parliament, or single council whatever it be called, with power (subject only to the royal assent) to frame laws over the whole sphere of public right. [89] For as for our laws governing private rights, this treaty ensures they will remain intact, unless we wish to change them for our greater advantage.

'One further point. The notion that this article does any kind of outrage to the people of Scotland cannot be maintained without accusing ourselves of deplorable inconstancy. Let me quote from the letter already referred to which the estates of Scotland addressed to King William in 1689:

> We are most sensible of your Majesty's kindness and fatherly care to both your kingdoms in promoting their union, which we hope hath been reserved to be accomplished by you, that as both kingdoms are united in one head and sovereign, so they may become one body politic, one nation to be represented in one parliament.[1]

Why then this sudden change? Why should the same nation, indeed almost the same men as subscribed that letter, be so fickle and light-minded as now to take the opposite view? If they then thought a union of parliaments would so greatly strengthen both kingdoms, why now see it as the ruin of ours? But however that may be, let every person here be persuaded of this, that the condition of our country now forces us to choose. Either we must embrace the terms of this fellowship under the rule of one king and one parliament, or remain for ever in a state of separation as before. I mean that state in which, for a full hundred years, we have been beset by all kinds of wretchedness, and from which (worse still), as our problems increase, there will be no way out.'

After these and other speeches in similar vein, the matter was at last brought to a vote, but not before the marquis of Annandale entered a protestation as follows:

[89-90] Here Clerk translates Annandale's protestation 'on the foot of his former Resolve' (*APS*, xi, 328).

The entire Jacobite and Hamiltonian party [91] adhered to this protestation, after which the decision was reached in a full house that there should be a single parliament in the united kingdom. Since the day's debate had as usual lasted

1   *APS*, ix, 60 (modernized text).

until nightfall, some troublemakers endeavoured to excite the mob to further misdemeanours, thinking the time was ripe to renew their attacks on unionists and the Commissioner in particular. As these men were making their way unsuspectingly home, stones were flung at them and curses heaped on the Commissioner and even the Queen, until finally the Commissioner, in peril of his life, managed to escape into Holyrood Abbey with the help of the guard. The crowds in the streets applauding this disgraceful behaviour were so vast that the whole population seemed to be in a conspiracy.

The Lord Chancellor spoke out against these outrages in parliament next day:

'Scotland has always revered her parliament, her chief governing body, the Grand Council of her monarchs, represented by the Lord High Commissioner. In the person of the Commissioner we honour the Queen's majesty; any injury to him must be deemed to have been offered to the Queen herself. But should you care nothing for the royal majesty or the Commissioner's dignity, provide at least for your own safety, for dangers surround us all, day and night. I have a shameful report to make to you. Last night an attempt was made on the lives of the Commissioner and many of our members. Must we then constantly expect a dagger in the ribs, [92] even in the safety of our homes? Are mobs of ruffians to be left unchecked? Premeditated crimes, murder and arson are upon us; a breakdown of law and order seems close. See how the storm-clouds are gathering. Soon we shall be threatened, not by the secret ambush or riot in the night, but by open attacks in broad daylight, and neither the Queen's majesty nor the dignity of this house will give us any protection. It is not the mindless audacity of faction that we are up against but a bare-faced conspiracy of desperate criminals. I urge you, then, to act with firmness and diligence, for the sake of the Queen's majesty, the Commissioner's honour, and your own and the people of Scotland's safety, to ensure that in our country such flagrant atrocities and contempt of authority are not seen to continue or go unpunished. The hope of impunity is what breeds effrontery and lures men to crime. It is for you to put a stop to this evil.'

The danger to everyone stressed by the Chancellor and other speakers lulled party strife to some degree. Hostilities laid aside, an enquiry into the mob riots was set up. To ensure that the job was done thoroughly, the parliamentary committee which had been given the task[1] of examining the equivalent to be paid to Scotland by way of compensation was instructed to uncover the ring-leaders and recommend measures to protect the public and the dignity of parliament. Some of the malefactors were later arrested and imprisoned to await sentence, but through the Commissioner's leniency [93] were released unpunished.

1   Reading *negotium* MS 1. MS 2 *negatum*.

Following the debate on the united parliament, the question was raised of where in Britain it should meet. The opposition wanted it to meet in Scotland at least one year in three; anything less, they claimed, would be unjust and an affront to our national dignity. Major disadvantages would result if the British parliament always met in England. Our delegates would take money, trade and employment with them into England, leaving Scotland to face a future of intolerable poverty to add to her shame.

The answer to this was that Britain's monarchs had the right to summon parliaments wherever they wished. That was the main reason why this proposal—fair and just in itself—had not been put to the English; it must necessarily be left to the discretion of the monarchy so as not to detract from the royal prerogative. So parliament conceded that the place, time and manner of holding parliaments were for future monarchs to determine.

Article 4, on the sharing of trade, came under discussion next, though not before the opposition reverted to stalling tactics by demanding a preliminary enquiry into the kinds of trade to be shared.[1] This of all the articles seemed the most useful to Scotland, the most likely to prove beneficial beyond any that human wit could devise, and the least likely to occasion more controversy. It was none the less the object, [94] like all the others, of a considered attack, thus:

'The advantages we shall derive from this article are either negligible or non-existent or incompatible with the freedom and honour of the kingdom. No doubt our trade is poor, but one may well wonder if this article will enrich it, since England's commerce is entirely controlled by a few individuals, or by companies trading to the West and East Indies and Africa, who would exclude the Scots as they do other aliens. For the rest, free trade with England will be damaging to Scotland. Our manufacturing industries are bound to collapse as English manufactures—from flax and silk, for example—are imported and sold here more cheaply than ours can be produced. Many an act has been passed in Scotland to protect and promote these industries: all must be repealed as a result of this article. It means that vast sums of money invested by individuals in men and equipment must go to waste, and ruined mill-owners be forced to earn a living from the soil. Nor must we forget that by prohibiting the export of raw wool, as in England, we cripple the sheep-farmers and wool-merchants who contribute a large share of Scotland's annual revenue. This is a necessary consequence of our being bound, in terms of this article, by the same trade-laws as the English. As for the community of privileges [95] promised by this article, don't let false colours deceive you. These much-vaunted privileges are of two

1   'Salton had a long discourse, showing the Disadvantages of the Communication of Trade with England. Sir Dav. Dal. had a long discourse of the benefits thereof. Salton alledged, There was a heap of 20 particulars spoke to, and moved they should speak to distinct branches severally' (Hume, *Diary*, 184).

privileges are of two kinds, either useless or positively harmful. An example of the first is of trading to the Indies. What do we derive from that? What gold-mines or silver-mines do the English have there to share with us? None, unless the Spaniards hand them over. So what privileges in those areas are they talking about? Possibly the right to bring in treacle or that American weed called tobacco. But where do we find the money to buy these things and the ships to import them? And even if we do get them here, to whom shall we sell them? Every market in Europe is glutted with such stuff. Among the positively harmful fruits of free trade is the prospect of more lucrative employment in England. We must migrate to England, it would seem, leaving our homes empty, abandoning our possessions, giving up for lost our spiritual heritage and the land of our fathers. Do you call these privileges that contribute to the death of our country? No, they are plagues rather, snares, fetters of gold that we shall soon regret. Recognize this. To match England's prosperity lies within our grasp. What we need is, not union, but sound legislation here in this house and the sound Scottish virtues of skill and hard work.'

These specious arguments were answered as follows:

'Can we never put a stop to cavilling [96] or a limit to disputation? It is sad when men have to impress the crowd by confusing fact and fiction, subordinating the public good to their own objectives by fair means or foul. Why this sudden change of mind, to repudiate what we once demanded now that it is offered? Can we have forgotten the parliaments of 1703 and 1704, how for almost two years we sweated over legislation that might win us communication of trade? In those days, that was what we worked and schemed for as the only cure for our ailments. To deny its all-importance now casts a slur on the serious and honourable aims of those parliaments. So we on this side ask pardon, and our opponents should not be upset, if we touch only lightly on the great issues of that time. Early in her reign, the Queen was at pains to console the Scottish people, her ancestors' most ancient subjects, in their suffering and despair after the Darien failure. She summoned parliament, giving us full scope to act, and we, stirred by that disaster, and with love of our country and care for our freedom in our hearts, set ourselves eagerly to enact wise measures for the good of ourselves and our posterity. One, the much-cited Act of Security, contains the provision that [97] the same monarch should not succeed to both thrones unless the Scots were granted full communication of trade, freedom of navigation, and the privilege of trading with England's possessions in the West Indies.[1] Don't forget how desperately we sought the royal assent to that act, which was not granted until the following

---

1   Clerk's marginal note on 4, fo. 150 (trans.): 'These words were certainly, by one of the court party and the negligence of the opposition, either omitted or deleted later, for they are not to be found in the Act as now published.' See also 'Testamentary Memorial', Appendix C, p. 186 below.

year, and then grudgingly, after much intercession by the Queen. You see how highly we valued these privileges then, that we made the succession conditional upon them.

'As for free trade between the two kingdoms, how strange to argue that it would damage our industries. You have just been praising a federal union to the skies: don't you see that any kind of union presupposes free trade? Or are you proposing that the Scots should have unrestricted access to English markets and the English no such rights here? They would sooner be beaten in battle and enslaved than agree to such terms. We ask you to face the familiar fact that, like it or not, our country's fortunes depend on England; the only wealth we have comes from the horses and cattle we sell there. [98] With other countries, as will later be shown, we have a negative, indeed a ruinous, balance of trade. So if we ask the English to maintain or increase the level of their imports from us, we must in fairness reciprocate.

'And now to be more specific. What industries do we have here in wool, linen or silk that will be hurt by imports from England? We must be blind if we suppose that the goods sold as Scottish in our shops are all made in Scotland. Most of our men's and women's clothing is made south of the border. We do of course make some cloth in Scotland, of inferior quality, but that only makes it easier for our shopkeepers to evade our present laws by selling English goods as Scottish. And notice, by the way, the leniency of the English in allowing us to send them, not only cattle and horses, but any of our manufactures, while we restrict imports from them. Even if everything sold in Scotland were actually made here, it still would not follow that free trade with England would damage our industries, because English wool and silk would be available for us to make up. And the fact that our better-quality woollen and silk goods contain a mixture of English and Spanish raw material reinforces this argument, [99] because nothing but laziness stops us from using material brought in from overseas as well as the English do, particularly now that we have freedom of navigation to look forward to. But you say that the import of such wares from England will hinder the sale of our own, it being cheaper to buy these things there than make them here. Does that mean you would sacrifice the public good to protect our inefficient weavers? There is nothing made in England that couldn't be produced here more cheaply. After all, everyone knows that Scottish workmen eat less and live more frugally than their English counterparts, and will also pay lower taxes under the terms of this treaty. So, since they are sound in mind and body, why encourage them to be idle? Competition from English imports will make them raise their standards and increase their profits. If they want to live as well as the English workmen, they must learn from them how to work; and if they don't want to work, they must put up with being poor.

'Linen is another matter. We make our own, and this industry will certainly prosper with free trade and freedom of the seas. But a particular advantage under this article is the chance to export our linen to England's colonies in the West Indies. Ports [100] formerly closed to us will be open to our traders there, and that is a region where enterprise will be rewarded and even the sluggish may find opportunities. You scoff, some of you, at the prospect of bringing back treacle and tobacco from those parts. Why then have we made such efforts, ever since the union of the crowns, to acquire the right to do precisely that? You risk being mocked for inconsistency as well as stupidity. If we could read the thoughts of the most successful English traders in these commodities, we would find them alarmed by this concession which could divert to Scotland goods that now come into England only. One hears it objected that England's commerce is carried on by the companies trading to both the Indies, and that therefore free trade cannot give Scotland what it hopes for. But that objection, we very much fear, is more mischievous than ignorant. For nobody even slightly familiar with British commerce can fail to be aware that those companies control only trade to the East Indies and Africa, and that in England trade with all other areas is open to all. Moreover, in the constitution of those companies, there is nothing that prevents them from taking on new partners. So, particularly under free trade, they cannot shut us out of the West Indies or America which [101] will be a common market for all British citizens.

'You also complain that, once English trade-laws take effect in Scotland, we shall lose a main source of income from exporting raw wool. As though we ourselves had not legislated against this pernicious practice before, or had forgotten that it was only recently permitted through our countrymen's infirmity of purpose! The wiser ones among us hoped that, sooner or later, union or no union, we would return to our senses and renew that embargo, thus guaranteeing a supply of raw material to our weavers and ensuring that the labours of the poor served the public good. Look around the world, you will hardly find another people so profligate, so slack, so lethargic as to countenance an export policy that disadvantages its poor and lets foreigners reap the fruits of their honest labours.

'As for the harm you declare will come to Scotland from making places and pensions available to citizens of both nations, there is no denying that major advantages carry problems along with them. But would any of us here strike such a moral pose as to refuse a benefice for being tainted with a whiff of false religion? No one, surely, will turn down union for that.

'Finally, a word about the answers to our problems which you say lie in sound legislation, hard work and skill. We all recognize the universal truth that a nation's happiness depends on its virtues and the laws it enacts. But how long must we keep on legislating, how long must we combat our countrymen's torpor and sloth? [102] We have tried every measure, and every measure has failed, as you know, because at home we must contend with poverty and abject need, abroad with the rivalry and ill-will of our neighbours. This, in reality, is the snare we are caught in. Are you then willing to liberate yourselves and your descendants, to find a wider field for the exercise of virtue, open new avenues of trade, give skill and hard work better opportunities? All these lie within your reach. This article opens up a road which will carry this country to the heights it dreams of.'

The opposition's arguments thus confuted, the article was approved, to the considerable satisfaction of many men of business who could benefit at last from privileges they had long despaired of acquiring.

Parliament then moved to Article 5, on privileges to be afforded and restrictions applied to Scottish shipping. The opposition found plenty to carp at here:

'The privileges this article grants us are in fact restrictions, curbs on our merchants' ability to carry on business. But perhaps all the rights we enjoy under the Laws of Nature and Nations should be reckoned as privileges, in so far as we are able to enjoy them without damage to England's interests. No doubt we should count it among our blessings and privileges that we are allowed to draw water and kindle fire and breathe the same air as Englishmen. The previous article gave us free trade; [103] this one ensures that we shall lack ships to carry it on. What else can we make of the stipulation that our merchants must register in London the ships they own at present if they want to share the rights of English shipping, and, what is worse, prevents them in future from chartering or building ships abroad? Remember that in the recent war around two hundred of our merchant vessels were seized—not one of our greatest disasters, perhaps, but quite enough to cripple our commerce. Now the English aim to cripple us further, knowing we have neither money nor timber to build ships for ourselves. What is the value of trading privileges that we are prevented from using? You will say we can get our ships from England, but any trade depending on English goodwill will be precarious indeed.'

The unionists replied:

'Anyone who examines this article objectively, unemotionally, rationally will acknowledge not only its essential fairness but its peculiar fitness to British conditions. When the English freed themselves from tyranny in the twelfth year of Charles II's reign, they determined to revive their flagging commerce, passing an Act of Navigation in 1661. [104] This allowed English ships many privileges denied to those of other nations. The act had three principal aims. First, to promote navigational science. Second, to develop an import policy that would benefit the English rather than foreigners by restricting imports of what England could grow or manufacture itself. The third aim was to encourage merchants to build their own vessels. The result of this today is that many thousands of Englishmen are employed in shipbuilding, rivalling even the Dutch. From the success of that industry their neighbours benefit, but the pleasure it gives us must be tinged with envy, and to dwell on it is useless unless we bestir ourselves to imitate their prudence, frugality and skill. It is not only wise but essential that we implement a similar policy for our merchant shipping. That we have so few ships is deplorable; that we have insufficient trade to fill them is more so; but the lesson to be drawn from these and all our misfortunes is how much we need union with England. Should our commerce require [105] more vessels than we have, England can supply us until such time as we give shipbuilding greater attention.[1] And meanwhile, if the time-limit allowed by this article for registering our shipping seems insufficient, we are free to extend it as far as can be done without detriment to Britain.'

The limit then came under discussion, most members thinking it too short.[2] Some proposed a six-month period during which the Scots could procure ships from any convenient source. Others wanted the time-limit to run, not from the date of the commissioners' agreement, but from the date of Scotland's ratification of the treaty. Others still proposed the date when the treaty was ratified by both parliaments. The date of Scotland's ratification was judged to provide sufficient time. The key issue was whether ships were to be procured from England or overseas. If the latter, England's deadline would have little meaning. But England had always allowed us to get ships from her, and now, with union in the offing, it seemed good British policy to continue the practice.

An addendum to the article was moved that for seven years Scottish seamen should be exempt from the imposition, common in England, of being pressed into the navy in wartime against their will. This idea was rejected on the score that, in fairness, Scots should take the rough with the smooth if they entered into union. It would also prove counter-productive in that it would force many thousands of the unemployed seamen with which Scotland swarmed to go abroad to earn their living, taking service with the navies or merchant fleets of foreign countries to the detriment of our own. One may note here in passing how the most trivial matters engendered fierce parliamentary disputes. Yet these serve to illustrate the opposition's reliance on long speeches and far-fetched, time-wasting arguments as their best hope of wrecking the design. It

---

1   Reading *impensius animos applicaremus* MS 1. MS 2 *impertius*.

2   Here, as often under subsequent articles, Clerk assumes that his reader will refer to the text of the draft treaty translated in Book 5. Without it, his summary of the debate is none too clear. Defoe, whom he is here following perfunctorily, provides a fuller explanation of the issues (*History*, 'Abstract of Proceedings', 84, 86-8).

need come as no surprise to the reader to perceive that this was their primary objective throughout the session.

At the next sederunt, November 26th, addresses were read from various shires, cities and towns, all much to the same purpose, urging parliament to change course and abandon a treaty hated by the whole kingdom. These, like previous ones, were rejected quite disdainfully. Then petitions of a different kind were received from the burghs of Dundee, Aberdeen, Kirkcaldy and St Andrews, among others, for permission to levy a tax of two pennies Scots on beer consumed locally to defray their necessary expenses. This was taken as a sign that these burghs would react better than predicted to taxes arising under union. [107] Accordingly parliament agreed to the legislation requested and gave it an immediate first reading.

So to discussion of Article 6, which provided that trade throughout Britain, both export and import, should be subject to the same prohibitions, restrictions, encouragements, customs and duties as under English law. It was opposed in general by the anti-unionists on the following grounds:

'Terms of slavery are easier to bear when understood in advance and accepted in full knowledge of the suffering they will cause and the oppression they involve. We must therefore learn precisely what these prohibitions, restrictions, duties and customs are before subjecting our trade to them. But the general picture is clear: we are to shoulder heavier taxes than any we have hitherto known or can bear; heavier, indeed, than the English themselves with all their riches could bear if suddenly imposed by a single decree. That is why England imposed them gradually; they would otherwise have caused riots, if not bloodshed. Now we are to experience, at one blow, burdens which the English after many years of training can scarcely sustain. Legislation so weighty should be handled with some sense of natural justice and introduced by stages, so that our shoulders can learn to bear greater loads than they are used to. [108] Not even the creatures God gave for man's help can be treated like this: beasts of burden must be made to bear gradually, according to their strength. Perhaps to English eyes such treatment of the Scots would be over-indulgent; we should be taken by surprise, broken down and crushed.

'But in any case why talk of gradually imposing English taxes and duties which are totally unacceptable to us? They have brought about a rapid decline in England's trade and would certainly be the death of ours. We are told of new commercial fields to be opened up by union, rich pickings from the new world which would enable us to bear any load of taxation. But do you not see that our shortage of ships and our growing poverty put such things out of our reach? If we are not allowed to trade within our means, we might as well be forbidden from trading altogether.'

The answer to this[1] was that 'terms of slavery' was a misnomer, since the English, who were known throughout Europe for their love of liberty and commercial expertise, had willingly imposed them on themselves. 'We would all prefer lower trade tariffs, or none at all, but there is comfort in the fact that almost all these apply to the import of luxuries, affecting only the rich, luxuries which in our view deserve to be heavily taxed or banned altogether. [109] Most discussions of trade go astray through an exclusive concern about profit and loss. So we need to make a clear distinction between trade that genuinely benefits a people and such as caters only to luxury, for much that is harmful to the people as a whole makes a profit for traders, who conversely may make little from trade in essentials. Examples of inessential luxury imports are French wines and spirits. In England these, along with goods from the East Indies, are therefore subjected to the highest tariffs. But to take an opposite example, woollen manufactures, though sometimes sold at a loss by merchants (the same merchants who[2] made a profit[3] from the export of raw wool), are of great use to everyone and accordingly in England have the law's protection. Another point worth noting is that little or no duty is charged on the export of home-produced or home-grown items, or indeed on the import of goods from abroad that are intended for export, a practice for which inducements are offered. Not all imports are taxed at the same rate. Essential items, such as everything needed to build and equip ships, are taxed lightly, as also are a great many inessentials—Portuguese wine is an obvious example—where the object is to promote trade with particular nations. [110] In every branch of commerce the factor that determines prohibitions, restrictions and other regulations is the public good; trade is taxed or encouraged accordingly and always with due regard to British foreign policy as a whole. Scotland's trade should not be managed differently merely because some of our merchants have profited from the import of certain commodities or because landowners have benefited from exporting raw wool. Our poverty can be laid at the door of such people. Vast fortunes have been made from the import of French wine and the nation has suffered for it. Since we neither make nor grow anything that the French want to buy, we have sent them our money and got wine in exchange! Should not sensible men be ashamed of wasting their substance on drink?[4] And much the same can be said of exporting wool. We deprive the poor of the material they should work on to clothe their bodies and earn an honest living; we deny them the fruits of their labour and lead them into utter destitution. The English can

---

1   The following speech is attributed at the end to Stair.
2   Reading *qui*. MSS *quae*.
3   Reading *quaestum* MS 1. MS 2 *questum*.
4   Clerk has a diatribe on this in *Observations (1730)*, 199–200.

teach us in matters like this how to manage our affairs more wisely, and we must manage them exactly as they do if we wish to achieve equal success.

'You complain, however, that taxes after union will rise instantly rather than by stages: a tough prospect indeed. Two things may make them more bearable. First, as we said before, they affect mainly those who can pay,[1] [111] and thus cannot harm our manufactures, fisheries[2] and agriculture on which we absolutely rely. Secondly, since there was no way of avoiding them, acceptance may be easier where necessity compels. If we really do want this common market that we clamoured for so loudly a few years ago, both nations must bear their burdens in common; otherwise this union will be a sort of "lion's partnership" in which one party gets all the profit and the other all the loss. *Cujus est commodum eius debet esse incommodum* is a legal maxim,[3] and accordingly all Britons should share their fortunes whether good or bad.

'Give a thought to geography. There are many places where we are separated from England not by rivers or seas but by boundaries so uncertain that we cannot agree on the division of fields. Awkward consequences must therefore be expected from free trade without equality of customs and excise. Our traders will have free access to England—and indeed, from the nature of the border, cannot well be kept out—thus opening a way to bring all England's commerce to ruin and confusion. Items that the English tax more heavily than we do could be brought in from Scotland at great loss to them. And when they see the damage they suffer from unequal excise, we shall be the losers if they remedy their situation by banning or curtailing such imports. For on the day when our traders are denied access to England, on no matter what slight pretext, the whole concept of free trade will go up in smoke, and the whole benefit of union along with it.' [112]

All this the earl of Stair explained fully and clearly in his usual way, holding the attention of the whole house. And he added what is well worth recalling, that he was sure that even his adversaries would on second thoughts be reconciled to equal taxation, since they spoke so eloquently about the benefits of union, that federal union they so loved to imagine. Community of trade was the greatest benefit they proposed from it—the point kept recurring in their speeches and publications—and on that they had been perfectly right. But nothing of the kind could work without equal taxation. 'If these English duties bite, and we do not deny that they will, remember none the less that in any kind of union involving free trade equality of taxation is the mainstay on which the welfare of both countries depends.'

1   This is plainly the intended sense but the expression is ungrammatical and both MSS may be corrupt: *Prima est … superflua plerumque ab iis afficiuntur.*
2   Reading *piscationibus* MS 1. MS 2 *piscatoribus.*
3   'He who reaps an advantage must accept the disadvantage entailed.'

The matter of excise was long debated but, being little understood, was referred to a committee of the house who were to inquire into it and bring back proposals for any necessary amendments or additions to the article. They made a diligent comparison of the two scales of duties and finally agreed that except for duties on luxury goods and inessentials the English duties were not much heavier than the Scottish. They also later proposed the following additional clauses which they thought necessary for the encouragement of trade:

That no duty should be charged on the import and export of [113] goods specially exempted through private rights accorded to individuals.

That after union Scottish cattle sent into England should be subject to no duties, public or private, further than such as were commonly imposed on English cattle. (Some considered this provision pointless without the observation that some English landowners on the border charged private taxes to those who brought in Scottish beasts.)

That since among the kinds of grain whose export was to be encouraged no mention was made of oats or oatmeal, when the price of a quarter of English oats did not exceed fifteen shillings sterling, exporters of oats should receive two shillings and sixpence sterling per quarter for as long as the export of grain was to be encouraged.

That with respect to these premiums Scottish and English barley should be reckoned alike.

That since the import of grain from abroad into Scotland would prove harmful to Scottish agriculture, the embargo on such imports from Ireland and other foreign regions should remain in force under Scottish law until such time as the British parliament took more effective action against them.

These clauses were unanimously approved and added to Article 6.

The addition of these clauses gave enormous delight to the anti-unionists as though they had won some kind of victory. In particular, they had found out that the city of Carlisle [114] and certain individuals enjoyed the privilege of exacting duties on cattle brought into England. Whether it had been granted by English kings in ancient times[1] or was founded on custom over a very long period, they thought it would be hard to revoke. So they hoped that this or the other additional clauses would induce the English to repudiate the treaty. It was their constant aim, whenever they gave up hope of arresting the progress of union, to add hard or impossible conditions that would sink the treaty under its own weight. How vain their hope was they learned soon after, when, in order to remove all obstacles in the way of free trade, the English parliament bought back those privileges at an agreed price.

1   Reading *antiquitus* MS 1. MS 2 *antiquitas*.

They also sought to add a further condition, no less damaging to Scotland than to England, namely that the export of wool from Scotland should continue to be allowed as it then was. This pernicious practice, often banned before, had been authorized by the estates in 1703 in the main hope perhaps of making capital at England's expense, for the result was that vast quantities of English wool were brought into the country and exported along with the Scottish, there being no way of preventing cross-border traffic through mountains and isolated regions. Since a number of plausible arguments in favour of this condition were advanced by wool-owners and exporters, parliament saw fit [115] to remit it, like other difficult matters, to the select committee, which after meeting many times rejected it and censured its proponents for scheming the ruin of both nations. On receipt of the committee's report, parliament resolved to repeal the act allowing the export of wool regardless of the outcome of the union debate, taking the view that the profits of a few could in no way repair the harm done to many thousands of the poor who sought a living from wool-manufactures. This was one of many instances of how ignorantly, obstinately and maliciously certain people pursued their own private advantage beneath a cloak of public concern, choosing to see the kingdoms of Britain damaged rather than united.

Many other proposals regarding taxation which might be thought of little significance were none the less referred to the committee to avoid any appearance of forcing matters through unadvisedly. Everything had to be scrutinized closely and openly, and the right choices made from a confused medley of conflicting notions. This placed a severe strain on the committee, which accordingly co-opted two members from each of the estates: the earls of Haddington and Cromartie from the nobility, Sir Gilbert Elliot of Minto and Thomas Burnet of Leys for the barons, and Sir John Erskine and Sir Peter Halket for the burgesses.

The house then moved to Article 7 which provided that [116] English duties on liquors should apply throughout the united kingdom. These duties provoked much strife, particularly since a case could be made that they would mainly affect the poor. No wonder then that opposition speakers sought to alarm the mob by stressing heavily that 'tippeny ale',[1] the common drink of most of the people, would now be taxed at English rates and doubtless at the level of the best English ale. The English had two kinds of ale, first and second quality (or 'small beer'), made with different ingredients, while the Scots ale was of medium strength, taxed at two shillings sterling on the Scottish measure. The article did not specify what tax should be levied on this medium-strength ale, possibly in the hope that it would be classed as small beer. To prevent future wrangling, and avoid leaving the matter to be settled by inn-keepers

1   Latinized by Clerk as *cervisia vulgaris*.

and excisemen, parliament decided to refer it to the select committee, instruct-
ing it if need be to draft an addendum that would obviate the problem.

While this was under discussion, and the prospect of union seemed close,
the opposition redoubled its efforts to subvert the will of parliament by any
means available, using every kind of tactic to instigate a popular rebellion.
**[116–32] Here Clerk inserts a long narrative account of the disorders
in Dumfries and Glasgow.**[1]

[132] Finally, its fears dissolved, parliament was free to resume its discussion
of union and return to Article 7, dealing with the excise on liquors. This had
been referred to the select committee in the hope of reaching a settlement that
would seem fair to both countries. After diligent inquiry the committee
recommended the addition of a clause to the effect that the excise on liquors
should be the same throughout the united kingdom except only that the
English beer-barrel, containing 34 English and 12 Scots gallons, which now
sells in Scotland for nine shillings and sixpence sterling without tax [133] or
twopence sterling per Scots pint after tax, should not after union be liable to
higher duty than two shillings sterling. An alternative motion was 'that the
Scots ale which now sells for twopence a pint should be reckoned like the small
beer of England and charged no higher excise.' After a wide-ranging debate
these two clauses were voted on and the first was approved, though many
thought the second safer and better. The anxieties of the mob were allayed, if
not removed, and attention was directed to Article 8.

This related to salt taxes which were thought likely to have a strong impact
on Scottish trade and especially on the poor and those engaged in the fisheries.
Efforts had therefore to be made to alleviate them as far as possible.

Fishing is a commercial activity for those who catch more than they need
to live on, and one rightly likened to the mining of gold and silver.[2] Some
indeed think it superior in that fish-stocks are neither consumed nor diminished but are renewed every year and increased by harvesting. Moreover, it is
not the sort of mining that buries men alive, since fishermen grow in strength
and daring as they serve their country's needs and [134] gallantly carry out their
business on sea and land. So it comes about that for bravery, physical strength
and agility the British seamen are the best in the world. No country is more
blessed by the sea's bounty than the island of Britain, and no part of it more so
than our Scotland in the north. A carefully-managed fishery could bring us

---

1   The account draws heavily on Defoe, *History*, 'Carrying on of the treaty in Scotland', 40–3, 55–74, and
     esp. Lockhart, *Memoirs*, 273–85. Clerk adds little except on the role of James Cunningham of Ecket,
     whom he sees as an agent employed by Queensberry, a view more fully developed in his notes on
     Lockhart, 279–83. Since the political significance and impact of the risings are barely discussed, Clerk
     appears to have intended his account mainly as a narrative 'episode' to break the monotony of the union
     debate.
2   This excursus on fishing is the longest instance in Book 6 of undisguised expression of the author's views.

more profit than any other branch of commerce. Nor need we Scots seek our treasures from afar, from Indies West or East, since Nature has kindly given us the mastery of an almost world-wide trade. But it is a regrettable human failing to take little care of what comes as a gift. For many years Scotland's fishing industry was neglected or improperly managed. Then, to reverse its long and steady decline, parliament had enacted among other measures that herring, salmon and other fish common in Scottish waters should be preserved in foreign salt, either Spanish or French. It was therefore not surprising that members should make every effort at this juncture to annul or reduce the tax on salt agreed to in Article 8. But as a safeguard against hasty decisions the select committee had been charged to devise alleviating measures, and after long consideration it brought before parliament the following addendum, 'that to reduce the burden on merchant-importers of foreign salt, [135] such salt should be cellared and locked up under the joint custody of importers and excise officials, and released to the importer as required, not less than forty bushels at a time, on receipt of security that duty would be paid within six months.'

One might have wished for salt to be exempt from all duty, but since the English fisheries lay under that burden a slight and temporary relief for the Scots was considered enough. The clause cited, for what it was worth, received parliamentary approval, and it was left for a later and perhaps wiser generation to bring fresh help to Scotland's fisheries, her 'only hope' as it seemed at that time.[1]

Discussion then turned to the duty on home-produced salt. The suspension of this for a seven-year period had been agreed by the commissioners with much reluctance on the part of the English. But the opposition were dissatisfied, wanting a total exemption, and they advanced these populist arguments:

'The relief of poverty by all possible means is in the national interest. Our kingdom's strength lies in men, not in silver or gold, and men are more serviceable the better they are fed. Salt is not merely the best means of seasoning food: for the poor it is very often a food in itself, which they can no more live without than bread. And burdens placed on them are also burdens on our trade, since badly-fed men do bad work and bad work cannot be exported at a profit. The way to help our country to prosper [136] is by developing and encouraging skills. Taxation should be used to discourage or eliminate luxury and idleness.'

The unionists responded that in a true and perfect union both peoples had to be bound by the same conditions. We fervently claimed we were the equals

---

1   Cf. *Observations (1730)*, 197: 'Our salmon and herring fishings are much in the same state they were in at the time of the Union, yet there is this difference, that by the care of the Trustees for our fisheries and manufactories the credite of our herrings is somewhat better established'. Clerk was one of the original trustees, appointed in 1727 (*Memoirs*, 132-3).

of the English: that claim would be meaningless if we had to be exempted from taxes that the English paid. We might of course have framed this contract on an assumption of inequality, but that would have been no way to solve Britain's problems, since a one-sided contract would soon be bound to collapse, and peoples who had come together in friendship would end up worse enemies than ever. Why want to open and deepen such wounds? There were many details which had to be left for the legislature to deal with in the course of time, and notable among these were questions of what taxation one people or the other was able to bear.

Loud cries from the opposition at this.[1] 'Don't trust the British parliament for that! Would the English majority neglect their overtaxed constituents and turn a ready ear to our necessitous begging? The house might be governed by factions; the kingdom might be in some sort of crisis. There is no certainty of our getting even what we have been promised, let alone other things which we leave to the discretion of the English. Any [137] improvements we want in this treaty should be written into it now. If our claims are fully met, well and good. If not, we shall at least have the comfort of having tried to help our country.'

After this and other similar outbursts a clause was finally approved that, after the said seven years, Scotland should remain exempt from the duty of two shillings and fourpence per bushel of salt, as imposed by the parliament of England in the ninth and tenth years of King William III; and that, if the British parliament before or after the said seven years should substitute a new tax, then the Scots would pay their share of it but receive an equivalent as provided for in terms of the treaty.

This clause gave no small relief to the Scots, and perhaps more than was fair, since the English too have their poor to feed and industries to promote which suffer from salt taxes greatly. The inequality of these taxes was interpreted by the opposition as a major success, but since they did not consider it enough in itself to wreck union, they supported and wished to have published the duke of Atholl's protestation that, salt being a useful and necessary ingredient in all sorts of food, and duty upon it being likely to prove a grievous and unbearable burden on the common people, [138] the people of Scotland should for ever be exempt from taxes on home-produced salt. On its publication some cheered this wildly; others thought it absurdly overweight in view of the subject-matter and pointed out that similar arguments could be levelled against all taxation, which every political writer from Tacitus onward had agreed was

---

1   An altercation between Fletcher and Stair, each calling the other a liar, disrupted debate for nearly an
     hour at this point (Hume, *Diary*, 192). Defoe (*History*, 'Abstract of Proceedings', 144) implies that the
     row was connected with the issue raised here.

essential for embellishing peace, providing for war, and strengthening the state, in that peace requires armies, armies require pay, and pay requires levies.[1]

Further additions to Article 8 were made on the committee's recommendation:

And for establishing equality in trade, that all meats exported from Scotland to England or foreign countries, and all provisions for ships in Scotland and for foreign voyages, may be salted with Scots salt, paying the same duty as the same quantity of such salt pays in England, and under the same penalties, forfeits and provision for preventing frauds as are mentioned in English laws; and that after union all Scottish laws should remain in force with regard to the curing and packing of herring, white fish and salmon in foreign salt, without any admixture whatever of British or Irish salt.

The next dispute concerned encouragements to be given to fish-exporters. It was finally decided that ten shillings and fivepence sterling should be paid on every barrel of herring cured in foreign salt, and five shillings on every barrel of beef [139] or pork similarly salted, and in general that fish-exporters should be allowed the same encouragements, reductions and so-called 'drawbacks'[2] in excise permitted by English law now or British law in future.

Next came Article 9, the agreement on the land tax. In the whole of this great transaction there were no terms more favourable to Scotland than these, since her commissioners had taken the utmost pains to make the burden on landowners as light as possible. They had negotiated that where England was assessed at £1,997,763 8s 4½d, the Scots should pay £48,000, the proportion to remain the same as the circumstances of Britain dictated an increase or decrease in the levy on England.

This land tax was usually levied in Scotland every year, and quite often £36,000, called a six-month cess, was considered sufficient. So the unionists thought that the Scottish tax would be very far from grievous, since they foresaw that the sum mentioned in the article would rarely be levied except in time of war or necessity, and that instead Scotland's share would become progressively easier as union brought the hoped-for increase in her trade and wealth. The opposition saw [140] new grounds for contention here and argued strenuously that the Scottish share should not exceed £36,000, but after speeches from both sides courting popular approval it was decided to leave the article unchanged, members reckoning that Scotland would be disgraced if it contributed less to Britain's expenses than many English counties.

Articles 10, 11, 12 and 13 offered little room for dispute and created the impression of a truce. But where the parties loathed each other worse than

1   Tacitus, *Histories*, IV, 74.
2   MSS *retractiones* (Draubacks).

enemies it could not last long, and Article 14 saw hostilities resumed more savagely than ever. The leaders[1] of the Hamiltonian faction, seeking as always to please the mob, vehemently argued that Scotland should be granted a perpetual exemption from the malt tax. This tax, although very burdensome, was rarely imposed in England except in wartime, and accordingly gave the unionists little alarm, but the opposition more sensibly[2] strove for its total abolition. The misfortune here and on other occasions was that the unionists would have listened to some of the opposition's saner suggestions if its seemingly single-minded determination to wreck union had not made all its proposals suspect. Perhaps both parties were at fault: the one wanting fellowship with England too much, the other too little. As a result, the matter of the malt tax was only temporarily settled by adding a clause that the Scots should be free of it while the present war lasted. [141]

Then Article 15 engrossed everyone's attention, full of difficult, controversial material which gave the parties ample scope to belabour each other with calumny and abuse. The general sense of the agreement was this: that since the previous articles had made the Scots liable for taxes on liquor and trade which England had imposed to secure and pay off her public debts, Scotland should be furnished with an equivalent remuneration. So a calculation had been made to determine Scotland's entitlement, i.e. the amount by which her present tax-burden was to be increased in order to pay English debts, and the figure arrived at was £398,085 10s., to be paid as a lump sum. The article further stipulated that the Scots should be compensated on all future occasions when they might seem to be made liable for English debts.

Initially, then, the question that arose was whether English debts should be assumed at all. The Hamiltonians vigorously denied the obligation. They could not have hoped for a better opportunity to win popular support. Here, they thought, were fertile grounds for censure. In effusive speeches they resorted to every kind of demagogic rhetoric:

'Is it not enough that we must lose our freedom—that dear and lovely freedom [142] our fathers defended against all assaults—not enough that we must lose our parliament for ever, without also being subject to intolerable taxes to pay others' debts? O Scotland, ancient but impoverished kingdom, who would believe that you, who can scarcely meet your own obligations, would be coerced into meeting those of others, and especially those of England, the richest nation on earth, England that has always made a mock of your poverty? How shall we explain this to our children? It will scarcely excuse

1   Reading *principes* MS 1. MS 2 *princeps* followed by two plural verbs.
2   A rare concession, occasioned by hindsight after 1725 when threatened introduction of the tax provoked riots in Scotland. Perpetual exemption had been moved by Fletcher, exemption for the duration of the war by Stair (Hume, *Diary*, 189).

us to make the proud boast that from our meagre resources we volunteered aid to an arrogant and enviably wealthy nation, a people so spoiled by good fortune that they hardly realise it. But you tell us that England, all-powerful today, was once not just burdened but sunk and buried under loads of debt. What of that? Must we then rush to help those in whose shadow we have silently suffered for a century, those who have deafened us with the noise of their wars while we sought the pleasures of peace? And the facts concerning this English debt are in any case well enough known. Most of it cannot be paid off for a hundred years. All these duties and taxes that England has levied have gone as interest-payments on a sort of mortgage which, without the approval of her creditors, cannot be redeemed until its term has expired. So it is not only we who will be crushed by this debt: it will hang [143] inexorably around the necks of our children. And let us not be taken in[1] by the foolish view that the English are rich enough to afford it. Even now they are waging an enormously expensive war and contracting new debts daily to pay for it. And despite their continuing shortage of money they will go on to wage new wars. They have planted the seeds of some already and will find the most unlikely pretexts for others. How, then, and when will our miseries end? Debtors and their guarantors share the same fate. Beware while you can; take warning from your country's woes and your people's needs; listen above all to those most concerned, your posterity pleading to avoid an inheritance of dire destitution and burdens more onerous than any kind of slavery. Leave the guilty to suffer for their crimes and debtors to pay for their extravagance, and let Scotland, poor as she is, take pride in her long-preserved virtue, her public integrity, her record of unblemished independence. Those men are strong who hold the fortunes of their neighbours in their hands; nor are they poor whose only debts are to Nature for giving them an abundance of everything they need.

'As for the sum of money mentioned in the article, count it as the price of our freedom, a reward for betraying our country. Never believe in it as just remuneration for assuming England's debts, for nothing good or fair should ever be looked for from an old and bitter enemy. We beg you, therefore, we beseech you by the memory of our forefathers and the love we bear our children, let it never be said to the dishonour [144] of the Scots that they sold and subjected their country for gold. Let those who would rather be rich in slavery than free in honest poverty embrace their good fortune. Others, and members of this house above all, should learn *timere Anglos et dona ferentes*.[2] The traitors who have ambushed Scotland like thieves in the night must pay for their villainy, but in the meantime everyone here present, however corrupted and greedy for his reward, should consider if this bribe that has been offered

1   Reading *absit credulitas* MS 1. MS 2 *absit crudelitas*.
2   'To fear the English, even when bearing gifts.' Adapted from Virgil, *Aeneid*, II, 49.

for our freedom will ever be forthcoming. Who have promised it? The English. Who are to pay it? A nation of debtors. And if they default, what recourse do we have against superior numbers? Surely none at all. So be warned that all your hopes of wealth and fortune may miscarry along with our freedom. And if our predictions come true, if indeed we are tricked, every Englishman will say that we deserve no less, since those who betray their ancestral freedom should expect no worthier fate.'

The unionists replied:

'These provocative words might have strained our patience if we had not determined from the start to pursue a steady course, through riot and slander, toward our goal of a peaceful and stable Britain. Treating every gibe with contempt, we must hold firm to our principle of allowing no private interests whatever to interfere with those of the nation. It is to earn the thanks of posterity, not of the mob, that we have taken all this weight of odium upon us.

'Meantime your objections must be answered. Bear in mind that in formulating this union [145] our delegates took as a prerequisite of free trade that all Britons should pay as far as possible the same customs and excises. Otherwise, as we have already explained, English trade could be ruined by goods brought in from Scotland on which lower duties or none at all had been charged, and the English resentment which that would cause would put paid to union and spark off old hatreds anew. What is true of customs tariffs would be equally true of other forms of excise, notably on liquors, since trade can be affected by indirect as well as direct taxation—witness the time-honoured mercantile maxim that profits are highest where living-costs are lowest. Those in favour of free trade must therefore accept the general principle of equal taxation, and accept it (as we argued) as a necessary concomitant of any kind of union, full or less full, federal or incorporating. [146] Now, seeing that England carries a heavy tax-burden (mainly to enable her to pay off her debt at the end of the present war in Europe), and seeing that unions require both peoples to be equally taxed, it follows inevitably that taxes raised here must be applied to the same ends as those raised in England: to sustaining the honour and dignity of Britain as a whole and to paying off the national debt—whether incurred by England or Scotland is immaterial if it is in the national interest to pay it. But since equal taxes result from this union, nothing could be more just or right than that the English should grant us this equivalent to compensate us for the extra burden we must bear.

'It is useless to pretend that we could meet Scotland's needs by taxation raised here. Without this payment we would lack the resources to exploit the commercial opportunities of union and be quite unable to meet any of our obligations. At present we tell the poor to keep warm and well-fed but do not allow them food or clothes. The sum of £398,085 is to enable us to provide for such necessities, and it comes to us from England, not as a favour but as ours by right, not as a random concession won by our commissioners but as the product of disinterested calculation, measuring our present levels of taxation against those [147] that will obtain at the time of union. And since future taxes can never be predicted, our commissioners have bargained for a refund in future of whatever proportion of such taxes is required to repay English debts—debts, that is to say, contracted before union, since those contracted after will be British debts and the responsibility of all British subjects.

'Finally, a point which should perhaps have been given pride of place. We have heard our commissioners branded as traitors and this sum of money branded as the bribe they were offered to betray their country's freedom. The truth is that Article 15 is in all respects an honourable part of this treaty without which the rest of it would be ineffectual, and our commissioners would indeed have been traitorous and guilty if they had made us and our descendants liable to others' debts without ensuring that our share would be repaid. They would indeed have added to our woes if they had come home empty-handed, committing us to taxes we could never support. As things stand, however, why should these debts and these taxes cause such alarm? For with the payment of the sum that England has promised, all the bogeys raised against union in the public mind [148] will vanish into air. Let us therefore approve this article gladly. With it, the new world of trade is not only available but delivered into our power; wealth will no longer be a dream but a possession. If God so wills, and if our people will shake off their inveterate sloth, no bars or limits need be set on our future prosperity.'

Parliament then approved by a majority vote that on completion of these monetary arrangements Scotland would underwrite its proportion of the English national debt. As previously stated, James Gregory and Thomas Bower,[1] professors of mathematics in the universities of Edinburgh and Aberdeen, had been instructed to check the figures involved, and in a few days confirmed the accuracy of the calculations made in England by the commissioners of both nations.

Meantime the remaining clauses of Article 15 dealing with equivalent repayments due to the Scots were read and approved as promising to be highly advantageous.

While engaged in this business parliament had learned of new moves set on foot by the dissidents. Missives had been sent to all shires in the kingdom urging those whose supplicatory addresses against union had been dismissed by parliament to assemble in person at Edinburgh on a certain day. If their

1   MSS *Bruerio*. Cf. n. 2, p. 100 above.

F

speeches had no more effect than their letters, they were to [149] dissolve parliament by force. Like its predecessors, this plot originated within parliament itself, opposition members not scrupling to hope that cunning would prevail where legal means had failed, and that vast hosts of anti-unionists in Edinburgh would frighten parliament into dissolving itself. The Lord Chancellor revealed this development to the house and counselled care for the commonwealth against the tireless efforts of disaffected persons to disrupt union. Such riotous gatherings were, he said, bound to lead to acts of violence and public disorder by those who either knew no better or had been won over to sedition, more especially since such people were so unimpressed by the royal office and the dignity of parliament that they would never accept the parliamentary record as an answer to their demands. The Chancellor's statement was endorsed by the High Commissioner. He said the source of this latest outrage was sufficiently clear to him, but warned its authors not to be emboldened by the leniency of the Queen's ministers. He was aware[1] how hard his adversaries had laboured to produce these addresses to parliament and how deviously signatures had been solicited, nor was he blind to the way all the terms of the treaty had been grossly misrepresented to arouse public anger. He himself stood ready to condone such wrongs if only he could see signs of penitence in his adversaries, if only he could feel sure they had acted out of ignorance more than ill-will. But conversely, if their tactics reached such a point of madness as to aim at a dissolution of parliament, they should all take warning [150] that it was his business to protect the Queen's majesty and the authority of the house.

After these speeches parliament approved a further proclamation against riotous assemblies. This was opposed by George Lockhart of Carnwath who protested that any proclamation forbidding barons and other free subjects from coming to Edinburgh was unjust and could in no way detract from their rights under the laws of the kingdom. To this protestation all the Hamiltonians adhered, but one may note that, had they not been so eager to protest, they would have found no cause of offence in the proclamation, which denied nobody the right to go where he pleased but merely forbade riot and the misuse of arms. The names of the protesters were recorded in the usual bid for popular support, but their opponents were universally relieved that this second edict against riotous assemblies had cut at the roots of sedition.

While the Hamiltonians were stirring up the laity like this, they lost no opportunity to inflame the minds of the clergy. Some of the opposition were as hostile to presbytery as they were to union, yet kept affirming their concern over what they called an imminent threat to the kirk. The more credulous of the brethren were deceived by this pretence to the degree of supposing that

1   Reading *gnarum se esse* MS 1. MS 2 *quarum se esse*.

union would spell death to the Church of Scotland. To allay this anxiety, the Commission of the General Assembly wrote to the presbyteries, and their success can be measured by the fact that thereafter in no part of the kingdom did ministers meddle publicly with the union question. [151] Of the sixty-eight presbyteries I find that only three sent addresses to the Assembly against union, and those were expressed in quite moderate terms, asking parliament to pass no act affecting the kirk without first obtaining the Assembly's approval. The three presbyteries were Hamilton, Lanark and Dunblane, influenced by noblemen who had opposed union from the start. But this is to digress, and we should return to the discussion of Article 15.

Parliament next went on to consider how the equivalent should be used. It enacted first that individuals should be indemnified against losses arising from the replacement of the Scottish coinage by the English, as provided for in Article 16. Because of the shortage of coin in Scotland, the universally-damaging remedy had been devised of accepting both Scottish and foreign coins at more than their intrinsic value, almost a twelfth part above their true worth in gold or silver. This excess was to be covered when coins were withdrawn from circulation. Secondly, share-holders in the Company trading to Africa and the Indies were to have their money refunded at the usual rate of interest and within the year, after which the company was to be dissolved. This measure seemed harsh to the company's officers and was accordingly challenged.

For a great many years (so the argument ran) we had clamoured for such a company, [152] finally securing it under King William after long pleading on our part and much hostility and dragging of feet from the English. Since then, the company had cost Scotland dear in money and bloodshed, but had withstood the threats and machinations of its enemies and survived to this day. To allow it to capitulate to the English companies would be a national disgrace. Now, in particular, with our trade supposed to increase under union, the nation might finally expect some return for all that the company had cost it. The best way of proving the advantages of union would be to let the company reap the benefit of this much-vaunted free trade. Without such organizations in place, our efforts to improve our trade would go for nothing, since they were in a sense the cradles of commerce. Under their auspices, merchants would be able to serve Scotland better, since they had no hope whatever of gaining admission to their English counterparts.

These fine-sounding arguments were answered thus:

'It is true that this company has cost us dearly—what is dearer to any nation than its wealth and its blood? Nor would we deny[1] that difficult births should be actively fostered, except only when they cause more trouble each day. We ought to have misgivings about a company which has hitherto proved so unprofitable to its share-holders: roughly half of its capital spent already with no visible return, and the balance under threat, particularly in view of the uniform taxation that will be applied to every company in Britain after union. As we all know, this company, when founded, was granted certain privileges, including tax-immunity, which are [153] inconsistent with union as proposed. So surely no one with any business sense should expect that, having failed so wretchedly in spite of these privileges, it could do better without them. For our part, we cannot think that Scotland's interests and the needs of private citizens could better be served than by refunding to its share holders the vast sum of money they have lost and by winding up the company before things get worse. As to the matter of national disgrace, members who have grown accustomed to this charge, on issues where it might be more sensibly urged, are unlikely to be bothered by it here. We have learned to put the public welfare first. But squeamish individuals may need to be reminded that our company is not capitulating to the English ones but they to it. At present we Scots are barred from them as foreigners, but from the date of union nothing stops us from joining them, since all British companies will be open to Scots as to English. Their rules and conditions will be publicly revised to eliminate any discrimination between Britons; there will be one people only, one in body and spirit. On the other hand, if the company's future were to be settled otherwise, its share-holders would need to watch out, and so would every patriotic Scotsman. Under union it would be crippled by taxation and its own inefficiency. And if there is no union, not all the strength and resources of the kingdom would suffice to protect it from the spite of our neighbours.' [154]

These arguments strengthened the resolve of the majority to allow the company to be dissolved within the year after refund of investments. Certainly, nothing more disastrous could be imagined than that similar companies should operate within Britain, each owning different colonies in the new world, each trading separately at the other's expense with a consequent souring of relations between them, and all this at a time when the English merchant companies were to be opened up to investors and their partners permitted to extend their rights and privileges to others, and when union was to give the Scots equal access to trade normally restricted to English citizens.

Parliament then ordered the company's directors to give an account to the select committee of what funds had been spent and who should be reimbursed.

1   Reading *inficiandum*. MSS *inficiendum*.

It went on to authorize, as a third charge on the equivalent, the repayment of all public debts. Here again the committee was ordered to inquire and report. A further provision included in the article was that £2,000 sterling should be allocated annually for seven years to promote the manufacture of coarse wool in regions producing such wool, the first payment to be made not later than Martinmas next. Finally, after meeting all the charges aforesaid, the balance of the equivalent was to be devoted to encouraging fisheries, developing manufactures and other such projects for the good of the nation.

To the last clause of Article 15, appointing commissioners [155] to supervise the implementation of all its provisions, no changes were made. The article as a whole was therefore put to the vote and almost unanimously approved.

Article 16 passed with the added stipulation that officers presently employed in the Scottish mint should continue in office, but subject to such conditions and laws as the Queen or her successors or the British parliament should approve.

No additions were thought necessary to Article 17, establishing uniform weights and measures throughout Britain. So the house moved to Article 18.

This involved a matter of major significance, the legislative powers of the British parliament. Some wanted Scots law in respect of private rights to be declared immutable. The case for this seemed badly thought out, and indeed a sad future would await the Scots if some of their present laws were to remain in force for ever. As all things in nature are subject to change, and pressing needs often require them to be changed, a ban on law reform would have been excessively constraining. So the Scottish commissioners had sensibly added a clause to the effect that, while the Scots were to be allowed to retain their system of private law, it could none the less be changed to suit their advantage. Others moved an addendum excusing Scots from taking the English Sacramental Test, not only within [156] Scotland but also throughout Britain and its colonies, to enable them to qualify for public office without swearing an oath that had been designed to protect the Church of England.

This was the same cause that the opposition had strenuously argued in relation to the security of the Church of Scotland, and their purpose was the same here also, to frustrate union by imposing tough conditions which appeared on the surface to be honourable and fair. They rightly judged that their addendum would be totally unacceptable to the English, who relied on this Test above all others to protect their church from the assaults of the wicked and to keep dissenters out of office. The more tightly the English appeared to cling to it, the harder the opposition tried to present it as a shaming irrelevance to Scotsmen, whose release from it they urged with great persistence. Unionists were generally sympathetic to their motion but none the less rejected it as involving such a revolutionary challenge to the Anglican position that it would put union in danger.

While these discussions were in progress, parliament received an overture containing proposals for covering loss to individuals on the withdrawal of the Scottish coinage. To avoid interruption of business, this was referred to the committee with an order to consider it immediately. The whole country then focused its attention on the committee. Many wanted [157] losses to be covered not only when Scottish and foreign coins were handed in but also on English coins already in the country which had come to be valued above their true worth. For the English shilling, to cite just one example, was worth twelve pence in England and thirteen in Scotland, with the result that in the standardization of the coinage Scotsmen would lose one penny in thirteen. Different opinions were expressed about this, but the committee recommended making up losses on both counts. And to forestall the speculative import of English coin when their recommendation became known, they added that, before a certain date, holders of all denominations of English coin should present their coins for counting by overseers charged with this function at appointed places in the kingdom, receiving a certificate of the amount of their holdings and the loss to be repaired.

At this time also parliament ordered an adjournment[1] of the law-courts so that judges should be free to give their full attention to the matter of union and especially to the future of the College of Justice under Article 19.[2] (The courts were normally required to sit while parliament was in session.) No additions to this article were thought necessary apart from the following stipulation which, though subject to change by the British parliament, [158] is so essential to the dignity of our judges and advocates that everyone hoped it would be permanent. This was that in future no one should be raised to the bench by the Queen or her successors who had not served for at least five years as an advocate or principal clerk or ten years as a Writer to the Signet, and that a Writer to the Signet must be privately and publicly examined in civil law by the Faculty of Advocates and declared by them fit for judicial office two years before being promoted.[3]

From speeches made under Article 20 it was clear that the provisions it made for heritable offices and jurisdictions satisfied the members of the court party

---

1   Reading *institium* MS 1. MS 2 *justitium*.
2   Correcting MSS *decimo octavo*.
3   Cf. Clerk's letter to his father, n.d., referring to discussion of Article 19 (SRO, GD18 3131/1): 'Very bitter things were said by the Dukes of Hamilton & Argyle against the custom of admitting Lords of Session of late years, that were fitter for the plough than the bench. These reproaches confounded some of our new Lords particularly the justice Clark & Forglan, and all their patrons. These things were like to create a scism amongst us, for the D of Argyle spared no body, but ran down all forfoot, & made some people about the throne tremble.'

whom they had plainly been introduced to please.[1] But the same party also moved an addendum to retain 'superiorities', the age-old rights of feudal superiors. It would have been a happy day for Scotland if this had been omitted or left to be settled by the parliament of Britain. The Scottish love of freedom could not have been better shown than by abolishing those forms of bondage which barbarous nations first introduced into Italy and which later spread to the remainder of Europe. The extent of public harm done daily in Scotland by these feudal superiors is generally acknowledged, and their authority to exact military service from their vassals had often proved a serious threat to Scotland's kings. [159] The commissioners for union had taken no account of these feudal rights, assuming that Scots and English should enjoy equal freedom in all respects, and that the former would not have to go on suffering from feudal laws so totally alien to the latter. But now, by the addition of a single word, the liberty of the majority of Scottish subjects, especially in the north of the country, has been rendered precarious, and the fortunes of many made to depend on the power of their superiors.[2]

A similar matter came under discussion in Article 21,[3] which maintained the privileges of royal burghs. This was welcome to those burghs and their representatives but unwelcome to others, for many of their privileges and rights go against the best interests of Scottish trade and manufactures and indeed of their citizens themselves. For example, a burgh could restrict to its citizens the right to carry on trade or manufacture, a restriction made particularly harsh by the difficulty of obtaining citizenship. To relieve the commissioners of blame, however, one must note that, even if they had detected the flaw in such a privilege, they would still have been obliged to humour the burghs and make a case for its usefulness, because the burghs' representatives formed the third estate of parliament and to have turned them against union would have been bad tactics. So the commissioners had hoped that when this article came before parliament it would be either rejected outright or referred to the parliament of Britain. During debate on it [160] a motion was duly put to make it subject to change, but to no avail, as although many burgesses saw much in it inconsistent with union and personal freedom they would not risk offending their constituents by amending it, arguing instead that the burghs themselves would amend their laws if their trade suffered. At present Scotland's burghs retain all their old privileges, engaging in monopolies and other practices which in no way serve their own interests. Sometimes, indeed, they issue

1   Clerk's distaste for these feudal relics makes him distance himself from the court party here. Cf. 'Testamentary Memorial', Appendix C, p. 196 below.
2   Clerk's late marginal addition (trans.): 'Feudal laws in Scotland have been greatly modified since 1750.'
3   Correcting MSS *vigesimo*.

formal diplomas conferring freedom on selected outsiders, but these are honorary favours that bring them no practical advantage or profit.

Article 22 dealt with the constitution of the British parliament and stipulated among other things the number of Scottish nobles, barons and burgesses who could vote in it. The embers of controversy, having seemed to die down somewhat in the preceding debates, now burst into flame, the whole house wracked with grief and indignation, patriotic fervour and partisan zeal. At first a deep silence settled over the chamber. The party leaders, like gladiators about to do battle in the arena, hesitated between attack and defence, whether to give or receive the first blow. At length, seething with anger, the opposition broke out as follows:

'That the die had been cast for Scotland, and her fate sealed for ever, [161] all good men knew when they saw that this house had passed Article 3, nor can they recall that unutterable woe[1] without tears and groans even today. So where do we stop? Having crossed that Rubicon, must we wade deeper into crime? Have we so little sated England's greed and ambition by agreeing to this calamitous union of parliaments that we must also deliver a maimed rump of ourselves into the ambush that awaits us? For that is what this article means: that we butcher and dismember the venerable body that so long and so honourably has sustained our monarchs' dignity and our country's freedom. Even at full strength, we have rarely been a match for the English, so how shall a few of us resist them? Who will stand up for Scotland when the English see that her parliament, her glory and her bulwark, has been utterly demolished? And where shall we turn for help? Must we carry our grievances and complaints to the parliament of Britain, and rely on it to settle our disputes and grant us every favour? She will prove an awkward and cruel stepmother, you may be sure, deaf and tight-fisted, ready to unsay and undo after union all she has said and done before. Were the parliaments to enter union with their full numbers intact, they might yet salve their honour and dignity. Otherwise we face nothing but ignominy and reproach.

'Our opponents have told us [162] that fair and equal terms are the basis of a true and perfect union. By what standard of fairness does the English parliament retain all its members, while this august body contributes a mere sixteen nobles and forty-five barons and burgesses? We should learn from the English to be fair to ourselves, for if we betray our own interests as shamefully as this we shall not be thought worthy of sharing the government of Britain. Not one single member were they willing to give up out of all the vast throng in their two houses, and yet, without a blush, they tell us to reduce our small numbers still further. For such effrontery the only explanation is that they saw

1   See n. 1, p. 111 above.

they were dealing with faint-hearted cowards from a servile race that could easily be led to swallow any indignity.

'But the most monstrous and horrendous aspect of this affair is that the commissioners to whom we entrusted our fortunes had the face to plot our destruction. We appointed them, empowered them to negotiate union if fair and worthy terms could be obtained, and we gave them this primary mandate: to uphold Scotland's honour and dignity and to strengthen and secure her as best they could. We by no means charged them to abandon and destroy our rights and privileges, our freedom and all we hold dear. Now if we had given this momentous charge to men of no knowledge or ability, the blame [163] for their actions should have fallen on ourselves or on the royal office. Or if, through inexperience of the English character and constitution, they had made certain trifling mistakes, these could have been pardoned. But since in fact the matter they were negotiating was not at all new but the subject of many similar attempts in the past and of numerous conferences and embassies, they seem to have been guilty, not of mistakes, but of wilful conspiracy. Why else did they not steer clear of those reefs which their predecessors carefully and shrewdly avoided? There have been moves toward union under every monarch since the crowns were joined, and all came to nothing because our delegates always kept the dignity of our kingdom and parliament in mind, determined to guard it in their councils as they would on the battlefield. A recent example could have taught our commissioners how their predecessors cherished what they sell so cheap. In the discussions on union under Charles II, when the English proposed a single parliament, what did our representatives do? Did they yield to such ignominy? Not for the world. They replied that, under the second act of the eighth parliament of James VI,[1] they would be guilty of lese-majesty if they threatened the dignity of the Scottish parliament or in any way abrogated the authority of the estates. Among them, Sir John Nisbet, then Lord Advocate, was not averse to a joint meeting of the two parliaments at full strength; he judged that, even if the kingdoms remained separate, [164] a British monarch could lawfully call both parliaments together to give counsel on matters of common concern without impairing the honour and dignity of either. But that excellent man always strongly opposed the sort of unification proposed in this article, and all our later lawyers of note have concurred with him. So what breed of men has our own age produced? What vipers do we nourish in our bosoms who scorn the authority of the estates and the judgements of the learned by seeking to injure and disgrace us like this? Will the walls of this hallowed chamber see anyone so lost to all shame as to let them have their way? Shall we offer our necks to the assassin's blow? May Heaven

1   *APS*, iii, 293, c. 3.

forbid it and incline us to wiser counsels, for the health of our nation, its hope and security, are at stake in this issue alone.'

After speeches of this kind some members urged that the commissioners who were present should be impeached for lese-majesty forthwith. They were obliged to desist, however, on finding support only among manifest enemies of union. So they resorted to indignant rhetoric:

'In the midst of this dire calamity, when the honour and dignity of this venerable senate are in the gravest danger, it is an indelible reproach to the name of Scotland that so few can be found who will dare to vindicate its authority. What? shall the British parliament contain only sixteen of our nobles, whose birthright it is to give counsel to our kings and be their faithful servants in governing the realm? [165] Are the heads of the oldest families in this island to be barred from Britain's councils unless newly elected and co-opted, as though restored to favour after banishment from court for some crime against the state? Are those whose forefathers earned advancement to the highest rank by the deeds they performed and the blood they shed for their king and country to be reduced once again to the rank of commoners? And shall our barons and burgesses also be stripped of their honour by this wrongful reduction of their number to forty-five? How have our shires and burghs merited to lose the representatives who served them so well in our assemblies? And who will look after their interests when in the British parliament they are left at the mercy of their old enemies? The hard future they face is one they well might bear if they had agreed to these changes, but let us not forget how firmly and constantly they have pleaded against union in their addresses, fearing lest their silence be taken for consent.

'And consider what these changes involve. In the English parliament the barons and burgesses do not enjoy the rights that ours do here. Ours, when they join them, will form a Lower House, and will in many ways be treated as lower than the nobility. They will not have the right to judge appeals or impeach for lese-majesty, [166] except when they appear before a tribunal of the Upper House, where they would act as prosecutors, not judges. But here they have equal rights with the nobility. They sit and vote in the same chamber, have an equal voice in appeals and legislation, and generally yield to the nobility in nothing except titles of honour.

'The changes which must come with this British parliament are not to be thought about, let alone borne, with equanimity. It is painful to talk of them. But a different point to be remembered is what will follow from this mass migration of our elected representatives to England. Crippled by their expenses, they will return home empty-handed beggars. Not only will their rights and dignities be impaired, they will also have the pain of seeing their families, even the memory of their families, utterly extinguished by poverty and need. For this is the wretched future we foresee for our delegates, that if they do go to England to attend the parliament, they will either come back paupers, as we said, or, worse, break faith with their country and flourish on ill-gotten riches; and if they do not go, they must leave Scottish affairs to be settled as the English please. We hold in our hands our country's honour, our parliament's authority. Let us therefore be wary of this union. Let us reject all its terms, but especially this, the most injurious of all.' [167]

The anti-unionists then received this answer from the earl of Stair and others:

'We must first ask members' pardon for repeating some points made in earlier debates, but the issues raised here make this necessary, and we believe we shall be able to bring forward arguments which will make this article acceptable to most. Serious and seemingly insuperable objections have been made to it; no opportunity has been missed to discredit it. But if prejudice is laid aside, many objections will disappear, others will lose force, and the rest can be weighed against union's advantages.

'At the outset let us be clear that in their discussions with the English our commissioners made every effort to meet the wishes of this house. They therefore pressed hard for a body that would unite the full strength of both parliaments, and when that effort failed, for the best possible representation of ours. Sixteen from our nobility, thirty-eight from our barons and burgesses was the original English proposal, to which they clung so tenaciously that it took several days of public and private negotiation to persuade them to raise the latter number to forty-five. Why they would not raise the numbers further should be understood and we shall now explain. First, they contended that [168] each country's suffrage should be determined by its contribution to the revenue, though they were willing to allow us one twelfth of the seats in parliament in spite of our contribution being only one fortieth. This principle we opposed on the principle that it had never been applied in England, where certain counties return more members than their revenues warrant. Further, relying on the prospect of our revenues increasing with commercial prosperity under union, we argued that Scottish representation should be based on our estimated future contribution, not our wealth at present. But the English had a ready answer to that, namely that in certain articles, such as the ninth on the land tax, it had been agreed that levies on Scotland should never be increased beyond a fortieth part of the British total, and by the same count in Article 15 that Scotland should be compensated for any increase in taxation that was required for repayment of English debts. Look at it as you will, they said, you will find Scotland's share of the tax burden fixed at not more than a fortieth.

'Their second argument, which [169] weighed with us most heavily, was that our resources would be drained by sending a larger number of delegates to England, since we would find it hard enough to pay the expenses of the number proposed. They feared that concessions to our national honour would turn out to be costly. Here one must point to a swarm of contradictions in opposition speeches. Sometimes they complain that all our members are not to be admitted; at other times that a united parliament will cripple us financially, our delegates returning home penniless. So what remedy do they propose? Surely the only way out of the dilemma is to limit our representation as the article does. And do not suppose that no precedents exist for such an arrangement. You will find many such in the oldest unions. According to Strabo, when Lybica united with three neighbouring cities she was allowed two votes to their single one each on the score of her much greater revenue. And in a union of twenty cities in Lycia he reports how some had three votes, some two, some one, according to the tax-levies on each.[1] Philip of Macedon, after the [170] Phocian war, when he and his descendants were admitted to the Amphictyon assembly, took over the Phocians' double vote. Saxony had two votes in the league of Schmalkalden. But examples are needless for something that so evidently accords with natural justice, even if sometimes a powerful state does offer equal suffrage to a weaker neighbour in order to woo it into union.

'But you ask why the English would not reduce their numbers to parity with ours. In case of urgent necessity they would no doubt have done so, but they had not sunk so low that they needed us to tell them what to do. You cannot force your will on those stronger than yourself. In the flourishing condition of England today, who can imagine persuading fifty or so members of its lower house to give up their jobs and hand over their authority to others? Had such a thought even entered the heads of our commissioners, union would have been done for, or I am much mistaken.[2]

'We detect some grumbling[3] to the effect that parliaments should meet alternately, or every so often, on Scottish soil, so that the wealth of Britain might circulate. That would have been an excellent proviso, we agree. But how can one challenge that foremost among royal prerogatives, that of summoning assemblies? Think of the injustice of imposing such an unprecedented limitation on our monarchs, who have always been free to call parliaments at need, whenever and wherever they pleased. Had we [171] not been a monarchy, had this union been one of republics, it might have been appropriate to make such a condition, but in a kingdom the case is quite

---

1   The references to Strabo were made by Seton of Pitmedden, citing Grotius, in his speech on Article 3 (Defoe, *History*, 'Abstract of Proceedings', 79).

2   *Ni fallor*. The singular verb, elsewhere avoided by Clerk in 'composite' speeches such as this, suggests he wrote with a particular speaker, presumably Stair, in mind.

3   Reading *mussitare*. MSS *muscitare*.

otherwise. Nowhere, however, not even in the unions between European peoples that we witness today, have we found it laid down that any single city should be the capital and seat of government. And before going further let us make the point here that in advancing this kind of argument our opponents are being sly; they are not showing thoughtlessness or ignorance. For they care little what they come out with,[1] so long as it contributes to their goal of foiling or delaying this union, and they would act more honourably and fairly by showing to this house what their true feelings are than by resorting to arguments which children could refute.

'Now let us turn to the crime for which they wish to impeach our commissioners, that of acting to the prejudice of parliament in contravention of VI James, 8, 2. It is wearisome to repeat what we have said before, but our opponents have brought a grave charge. So take note that our commissioners were given full powers to negotiate terms at their discretion, and remember too that when it was moved in parliament in 1706 to debar them from negotiating any union detrimental to the laws, privileges, rights, liberty and dignity of parliament and the kingdom, [172] we voted down that motion, because the English commissioners had been given a free hand and we considered that ours deserved the same, more especially since none of their transactions would be binding on the kingdom but would require to be ratified or rejected by parliament in the national interest. To this moment, then, no crime has been committed. Our commissioners did as they were bid. They met their English counterparts, talked about union, and drew up the treaty which they have brought to us here. If we approve it, well and good; but if not, those who undertook this task for their country deserve our thanks, not malicious accusations.

'And how could they ascertain the will of parliament and people except from the parliamentary record? In the matter of union, where should they look but to that previously cited address to King William of 1689 that petitioned for a single British parliament? So surely our commissioners had every reason to agree to such a thing, since nothing we have enacted or legislated since then shows the least indication of a change in policy. It is a mystery to us why the concept of a single parliament should now be opposed by many who at that time, in this very house, sanctioned it as absolutely essential for Scotland and for Britain as a whole. But times have changed, and minds have changed with them, and not for the better, you will notice. For in those days they left it to the King alone to sort out the problems of union. [173] Now they are unwilling to give this trust to the Queen and parliament itself.

'But to leave that aside and answer further complaints, you say that all who try to injure or diminish parliament are guilty of treason. Our position is that

1   Reading *parum curant quid proferant* MS 1. MS 2 *parum curant proferant*.

any such attempt by one or more persons would indeed be a sort of lese-majesty; by plotting such a crime they would contravene private law. But it is quite another matter when private individuals, acting with the tacit or expressed consent of parliament, or here in the parliament chamber itself, bring forward new proposals to be passed into law. For it is everyone's duty to speak freely and openly on matters of state, and no one can be prosecuted for submitting his views to a parliamentary vote. As for parliament itself, for its laws and decrees it is answerable only to God and the eternal laws of Nature. And did it not quite lately, in the session of 1689, eliminate one of its three estates when it voted to throw out the bishops entirely and divide into two the estate of barons and burgesses? And were our forbears afraid of "diminishing" parliament when (witness Act 102 of the seventh parliament of James I) they removed the right to vote from all the barons in the land and gave it instead to their representatives from the shires?[1] It is a mistake to interpret that act as being merely a dispensation excusing lesser barons from the obligation to attend, for in later years they were denied admission when they asked for it, nor was their consent ever formally required, as it would need to have been to justify the requirements which our adversaries insist on for ratifying union. And as the number of members has been reduced from time to time, so [174] also from time to time it has been raised, as we ourselves instanced by increasing the representation from some shires. The sum of the whole matter can be stated like this, that although our parliament is founded on law and flourishes by law, yet by law it may also be dissolved. Our authority over it is total. We in Scotland, unlike the ancient Persians, acknowledge no laws or constitutions as binding for ever.

'A few words finally arising from the matter of appeals. We form in this house a supreme court of appeal where any Scottish subject may seek redress against the judgements of lower courts. Sitting as such, our barons and burgesses wield equal power with our nobility, and you note that under union they must lose this prerogative which will be transferred to the British House of Lords. But in this they will share the lot of their English counterparts, and should recognize that this will compensate them fully for any loss to their honour and dignity. The privileges of the British Lower House will be so great that such trifles can well be exchanged for them. Will they not have full power in financial matters, over levies and taxes? Proposals for these may need the royal assent and the approval of the Lords, but it is usually in the Commons that they originate. And will it not make up for the loss of that small prerogative, and for other such detriments and deprivations, that they are to share in the honour and dignity of the British House of Commons? Weigh its authority against that of our parliament. [175] We might wish to ascribe some slight

1   APS, ii, 15, c. 2.

worth to ourselves, but the world does not know that we exist. Since the union of crowns, such prestige and renown as our kingdom once enjoyed have been credited to the English. It is they who hold the balance of power between all the states of Europe; they who can justifiably boast of being guardians of every people's freedom; they whose light has not merely darkened Scotland's but extinguished it completely. And yet there is a way of coming at the fame for which we seem to be so avid, an easy, peaceful and direct route to restoring our former reputation. All the honour and dignity, the fame and reputation, the rights and privileges that the English possess will accrue to us by right. The union of the kingdoms means an equal partnership in all things, a sharing of fortunes in good times and bad.'

These speeches heartened the majority, and a crowded house then proceeded to vote on the first paragraph of the article. Some wished to enter protestations, however, including the duke of Atholl and the earl of Buchan from among the opposition nobles. The duke expressed dissent on grounds already recorded in his speeches against previous articles. The earl protested that the rights and privileges of the Scottish nobility should remain in force notwithstanding the articles of union. George Lockhart from the barons and Walter Stuart, the member for Linlithgow, also protested along similar lines. But others followed the earl of Marchmont, a recent Lord Chancellor, in protesting against those protestations, objecting that their terms were in breach of parliamentary decorum by proposing the continuation of rights and privileges 'notwithstanding union'. [176] As the earl remarked, 'Since the edicts of this house are sacrosanct and binding, it would be unworthy of us and indeed ridiculous to admit protestations that defy our own laws.' There was a long dispute over whether to admit them, but when everyone became thoroughly exhausted by the uproar it was agreed that the protestations should be entered in the record but not in the published minutes. There is indeed not much difference between the record and the minutes, since the former is open to inspection by anyone, and so the anti-unionists thought they had won no mean victory. Further protestations were made by the earl of Errol, Lord High Constable, and the Earl Marischal, the first that the office of Constable should continue to be held by himself and his successors by hereditary right, and the second that the office of the Marischal, together with all honours, dignity and emoluments belonging to it which he and his ancestors had enjoyed for almost seven hundred years, should not be affected by union. These protestations admitted, it was finally moved and agreed between the parties that the names of those voting on both sides should be printed. I have decided to subjoin them here because in giving an account of this momentous struggle it should be made clear whose votes determined the present form and constitution of the British parliament.

[176–81] Lists of voters (*APS*, xi, 388–90).

[182] The house now turned to the remainder of the article on the manner of appointing the British parliament and summoning the Scottish nobility and other representatives. Some wanted the method of electing the nobles to be laid down in the article; others were in favour of a simple provision reserving to parliament the right to determine this matter through new legislation which would have the same force as if it were part of the treaty. The latter view carried, and a clause containing that provision was added to the article. Otherwise the article caused no further problems, but four motions put by the opposition held up proceedings briefly.

First, with regard to triennial parliaments, was a motion that once in three years the British parliament should meet in Scotland. There was no dispute over triennial parliaments when it became known that English legislation had already provided for them, but like all other arguments with a popular appeal, the idea of requiring British monarchs to summon parliament in Scotland every third year caused a measure of perplexity. Finally, after carefully weighing the points made above about the crown's prerogatives, the house decided to leave them unchanged.

The second matter concerned the so-called Abjuration Oath, to be required of all members of the British parliament and placing certain conditions on their right to hold office. The motion was to have it either totally abrogated or modified to suit the Scottish situation, but this struck some as excessively captious and it was therefore laid aside. One wishes [183] it had passed, since this neglected opportunity sowed endless seeds of future discord among the ministers, some of whom argued that the oath endorsed church-government by bishops.

The third motion was to exempt holders of public office in Scotland from the Abjuration Oath. This was supported mainly by the Jacobites, since it was their prince whom the oath abjured by declaring that the right to succeed belonged to the Hanoverian line alone. But the opposition was far from united behind it. Not all were Jacobites or publicly willing to uphold their cause. So the motion caused embarrassment and had to be dropped in the interests of unity.

Fourth was a motion that what the English call the Sacramental Test should not apply in Scotland; also, that for so long as it had force in England, all persons holding public office in Scotland should be required to swear as follows: 'I, A.B., in the presence of God, declare that I acknowledge the presbyterian government of the church as now by law established to be the only lawful government of the church,[1] and that I shall neither directly nor indirectly attempt to subvert it or to alter anything in its worship, discipline or govern-

---

1   The actual wording was less exclusive: 'to be a lawfull government of the Church' (*APS*, xi, 397).

ment.' Every attempt to pass the first part of the motion was defeated. Over
the second part, containing the oath, there was widespread disagreement with
few thinking alike on the subject. Some inveighed against every kind of oath;
others wanted this or that wording; many hoped that under the last article of
the treaty the Sacramental Test would be abrogated by the English as [184]
contrary to union; a few, privately preferring the Anglican rule and regarding
the oath as its strongest bulwark, wanted it preserved intact. As often happens
when views are so various, the result was a stalemate. The article itself went
through.

Next to be read was Article 23, on the privileges of the Scottish peers. The
first of several addenda moved was that they should renounce the privilege of
enjoying personal security from their creditors. Some grudging individuals
were indignant that the nobility, under union, should have more and greater
privileges than before, for previously all Scottish members of parliament had
been equal except in title. The motion was meant to satirize noblemen who
had been commonly seen as over-zealous for union, and so their enemies
amused themselves with comments like this:[1]

'From now on, noble lords are not to be trusted in matters of business. They
can borrow without shame to stuff full their tottering palaces, knowing that
the law has made them free of their creditors. And how are the debts they have
already contracted ever to be recovered, if the threat of a squalid prison is lifted?
Removal of the penalty will seem to remove the obligation to pay.[2] Is there
then to be a new set of laws for the nobility, as there was at the time of the
Roman conspiracies?[3] And is this the privilege they covet so greedily, to be
free of their creditors? Their creditors should be warned [185] to look after
their interests while time permits.'

These taunts, however, though ferociously uttered, had very little effect on
the peers, who clung more tightly than ever to the privileges they would have
under union and were willing to give way in nothing. Then some of them
moved that the whole estate of the Scottish nobility should have the right to
sit covered in the British House of Lords when their affairs made it necessary,
in spite of the fact that only sixteen of them could vote. Others doubted the
value of this motion, foreseeing that the dignity of the Scots peerage would
hardly be enhanced if disenfranchised members were willing to enter the
chamber.

1   The 'ferocious' satire of these remarks strongly suggests that Clerk was recalling an actual speech. The
     speaker, clearly an outspoken independent and not of the nobility, could well have been Fletcher.
2   *Cessante poena soluta videbitur obligatio.* The neat phrasing suggests a legal aphorism.
3   A barbed thrust, hinting at a 'conspiracy' of union magnates analogous to that of Roman aristocrats who
     hoped to profit from the destruction of the republic by Catiline. The 'new set of laws' alludes to Cicero's
     disregard of the law by concealing the complicity of the well-born and powerful Caesar and Crassus
     when punishing the other conspirators.

When finally that clause of the article was reached which gave English peers created before union precedence over Scots of the same rank, the Hamiltonians began to remonstrate:[1]

'Have we not amply sated English ambitions by giving the vote to only sixteen Scottish nobles? Must all the others too be stripped of their honours and dignities? Think, my lords, of your ancestors, of their virtues, of the renown you inherit from their great deeds at home and abroad. If you cannot be moved by love of our country, or the greatness of our kingdom, or the majesty of our kings, or the integrity of our parliament, or the welfare of our people, yet surely at least the antiquity of your line, the splendour of your seats, and the happiness of your posterity should detain you. Everything that distinguishes noble blood from mean, those qualities that all races, even the most savage, so zealously cultivate, do they matter to you so little that you are willing to give them up for this calamitous union and exchange them for folly, iniquity and bondage? [186] Will you trade certainties for uncertainties, the hereditary rights that belong to you for precarious honours and dignities? And why mention those, indeed? As soon as this nefarious union takes place you must lose them too and be reduced to slavery, poor bondsmen of the English, you who were free men and scions of a nobility unsurpassed in Europe. God does not always grant us honours and dignities and riches for ourselves alone: sometimes these blessings are bestowed for the sake of our successors. Remember that, and be worthy of your children and defend their birthright, and let their credit be the greater that you were their fathers. The definition of true nobility is this, that only the path of virtue leads to the summit of honour. So learn to despise false and ill-gotten greatness, and strive with all your might to fulfil your ambitions by any other means than this mercenary alliance. You do not have the strength, you say? Ah, but you do, if you also have the will, for Nature herself will show the brave and the active how to repair their fortunes and restore their country to the heights of its ancient glory. And meantime let the English learn more restraint in the use of their riches; let those upstarts[2] learn from us how true nobility can be won.'

These grandiose words received a short answer:

'Honours and dignities and all that men prize must yield to the good of the country and its people. As for the nobility of England, you wrong them by calling them upstarts. Many of their families came to Britain with William of Normandy; [187] many were here before he came, and still to this day flourish nobly and honourably to the credit of England, and show that their Saxon lineage can rank with the most famous in Europe. But if there are indeed new

1   The speech shows Clerk's talent for irony at its best. See Intro., p. 24 above.
2   Translating *novi homines*, 'new men'. The gibe, often directed at Cicero in particular, maintains the Roman parallel, to be enforced in the answer below.

men among their peers, as there are among ours,[1] call to mind that it was the counsels of such men, their service and their worth, that upheld the Roman republic. Lucky the race that can bring forth and rear such men every day.'[2]

With speeches such as these the debate continued almost until nightfall, with no pause for breath until the vote was taken and the article approved. The status of the Scots nobility was radically altered by Articles 22 and 23 and it is hard to determine if the change was for better or worse, since they both gained and lost many privileges. The reader must decide for himself, but we can tell from the recorded votes that they brought their losses on themselves: forty-five peers supported the motions and only twenty-three opposed them.

After the debate, on the same day,[3] died John Dalrymple, earl of Stair. Renowned for wisdom and eloquence, throughout his life he had promoted union in all he said and did, and persevered right to the end. For some months he had suffered from weakness of the lungs, but did not fail to be present in the house every day, supporting in forceful and outstanding speeches the cause which he saw as the only remedy for all his country's woes since the crowns were joined. [188] It is to this great man above all that Britain owes whatever good it sees emerging from union.

To Article 24 parliament voted to add two clauses. One was to leave to the Queen to determine the precedence under union of Scotland's chief herald, called Lyon King of Arms. This was to gratify John Erskine, then holder of that office. The other was that the royal insignia—the crown, sceptre, and sword of state—together with all public records should be kept in Scotland. As for the regalia, nothing could have given the people more pleasure, because of their mistaken belief that they had adorned Scottish monarchs from very ancient times. Some were glad because they hoped for the restoration of Scottish independence. Others saw a symbol that Scotland was not yielding her sovereignty to England but entering into an alliance.

When the final article had been read, providing for the repeal of all laws in both kingdoms that ran counter to union, the motion was put to approve all the articles as amended. At this the Hamiltonians, like men struck by lightning and about to expire, made speeches like this:[4]

1   This rebuke to aristocratic snobbery shows Clerk preparing for his tribute to Stair below. The Dalrymples
      were prime examples of 'new men': Stair's father was made viscount in 1690 and his own earldom created
      in 1703.
2   *O fortunatam natam gentem quae tales quotidie parit nutritque.* Clerk clinches his sequence of allusions to
      republican Rome with an echo of Cicero's notorious verse-line commemorating his role in saving the
      republic: *O fortunatam natam me consule Romam.*
3   Not so. Article 23 was debated on Mon. 13 Jan.; Stair died on Wed. 8 Jan. after attending the debate on
      Article 22 the day before (Hume, *Diary*, 194; Defoe, *History*, 'Abstract of Proceedings', 207). See Intro.,
      p. 24 above.
4   *APS*, xi, 402, mentions 'some discourse' when the Act Ratifying the Treaty was first read on 15 January,
      but there is no evidence that major closing speeches such as Clerk provides were delivered. Defoe

'And so the darkest day in Scotland's history has finally arrived. The point of no return has been reached, and nothing is left to us of Scotland's sovereignty, nor her honour or dignity or name. Pause a little while and consider. Spare a thought for your country, your destiny, your children, before raising guilty hands to this execrable murder. It has often been said, and you should not forget, that this parliament of ours was set up to protect the welfare of our kingdom and people, not to bring them to ruin and destruction. [189] We are the servants of the state, not its masters; fathers and guardians, not tyrants or traitors. Cast your eyes round this assembly. You will see how many foes to the peace of Britain your policies have brought forth; but pay attention too to this throng from all ranks who prayerfully and tearfully oppose them. Look at that pile of supplicatory addresses: far away from here, people are begging us to learn sense at last, while time still permits, and not to let our factions and quarrels be the shipwreck of everyone's good. If you will not be moved by concern for your country, or the memory of your forebears, or care for your posterity, let us at least check this mad rush into suicide.

'To good and upright men it is freedom that gives relish to life; slavery and death are one and the same, unless it be that patriots sooner would die than see their dear land enslaved. It is true that a Cato or a Curtius[1] is rarely to be found, yet many a Brutus and Cassius is among us, many a Bruce and Wallace who would champion Scotland against England's vile yoke and restore to her her ancient freedom.

'History will be right to hold us responsible for the miseries and misfortunes that must stem from this day. Not just the shame of this enslavement, but the wars and divisions and hatreds whose seeds we now sow. Children yet unborn will deplore this day's madness—the day itself will be counted as unlucky—and they will hate and curse the memory of ancestors whom otherwise they should have revered.

'You who keep thanking our Queen for all the benefits she has done us, consider [190] how basely your policies betray her. She entrusted her government to you. She longed impatiently for a union of her kingdoms, provided it could be achieved in peace and without impairment to the honour and dignity of herself and her realm. Yes, indeed, she did call for her peoples to unite, but only on condition that they could do so wholeheartedly—not just in name, and certainly not against the universal wishes of one of them. So you go against her wishes too, or you keep her in ignorance of the facts, when you

---

(*History*, 'Abstract of Proceedings', 195) writes: 'The Act for the Union admitted now no Debate ... there was nothing to do but to put the Question.'

1   Marcus Curtius was a legendary Roman who saved his country by killing himself in obedience to an oracle. He and Cato seem to be linked here as patriotic suicides, while Brutus and Cassius represent more active resistance to tyranny.

push this union through, knowing full well that what you are doing is to turn loyal subjects into disaffected rebels. And as though these disasters at home were not enough, this action of ours will lead[1] to fierce wars abroad and disaffection among the Queen's allies. The French and the Catholics will be glad of it; our exiles will take hope from it; but the Confederate Princes will grieve to see Britons girding up their loins to attack each other and plunge into the chaos of civil war. You are madmen, you are fools, if you truly believe you are laying the foundation of everlasting peace between England and Scotland. You are rather tearing down the glorious bulwarks that have strengthened us till now both at home and abroad. You are placing in jeopardy our religion and the Hanoverian succession on which we rely.

'Must we then give up all our hopes, our laws, our destiny, for the sake of this union and a doubtful future? We say to you, be strong, have the courage [191] to beware of this yoke you are taking on yourselves. But if you will not, we call God to witness that we and our children will not bear the blame. We have told you what we think; our words are the pledges of our undying love for our country.'

Speeches of this kind angered the unionists, but they replied:

'Those who have fought this treaty every step of the way can be excused their intemperate language, and we must not let insult and slander deflect us from our task, especially in view of the benefits it will bring to our poor blind people. What have we not suffered in this arduous business to serve our country's needs? We have neglected our personal affairs to watch over the state. We have been scoffed at and taunted. We have been victims of plots and criminal assaults. But now we can only look for the long-awaited fruit of our labours. Since we have forecast already the many great advantages that union will bring, to speak further on the subject might seem useless. Yet we think it worthwhile to repeat a few points, and add a few others, if only to remove certain prejudicial notions that have impressed themselves on ignorant minds, and also to ensure that the stubborn are crushed, not by weight of votes only, but by arguments which will rob them of every excuse.

'We know that what chiefly prejudices our case is that we are commonly labelled courtiers and mercenaries, either because we are already profiting from lucrative offices, or because we have been bribed to support this business by a liberal dispensation of rewards and promises. Well, then, we challenge you; [192] make careful enquiries. You will find few placemen among us, and fewer still who would not gladly lose their places for the sake of this union. As for promises and pensions, these must be numbered among the slanders and false accusations brought against us, for there is no crime we have not been charged with to whet the implacable fury of the mob, as though we were monsters of

1   Reading *bella ... ex hoc facto ... eventura.* MSS ... *emptura.*

impiety, without families or homes or children of our own that we would wish to cherish and defend. We have no desire to boast of what we possess, but you must allow us to point out that the disasters you predict for Scotland would hit us harder than you, if only because there are more of us. We have no fear, however, of any such disasters, nor any expectations from a favourable outcome beyond those that can be common to all.

'So what remains to be said[1] in support of union? What persuasive rhetoric must we employ, now that every argument that might influence or sustain our hearers seems to have been exhausted? From our opponents we have heard fine speeches, timely (we would all have agreed) if uttered before the union of the crowns. Then was the time to urge that our kingdom's independence should be preserved; that our kings should rest content with the lot of their ancestors instead of removing to England and dragging us behind them into slavery. But since the joining of the crowns was both a natural evolution and a result of the political situation in Britain under King James VI, it would surely have been fortunate if the kingdoms had been united as well as the crowns. Fate worked against this; [193] so too did certain persons, who saw in the rivalry and discord of the nations and the factions of the people an opportunity for asserting absolute power. Yet in those days the wiser heads on both sides wanted union above all, and thought it reasonable that those who had a monarch in common should have all else in common as well. So now that a suitable occasion offers, now surely we should inaugurate and settle this league which the English especially have too long put off, which the court-party (one should rather say) has too long turned down.

'We have already shown how, after 1603, the glory of Scotland either perished entirely or faded in England's lustre like the stars at sunrise, so that the mere name of a kingdom was all we retained of our majesty and power. In answer you say that we kept our parliament, and were subject to no legislation or taxes which it had not approved. Truth that may be, but a specious truth not to be relied on: witness the fact that all our public laws and all that we attributed to the bounty of our sovereigns stemmed, like oracles, from their English advisers. And why talk of bounty, when we were refused free trade with England, and there were no British offices of state which we could share in or profit from?[2] The English wanted to control us, though indeed they allowed us to flaunt our royal ensign and other such gilded feathers. But as soon as they perceived that we had seen through their trick, roused

---

1   Reading *quid ... remanet*. MS 1 *quod ... remanet*. MS 2 *quod ... remanent*.

2   *Quum ... nobis communio munerum publicorum dignitatum & emolumentorum Britannicorum denegaretur* (lit. 'since community of British public offices, dignities and emoluments was denied us'). The reference is probably to diplomatic appointments. In foreign affairs the monarch exercised the prerogative on behalf of both kingdoms but rarely consulted or appointed Scots. Cf. 'Testamentary Memorial', Appendix C, p. 188 below.

ourselves from sleep and aspired to better things, [194] it became their necessary policy either to destroy us or to force us into union on well-defined terms. Choose, then, the role that Nature herself dictates to us. This union is not a thing the English want for themselves so much as an offer they are making, begging and beseeching us to become[1] not just trading partners but partners in their victories and triumphs, to share in their world-wide fame and the power that all Europe acknowledges and admires.

'And yet you declare that the prospect of this union gives pleasure to the French, delight to the Papists, hope to our enemies, as though they thought it would divide our kingdoms instead of bringing them together. Much rather it shocks and frightens them, and provokes them to envious cursing, while they watch from afar an immense increase in Britain's dominion. "Now tyranny is to be bridled," they exclaim, "and limits are to be set on the spread of Catholicism. Britain rides in triumph and leads captive all the foes of freedom and reformed religion."

'That would be the natural outcome of this union. But human predictions are never entirely reliable, and bad results stem from the best of causes. Religion itself has bred anger, hatred and intestine strife, for which the sinfulness of men, not religion itself, must be blamed. Change and uncertainty govern our lives; Fortune's wheel turns on a giddy axis; in human affairs there is always the danger of disputes and divisions and civil war arising. Union, however, is not to be blamed if fortune turns against us or if wicked men born for the destruction of mankind dare their utmost to wreck it. [195] Nor should it be laid at the door of union if our countrymen fail to bestir themselves, and Scotland remains always as needy and poor as she has been in the past.

'But be of good cheer: prosperity lies within our reach. The omens[2] for this league are propitious and happy, provided we can quell party factions and suppress those personal interests which constantly threaten public deliberations; provided also we can lay aside enmities and rivalries, and follow a policy of encouraging hard work and thrift and promoting religion and virtue. Meantime congratulations are due: first, to this entire assembly on being wiser than the people; second, to the nation, as with due resolution we bring to an end this great work, scorning the schemes of our opponents and the injuries they have done us; and finally, to all Scotsmen, who may now at last pursue

---

1   The logic of the previous lines is unclear. Is England or Nature dictating the terms of union? If the Scots are being forced into union, why do the English 'beg and beseech'? The sense must be: 'The Act of Security has forced England into forcing union on Scotland. So the English, who would otherwise not want union, must beg the Scots to accept the terms they are imposing. Both sides are under political compulsion, and it is through such compulsions that Nature dictates her ends.' In 'Testamentary Memorial' (Appendix C, p. 187 below) Clerk goes further by asserting that the Act of Security was 'invented or encouraged' by English ministers to frighten the English parliament into accepting union.

2   Reading *omina*. MSS *omnia*.

true honour and dignity and true freedom, freedom that is substantial, not a shifting shadow or an empty ghost. And now no more need be said, as Fame spreads her wings and announces to the farthest regions of the earth the good fortune that Britons will derive from this transaction. As for those members who through ignorance or misunderstanding or ill-will opposed it with all their strength, we must hope that in time, as the spirit of faction declines or the clouds are lifted from their eyes, they will come to their senses and acknowledge that Scotland, guided by us, has been led from the political wilderness on to the only true road to happiness and prosperity.'

Thereafter the articles [as amended] were read a second time, and on the next day[1] were approved by parliament and received the royal assent from the High Commissioner.

The remaining 66 sheets of Book 6 cover the following ground. Proceedings of the English parliament [197-205, 214-16]. The Scottish parliament debates procedure for choosing representatives [205-13]. The hostility of the Scottish people to union put down to anxiety for their church, mistrust of their rulers, and widespread Jacobitism, but 'true Britons, putting the good of Europe above national interests, predict that a stronger Britain will promote the cause of European freedom' [217-18]. Queensberry's satisfaction [219]. Text of amended treaty [220-42]. Last acts of the Scottish parliament [243-54]. Queensberry's welcome in England; service in St Paul's; the Queen's joy; first meeting of the British parliament [254-8]. Dissolution of the Scottish Privy Council [259]. The Jacobite expedition of 1708 [260-1]. Payment of the Equivalent; establishment of the Scottish Court of Exchequer; 'but this by the way, for the remaining history of the united kingdoms I leave to others' [262].

---

1   An error. The second reading of the Act Ratifying the Treaty and the final vote took place on the same day, Thur., 16 Jan. 1707.

APPENDICES

APPENDIX A
Memorandums concerning this History of the union written in Latine by me JoClerk pennicuik 3 novr 1746[1]

It was but a few years after the union of the two Kingdoms of England & Scotland that I thought of writing this history; & the motives I had for it, were these, 1° I observed that few, very few Men even of Letters & knowledge in our affaires understood much about it, they run away with a fancy that it was brought about by compulsion & corruption & gave themselves no farther trouble about it. They took things as they found them & relied on some silly accounts such as Mr Lockharts memoires wherein are sufficient Evidences that he did not understand what he was doing & that he was influenced only by the principles of the party he espoused. 2° y^t it was impossible for any man to entertain a clear notion of the union, unless he perfectly understood, the miserable circumstances, these nations were in, before we united. My 3^d motive was that it was fit that foreigners should have a competent knowledge of this great Transaction, that in case they stood united with their nearest nighbours, they might lairn to prize their own happiness & if they were not united, they should know wherin their true interest might consist. And my last motive was to vindicat my own conduct 'tho amongst wise people, especially such as deal in matters of State it will need no appology.

As to the facts related in this History, which preceeded my time, I was oblidged to take them as I found them handed down to posterity by others. Allowing still for English & Scotch differences & party views.

And as to such facts which fell within my own proper knowledge, these I affirm to be true, having been an Eye & Ear Witness to most of them, especially

---

1   SRO, GD18/3202/7. Holograph. Corrections and additions made in 1750 have been included.

what concerns consequences of the union of the two nations, these 43 years past having for so long a time been constantly emploied in publick business.

As to the Language, I take it to be Latine, except where by neglect, or bad habits I have made use of some modern words or phrases which strictly speaking, are not proper Latine; for modern Inventions & new words in several Arts & Sciences require great attention to be so exactly Latinized as to pass for true Latine. However, in such cases I have made use of such terms & words as are used by Buchanan & Thuanus or by Gronovius & Graevius in Histories or Orations, especially Graevius. The learned professor at Utrecht, some years ago.

And by the bye, I here acquaint my Reader that after I resolved to write this History, I bestowed at least Eghteen years in reading the Classicks, as vast collections of Latine Excerpts made by me, will shew, particularly from Livius Caesar Cicero Salustius Corn nepos Tacitus Suetonius & from other Authors both Latine & Greek see a particular List of My Authors here anexed. As to the Style, I endeavoured in most things, to imitat the easiness & plainess of Caesar, but it was impossible I cou'd do this in all particulars, as the subjects I treated, required often to be set furth in a different way & often in words & phrases of which there were scarcely any Traces in Antiquity.

I found great difficulties in Translations of Acts of parliament decrees & orders of state, in order to make them understood & therefor was frequently oblidged to use circumlocutions. But whatever Errors Escapes or neglects I have committed, such may be easily rectified from DeFoe's History of the Union a Book in folio, in the publishing of which, I contributed a good deal of assistence. In the mean time, if any Emendations be attempted I may venture to say that it will not be a matter in which one man of 500 will succeed; one must be as well acquainted with our History, Laws and constitution as I have been to make emendations. My business first as a commissioner of the publick accompts, next as a Commissioner of Trade afterwards as a Commissioner for the union as an Advocat & a Baron of the Exchequer, gave me great opportunities. I purpose, if God shall spare me for a few years, to make such Emendations, my self, & likeways to add some notes, for such I apprehend may be useful & necessary.

I purpose likeways for satisfying the Curiosity of my Readers to add a 7th book in order to shew the happy consequences of the union, such as that now we have lived in great peace & tranquillity with our nighbours of England for near 40 years except where hapned to be Insurrections or Invasions in favours of the House of Stuart, as in 1708 by the French who with the son of King James the 2^d. K. Of great Britain attempted an Invasion—& again in 1715, 1729 & 1745 for these misfortunes were not the consequences of the union; the succession to the Crown in the House of Hanover having been settled in

England many years before. I shall likeways demonstrat that since the union, the people of Scotland have incressed in Trade, except perhaps in these pernitious Branches of it which were carried on with France & Holand, in which the Ballance lay always against us. I shall shew that the vast incress of our Linnen Manufacturies is owing to our intercourse with England and the liberty of trading with the English plantations to which we had no access before the union & in speaking of the vast advantages which flow to Scotland from the plantation-Trade, I shall in course, shew that we have not only had our shares in these plantations, but that they have had many Governours from Scotland within these 20 years; and that the same advantages which the people of England had in their societies & factories to the East Indies, have likeways been communicated to us of Scotland. In a word, I shall shew, that every thing has been in common between us & our nighbours & that there was seldom or never any distinction made in bestowing of offices where it hapned that those of both nations were capable to discharge them. And that when such distinctions seemed to be made, they were owing to other causes than national distinctions, for that it was not to be supposed but that such as lived in or near the Court of Great Britain or were concerned in parliamentary affaires, wou'd always have more Interest than others living at a distance.

This History has been lying by me these several years so that I have had more time to consider it than Horace recommends for the perfecting of any work when he says

nonumque prematur in annum[1]

As to my Emendations, they were necessary either where words were left out in copying, or when they have been wrong spelt such for instance as concilio in place of consilio or the last in place of the first.[2] Several Errors were likeways in the Tenses, & some words as they stood, were not intelligible without some additions or alterations.

As for these Alterations I have made, I cannot positively say that they were always for the better, only in some cases I thought them necessary in order to the better explaining what was intended.

As to some Speeches used in this History: some of them I have delivered verbatim from the Authors who mention them for 'tho they were the inventions of these very Authors yet I thought the Reader wou'd be better pleased to have them repeated than to remit him to these Authors.[3]

---

1   'Hold it back for nine years' (*Ars Poetica*, 388).

2   Refers to Latin idiom for 'the former' and 'the latter'.

3   Only the speeches of Boudicca, Calgacus and Agricola transcribed from Tacitus in Book 1 belong in this category.

As to the Speeches I mention to be made in the parliament of Scotland when the Articles of the Union were under review: they are given with all the force & energy on both sides as they were delivered & 'tho some of them may seam to contain very rude & unpolished Expressions yet they are such things as were spoken with great freedom of speech for those who favoured the union were resolved to be offended with nothing but to bear all reproaches with patience, and as the adverse party knew that this was the case, they were far from being sparing in their reflexions.

As to the division of this History, I have made it in six books—the first treats of the attempts made by the Romans Saxons Danes & Normans to acquire the universal dominion of Great Britain. The 2^d treats of the bloody wars between England & Scotland in order to subdue one another & at last bring these nations under the dominion of one King and one Government. The 3^d book treats of the union of the Crowns of England & Scotland[1] & the attempts made to bring about the union of the two nations. The 4th treats of the attempts made for the same end from the Restoration of K Charles the 2^d to the end of King William's Reign. The 5th shews what was done under the Reign of Queen Ann for uniting the two nations & the sixth sets furth how the Articles of the Treaty of Union were past into a Law by the Parliaments of England & Scotland.

As to my final Intentions with regard to this History, if either I live to give the finishing hand to it or that a proper persone should be found to revise it, which I conceive to be a very difficult thing, I have no objection why it may not be printed & possibly I may even think of printing it in my own time if it be not that I know party writters on an opposite side, will lay out themselves to criticise upon some things in it, as I have no mind to make answers to them, being now too old for disputes of this kind; therefor, it is more probable that it will be left at my death as it now is amongst my papers. But this I think I am in duty to posterity & to my self that a fair Copy may be made and be presented to the Faculty of Advocates in order to find a place amongst their Manuscripts, but this I leave to my friends to do, or not, as they please.

John Clerk

On the 18 of Octr 1750 I finished a Review I made both of this History & this paper and think I have said & done enough.

---

1   In view of Clerk's claim to have revised Books 3 and 4 in Oct. 1746 (notes on manuscripts of 3A and 4), the inaccurate account of their contents given here a month later is remarkable.

APPENDIX B
A List of the Books I made use of in compiling this History besides those I used on account of the Latine language in which I was to write.[1]

Julius Caesar's commentaries,[2] Tacitus,[3] Suetonius,[4] Spartianus,[5] Herodianus,[6] Eutropius,[7] julius Capitolinus,[8] Dion Cassius,[9] Amianus Marcelinus,[10] Strabo,[11] Sleidanus,[12] Orosius,[13] Gildas,[14] Beda,[15] Pancirolus,[16] Nenius,[17] Eumenes Sozimus,[18] polidorus Virgilius,[19] Cronicum Saxonicum,[20] Gulielmus Malesburiensis,[21] Galfridus Monumetensis,[22] Albertus Cranzius,[23] Gulielmus Westmonasteriensis,[24] Gulielmus Lambardus,[25] Matheus Parisiensis,[26] Holon-

1   SRO, GD18/3202/8. In the following notes the editions probably used have been identified where possible from the Penicuik Library Catalogue (PLC) begun in 1724 (NLS MS Dept. 187/5), and failing that from *A Catalogue of the Library of the Faculty of Advocates, Edinburgh: Part the First* (Edinburgh, 1742) (ALC).
2   *C. Julii Caesaris Commentarii* (London, 1706). PLC.
3   *Tacitus cum notis Gronovii* (Amsterdam, 1673). PLC.
4   *C. Suetonii Tranquilli opera* (Amsterdam, 1661). PLC.
5   *Vitae Imperatorum*, in *Historiae Augustae scriptores sex*, ed. I. Casaubon (Paris, 1603). ALC.
6   *Historiarum sui temporis ... Libri viii* (London, 1639). ALC.
7   *Romanae historiae breviarium* (Paris, 1683). ALC.
8   *Historia aliquot Imperatorum Romanorum*, in *Historiae Augustae scriptores sex*, ed. I. Casaubon (Paris, 1603). ALC.
9   *Romana historia* (Basle, 1557). PLC.
10 *Ammianus Marcellinus cum notis variorum* (Leyden, 1693). PLC.
11 *Rerum geographicarum lib. xvii* (Amsterdam, 1707). ALC.
12 *De quattuor summis imperiis* (Amsterdam, 1586). PLC.
13 *Historiarum adversus paganos lib. vii* (Cologne, 1582). ALC.
14 *Historia de excidio & conquestu Britanniae*, in *Rerum Britannicarum scriptores vetustiores*, ed. H. Commelinus (Heidelberg, 1587). ALC.
15 *Historia ecclesiae gentis Anglorum*, ed. J. Smith (Cambridge, 1722). PLC.
16 *Commentarium in Notitiam utriusque imperii dignitatum* (Lyon, 1608). PLC.
17 *Eulogium Britanniae, sive historia Britonum*, in *Historiae Anglicanae scriptores xx*, ed. T. Gale (London, 1675). ALC.
18 Eumenius (Zosimus), *Orationes iv* (Geneva, 1625). ALC.
19 *Historia Angliae* (Basle, 1570). PLC.
20 Ed. E. Gibson (Oxford, 1692). ALC.
21 (William of Malmesbury), *De gestis Regum Anglorum*, in *Rerum Anglicanarum scriptores post Bedam praecipui*, ed. Sir H. Savile (Frankfurt, 1601). ALC.
22 (Geoffrey of Monmouth), *Historia de gestis Regum Britanniae*, in *Rerum Britannicarum scriptores vetustiores*, ed. H. Commelinus (Heidelberg, 1587). ALC.
23 Albertus Krantzius, *Regnorum aquilonarium ... Chronica* (Frankfurt, 1576). ALC.
24 Error for (Matthew of Westminster), *Flores historiarum, praecipue de rebus Britannicis* (London, 1570). ALC.
25 *Archaionomia, sive de priscis Anglorum legibus libri* (London, 1568). ALC.
26 *Opera, seu historia major* (London, 1684). ALC.

schedius,[1] Hovedenus,[2] Walsinghamius,[3] Pryneus,[4] Tyrellus,[5] Cragius de Hominio Successione & Unione,[6] Boethius,[7] Fordenus,[8] Joannes Major,[9] Lesleus,[10] Buchananus,[11] Barneus,[12] Froisardus,[13] Reymeri Foedera,[14] Traitez d'entre Les Roys de France & Angletere,[15] Drummondius,[16] Wilsonius,[17] Cambdenus,[18] Etchardius,[19] Andersonius,[20] Thuanus,[21] Abercromius,[22] Montrose's memoirs,[23] Acts of parliament several English Lawers, Acts & minutes of several Councils & a great many small treaties needless to be mentioned here. With most of the modern Historians.[24] And as to Classical Authors I think I have read them all & some of them several times over with some of the Greek Authors particularly Herodotus, Thucidedes & Xenophon. With Homer & most of the minor poets.

N.B. Having on the 18 of Oc^br 1750 revised the above List of Books I declare that it did not proceed from any Vanity or ostentation in me but honestly to account for the preparations I made before I wrote this History so that what neglects or mistakes I made were neither out of ignorance or design but hapned

---

1   R. Holinshed, *Description and chronicle of England, Scotland and Ireland* (London, 1587). ALC.
2   (Roger Howden), *Annales*, in *Rerum Anglicanarum scriptores post Bedam praecipui*, ed. Sir H. Savile (Frankfurt, 1601). ALC.
3   (Thomas Walsingham), *Historia Regum Angliae, ab initio regni Edwardi I ad obitum Henrici V*, in *Anglica, Hibernica, Normannica, Cambrica a veteribus scripta*, ed. W. Camden (Frankfurt, 1602). ALC.
4   William Prynne, *The History of King John, King Henry III and ... King Edward I* (London, 1670). ALC.
5   James Tyrrel, *General History of England ... To the reign of Henry IV* (London, 1696-1704). ALC.
6   See above, n. 1, p. 67. All three MSS are listed in PLC.
7   (Hector Boece), *Scotorum Historiae a prima gentis origine libri xvii* (Paris, 1574). ALC.
8   (John of Fordun), *Scotichronicon, cum supplemento & continuatione Walt. Boweri*, ed. T. Hearne (Oxford, 1722). ALC.
9   (John Mair), *Historia majoris Britanniae tam Angliae quam Scotiae* (Paris, 1521). ALC.
10 (John Leslie), *De origine, moribus & rebus gestis Scotorum libri x* (Rome, 1578) . ALC.
11 *Opera omnia* (Edinburgh, 1715). PLC.
12 Joshua Barnes, *The History of Edward III* (Cambridge, 1688). ALC.
13 Jehan Froissart, *Histoire et chronique* (Paris, 1574). PLC.
14 Thomas Rymer, *Foedera* (London, 1704-35). ALC.
15 Probably an error for 'Traittez entre les Roys de France & les Roys d'Escosse ... Années 1292, 1296'. MS. ALC.
16 William Drummond of Hawthornden, *Works* (Edinburgh, 1711). PLC.
17 Arthur Wilson, *The History of Great Britain, being the life and actions of King James I* (London, 1653). ALC.
18 (William Camden), *Annales Rerum Anglicanarum Hibernicarum* (London, 1615). PLC.
19 Laurence Eachard, *The history of England, from the first entrance of Julius Caesar to the conclusion of the reign of King James II* (London, 1707-18). PLC.
20 (i) *Historical essay, shewing that the Crown and Kingdom of Scotland is imperial and independent* (Edinburgh, 1705). PLC. (ii) *Collections relating to the History of Mary Queen of Scotland* (Edinburgh, 1725-28). PLC.
21 (J.A. de Thou), *Historiarum sui temporis ... Libri cxxxviii* (Geneva, 1626). PLC.
22 Patrick Abercromby, *The Martial Atchievements of the Scottish Nation* (Edinburgh, 1711, 1715). PLC.
23 George Wishart, *A Complete History of the Wars in Scotland under the conduct of ... James, Marquis of Montrose*, trans. W. Adams (London, 1720). ALC.
24 This note added by Clerk to his original MS, c. 1750.

purely by a certain *incuria* or inadvertency Let therefor my Readers follow the practise of Horace de Arte poetica,

verum ubi plura nitent in carmine, non ego paucis
offendar maculis quas aut incuria fudit
Aut humana parum cavit natura.[1]

1   'But in a poem where more things are fine, I shall not be offended by a few blots which either carelessness has caused or human frailty has failed to prevent' (*Ars Poetica*, 351-3).

APPENDIX C

A Testamentary Memorial concerning The Union of
the Two Kingdoms of Scotland & England in 1707
with a short account of the share I had in the
settlement of the present Government of Great
Britain.[1]

I desire that all my Children Brothers and Friends may be allowed copies of
this paper, but so as it the original may not be carried out of the House—and
if it be thought worth while as I believe it may be, 50 or so copies of it, may
sometime or other be printed off & distributed amongst my Friends. And to
facilitate this there is a copy of it written in a tollerable hand by Mr William
Ainsley my chaplain,[2] which will be found either in the great oaken chist in
the Charter Room of Pennicuik or in a little Iron chist in my Closet at
Mavisbank.

pennicuik house 20 Octob[r] 1744

Being now in the last Stage of Life and by reasone of my Age not far from the
Brink of Eternity, I shall for the satisfaction both of my own posterity and of
all others who shall take the truble to read this paper, declare my real, honest
and constant sentiments with regard to the union of England and Scotland, in
which I had so particular a concern, having been called by the providence of
God to be one of the Commissioners for Scotland in this great Transaction.

The true Grounds & reasons of the same have not hitherto been very well
understood, and consequently, it has been misrepresented by many, according
to their different views and prejudices. I happen at present, to be one of Three
now only alive of the 31 Commissioners for Scotland and therefor, judge it
my duty after a Tract of Experiences for thirty seven years to leave behind me
this Memorial. And I hope it will be received as a Testamentary performance
from a Man who writes according to the Light of his own conscience and the
knowledge he must have acquired in the publick affaires of Great Britain And
particularly of Scotland since the year 1703 down to the present year 1744. In
the first place I rejoice very much that it has been my Fate to be an Instrument
of so great a Benefite to this Island of Great Britain as I humbly conceive the

1   SRO, GD18/3243/1.
2   SRO, GD18/3243/2.

Union of the Two Kingdoms, is. Others, I hope, will be of the same mind, if they will seriously consider what is here subjoined. I am aware that it is a very difficult matter for Men of certain principles to be pleased with any thing that can be said in support of this Memorable Transaction & I know that some are even weak enough to lay great stress upon what they apprehend was due to the Honour of the Antient Kingdom of Scotland but true and disinterested Patriotism ought to extend it self over the whole Island of Great Britain, for her prosperity, in general, as the true *salus populi* ought, on all occasions to be considered as the *suprema Lex* and not the Welfare of any particular Corner thereof.

As I have frequently and I hope maturely considered the Histories of both Countries, I cannot help thinking that for many Ages past, down to the union of the two Crowns under King James the sixth of Scotland in the year 1604 our Forefathers have been in a most miserable situation; nothing but Thefts and Robries savage and bloody incursions into one anothers Borders were their perpetual occupations—in place of mutual good offices and that constant friendly correspondence which ought to have been between the two principal British nations, successive schemes of disorder and confusion displayed themselves, every where, to the great satisfaction of those nighbouring nations that placed their greatest happiness and security on our calamities.

This state of War in which we were constantly involved, appeared more particularly to proceed from the Politicks of France. Our divisions and animosities were constantly kept up and fomented by this nation in order to lessen that Power and Majesty which naturally belonged to Great Britain as Mistress of the seas and consequently the only proper Arbitrarix of peace and war in Europe. Hence it always hapned that when the Kings of England attempted, at any time, to assert their own Rights and privileges in the Kingdom of France, the Kings of Scotland & their subjects, were hounded out by the French to invade the nighbouring provinces of England with Fire & Sword.

After the union of the Crowns, above mentioned, took place in 1604 the Measurs of Goverment between Scotland and England altered much for the better, yet still Forreign princes observed with pleasure that this union carried nothing along with it that seem'd any accession of power, since the great Councils or parliaments of the two nations remained seperat & distract, and indeed this was precisely the case of the two nations for both of them lookt upon one another with jealous and invidious Eyes. The English from old resentments and prejudices cou'd not endure to see the Scots advanced to any offices of Honour Trust and advantage in any part of the Island and far less in England or any of the Countries and Territories thereto belonging; and on the other hand, the Scots considered the English as their greatest Rivals and

G

oppressors in every respect. Such were the constant sentiments of both nations during the Reigns of the above-named King James the 6th of Scotland and of King Charles the first King Charles the second, King James the 7 & King William and Queen Ann down to the periode in which the union of the Two Kingdoms, happily, took place, Anno 1707.

Thence it fell out that Scotland deprived of the Residence of her Kings came from time to time under the Government of such necessitous rapacious & mercenary Court-favourites as the Ministers of State in England thought fit to appoint. Those knew no better way to keep themselves in power but by innumerable Acts of oppression amongst their fellow subjects—a kind of uniformity in Religious matters was pushed on with the greatest severity and from thence a pretence was taken by many weak Enthusiastick disaffected Men to enter into conspiraces and Rebellions against the Government and consequently of falling under the pains and penalties which the Law inflicted on these occasions.

But the main sourse of jealousies on the part of England arose from the Tragedy which Scotland acted in the Reign of King Charles the first. The readiness which Her people almost generally shewed at that time to enter into a civil war & to assist the disaffected in England, served to demonstrate to the Ministers of State in that Country that Scotland wou'd no sooner acquire Richess & power by Trade navigation and Manufactories, than these wou'd be emploied to bring about dangerous schemes to the Liberty safety & Trade of England, therefor it was to be received as a settled maxim in the politicks of the Court of Great Britain or rather in the parliament of England, that Scotland was to be discouraged by all possible means whatsomever. Her people had a most flagrant instance of this in the year 1696 for when a Company was erected by the Authority of the parliament of Scotland for carrying on a Trade to Africa and the Indies, and after, at a vast expence, the Scots had made a settlement in the Isthmus of Darien, The English not only refused their assistence to them but without the least resentment, suffered the Spaniards to destroy the Colony with Fire & Sword.

I am, in the mean time, very far from thinking that this was a reasonable scheme with respect to the Scots, on the contrary, I always thought it not so much a foolish as a Rogueish project invented for the same bad purposes to which the Misisippi Company in France and afterwards the South Sea Company in England served, about the years 1720 1721 & 1722 namely for the benefite of the projectors and their Accomplices to betray and buble the innocent proprietors by raising the valew of their imaginary stocks & sinking them after these proprietors & their accomplices had sold out & gain'd Estates. But the Conduct of England towards Scotland, at that time, served sufficiently, as a profe that Scotland, in a seperat state, was not to enjoy the least shadow of property in any part of the World, which cou'd in any way interfere with the power, navigation & Trade of England: and the situation of our Country made it impossible for us to succeed in any thing that cou'd be of the least advantage to us in the way of Trade & Manufactories. Instances of this we had several times, for 'tho by the Authority of our own parliaments we erected diverse Kinds of Manufactories particularly for broad cloths and silks and guarded them by all necessary prohibitions and Regulations yet such importations were made over our dry Borders from England that all our endeavours were frustrated and great sums of money lost. The impossibility of guarding these Borders afforded dayly opportunities for Smuglers on both sides to destroy us.

Irritated by these misfortunes & constant disappointments we thought of various ways to redress our selves & distress our nighbours of England. A fit opportunity presented it self for the succession to our Crown coming in Question, upon the prospect of want of Issue of the Queens Body, we compiled that memorable Act in 1704 Entituled, a little improperly Act for Security of the Kingdom. This was however brought about with great deliberation both in the session of Parliament of 1703 & 1704. The whole Country of Scotland was to be armed upon the event of the Queen's death and a successor was not to be chosen unless upon certain conditions which depended altogether on the humours of the people of England. The most material clause in the s^d Act was as follows 'provided always that the same be not successor to the Crown of England unless that in this present session of parliament or any other session of this or any ensuing Parliament during her Majesty's Reign there be such conditions of Government settled and established as may secure the Honour & Soveraignity of this Crown & Kingdom, The Freedom frequency and power of parliaments, the Religion Liberty and Trade of the Nation from English or any forraign influence with power to the s^d meeting of Estates to add such farder conditions of Government as they shall think necessary the same being consistent with & no ways derogatory from these which shall be inacted in this or any other session of parliament during her Majesty's Reign. And farder but prejudice of the generality forsaid, it is hereby specially statute enacted & declared that it shall not be in the power of the s^d meeting of Estates to name the successor of the Crown of England to be successor to the imperial Crown of this Realm nor shall the same persone be capable in any event to be King or Queen of both Realms unless a free communication of Trade the freedom of navigation and the Liberty of the plantations be fully agreed to & established by the parliament & Kingdom of England to the Kingdom & subjects of Scotland at the sight & to the satisfaction of this or any ensewing parliament of Scotland or the said meeting of Estates.'

N.B. I have been the more particular in this clause in regard that I find in all our printed copies of the Acts of the parliament of Scotland the half of the clause is left out but it will be found in the Minutes of parliament on the 26 july 1703. How the clause was left out I cannot tell but it stood in it when it was voted & approven of in parliament. See the minutes of parliament 5 April 1704 and these minutes of parliament will be found in the laigh parliament house and in the Advocates Library.

By the above clause it was but too evident that the people of Scotland were to be utterly undone, unless in the Queen's life they could provide a sufficient Remedy. We were all to be, not only armed, but disciplined and every body the least acquainted with the affaires of the World, knows, that when Men get their Heads set upon Arms and military discipline it will not be an easy matter without Bloodshed to bring them to rights again. The liberty of the plantations purchessed by much English Blood Toile & Treasure was to be surrendered to us and all this without giving the English the least participation in our Government.

What could we then do but seriously think of an Union as the only Remedy cou'd be offered to that National Fermentation that was already begun amongst us. Even the Honour of our Antient Kingdoms behoved to give way to England on the best conditions that cou'd be obtained for if We had stood out to the last we must have submitted to the persone on whom the English nation had thought fit to confer their Crown or have made our Country a schene of dissolation Bloodshed and Confusion. It was impossible for us to have supported a different successor to our Crown from the persone in possession of the Crown of England and therefore must, at last, have shamefully fallen under such a Conquest as hapned to us under the Usurpation of Oliver Cromwell, when we did our outmost indeavours to support King Charles the 2^d against the superior power of this Scurge of God. England as being at least four times more numerous in people than Scotland wou'd have fund little or no difficulty in subdueing us except what wou'd have arisen from our Rocks & Mountains, and in treating us ignominiously & cruelly as a conquered province. We neither cou'd have asked nor expected assistence from our Antient Allies the French—their Religious concerns and ours were so opposite as to admit of no other tye of Friendship than what we observe amongst distant nations at this day. So that any tollerable conditions offered to us by the English had always met with a better Reception than possibly cou'd be offered to us by the French or any Forraign nation.

In the mean time, we were vain enough to think that no condescension on the part of England cou'd be too much for our Antient Kingdom, 'tho by the rest of the world we were no otherways considered than as a poor Antient Matron in Rags who always makes a very despicable figure. Our seperat and as we thought, independent parliaments were meer phantoms of power, and perfect Burlesques on free national Assemblies. They met always under the influence & direction of the Ministry of England and therefor nothing of consequence was transacted in them but what flowed from sign'd Instructions given to the King's High Commissioners who presided in their several sessions. For a full proof of what I here advance, I shall refer my self to the printed speeches of a very learned Gentleman, Mr Andrew Fletcher of Salton and which speeches were made in my hearing before the parliament of Scotland in 1703, 1704 & 1705. See likeways the above claus of the Act of Security.

I own indeed that some matters were, now and then transacted in our parliaments which in Appearance did not seem to be calculated altogether for the benefite of England, but still every thing passed under English Ministerial Influence to bring about some favourite point which the Court had in view, for their own particular interest & often to thwart the projects of an opposite party. The real and true benefite of the people of Scotland was no ingredient in their deliberations, as I cou'd demonstrat from many instances. The above mentioned Act of Security was of this kind, which 'tho concerted by the parliament of 1703 cou'd never have had the Royal Assent in 1704 if it had not been to intimidat the people of England & in order to make the succession of the Crown in the Family of Hannover, more necessary in Scotland and lastly for bringing about the union of the Two Kingdoms. This it did effectually, and in the mean time, gave rise to an Act of parliament in England in the 3^d & 4th year of Queen Ann intituled Act for affectual securing the Kingdom of England from the apparent dangers that may arise from several Acts passed in the Kingdom of Scotland. Such were the political views of the Ministry of England at that time. They themselves invented or encouraged a formidable Act in Scotland in order to frighten the parliament of England to provide a speedy Remedy against it. This Remedy as I have before noticed, was the Union, not so much, I believe, in compliance to the generality of the Whig party who above all things desired to see the succession in the House of Hannover secured as to gratify the Queen's own inclination. She, it is certain, from a real love to her people and from an ardent desire of making her Reign glorious to posterity had nothing so much at heart as the bringing about an Event that for many ages past had in vain been attempted by her predecessors since the first endeavours of the Romans to this purpose, down to our own times, for even those wanted above all things to settle their universal Empire in Britain but to proceed in my Reflexions on the true grounds & motives of the union, I shall for the satisfaction of my Reader put the case that the Ministry of England had been disappointed of their hopes in the above mentioned Act of Security, by the death of the Queen & that the Scots in pursuance of the

Act had been oblidged to make choise of a different King from England, wou'd not this have laid the foundation of a bloody destructive civil war? and let us farther suppose that this seperat King of Scotland had in compliance with the humours of his Country-men marched an Army into England & at last made conquest of that Country, as the small insignificant nation of the Tartars made, not many years ago, of the great Empire of China wou'd any other consequence have hapned to Scotland by this piece of Knight Errantry than what hapned to Tartary? wou'd not her King and his successors have deserted her & take up their residence in England, even as our own Kings did upon the Union of the Crowns in 1604? and had not the condition of the Scots been the very same they are in, at this day? wou'd not the great Metropolis of Britain, the city of London by its situation & natural advantages have been the center of Trade as it just now is? would not our parliaments have met there? wou'd not the Representatives for Scotland been settled and proportioned according to the valew of her Lands compared with these of England, wou'd not all Taxations on Land Trade & Manufactures been as equal as possible, that for the peace of Great Britain all her subjects might trade on a reasonable kind of Equality. No doubt all these circumstances had taken place, for to imagine that the Scots as the conquerors wou'd have had more extraordinary privileges than the English wou'd be as foolish a notion as to suppose that the future Governours of Great Britain cou'd not comprehend what was most for their own safety and interest. In a word, let the Scots put the case as they will on the most fortunat events that cou'd befall them, the natural situation of their Country wou'd in a very few years have put them in the very same circumstances with England in which they are at this day, & in which the conquering country of the Tartars is with respect to China, viz: to be poor & miserable.

I have, I think already shewn how necessary a measure of Government the Union of the Two Kingdoms was to all the Inhabitants of Britain, but to be a little more particular as to the Scots, I must add that 'tho they were the subjects of one King & in a good measure one People with the English yet they were constantly treated as Aliens and Mercenaries in all the publick concerns of Britain. In Embassies, for instance & Treaties with Forreign nations, we were seldom or never intrusted since the days of Oliver Cromwell. Once I think the Duke of Hamiltone was sent to France to congratulat Louis the 14 on the birth of his son the Dauphine, but other instances are out of my memory. In Treaties with forreign States & princes we had neither name nor interest 'tho we affected to act on the Stage of Life as the subjects of a different Kingdom from England. Our Troops were always considered as meer Mercinares and indeed not altogether without reasone since the Kingdom of Scotland did not contribute one farthing for their maintenance in forreign parts. All the offices & emoluments of the Colonies and Plantations both in the East & west Indies were intirely ingrossed by English Men, nor were our Merchants allowed at any rate, to trade there. In a word, all the privat views & advantages of Scotsmen behoved to center amongst themselves and their Gains were only to arise from pillaging & distressing one another.

Yet in all this I am far from arraigning the justice of England, on the contrary, if I had been born an Englishman with any interest or concern in their publick councils, I had acted the very same part which the Scots have so loudly complain'd of, for it was but too evident from the prejudices which the Scots entertain'd against the English, for many ages past, that all their acquisitions of power & richess wou'd have been emploied in distressing England & fomenting factions and party quarrels to her perpetual disturbance.

Was not then the union the only Expedient, which I in my poor Sphere of Life cou'd think of for establishing and securing the peace & happiness of my native Country? My own conscience persuaded me that it was, and therefor I shall proceed, with all brevity to explain my reasons & sentiments on each of the 25 Articles of the Treaty of Union.

The first Article of this important Transaction whereby the Two Kingdoms of England & Scotland became united into one, under the name of the Kingdom of Great Britain, gave in my opinion such a power and Majesty to the British Nations as they had never known before. That union of the Crowns in 1604 under king James the 6th of Scotland and first of England was meerly nominat, for our publick Councils and Interests continued as seperat as ever, yea in a great measure the s^{d} union of the Crowns lessened the power of Britain in the opinion of the World, since it was manifest that the jealousies and animosities between the two nations wou'd rather be incressed than diminished. So long as the Scots continued under the Government of their own princes they had no occasion to interfere with the English. The former might envie the prosperity of the latter, yet had no pretentions to Rival them in any thing. But when they came to be under one head, one Lord & Master the Scots thought they had a just Claim to an equal share of his favours, that it belonged in part to them to interpose in the affaires of Great Britain. From thence sprung the Grounds and reasons of the civil war in the Reign of King charles the first & King charles the 2^{d} with all the unlucky consequences that attended them. Besides, there was another event which was expected by all the political princes in Europe, from the union of the British Crowns, Namely, that the King of England wou'd make use of his Antient Kingdom of Scotland to enslave & subdue his English subjects. This Expectation came by various accidents to be disappointed for divine providence which watched over the liberties of Great Britain put it in the breasts of the Scots to oppose all standing Armies for supporting the honour and interest of the Crown as was pretended but in reality to curb and restrain the Liberties of the subjects of England. Frequent endeavours were used for this purpose particularly on the Restoration of King Charles the 2^d but the Scots, true to their own Liberties cou'd never endure any measurs of Government that had but the least tendency to infringe the Liberties of their nighbours. Now by this first Article of the Union the Scots have a more immediat concern in the wellfare of the English & therefor I hope will continue to be their best supporters.

The 2^d Article which settles the succession of the British Crown and dominions thereunto belonging, on the present Royal & Electoral Family of Hannover, needs nothing to be said in its defence. This succession had been before settled in England, and so became absolutely necessary in Scotland, even 'tho the two nations had not thought fit to unite together, what else could the Scots have done notwithstanding all the Grimace they made in the before mentioned Act of Security. The Family of Hannover provided to them the nearest protestant Heirs to their Crown while others of a different Religion were by the s^d act expressly secluded. Besides, I must say, he wou'd have been a very enterprising prince, who had taken upon him the Crown of Scotland in exclusion of the next protestant Heir supported by all the power & richess of England. In short I absolutely thought it a vain conceit in any sett of Men to fancy that the Scots even without the conditions they expected from England as a communication of Trade and the Liberty of the plantations wou'd so far declare themselves the irreconcilable Ennemies of England as to set up a different successor to their Crown. Most unhappy had the poor weak Man been who had accepted it. In fine what the Scots agreed to, in an honourable way, as a condition of the union was such a measure as they cou'd not possibly have avoided, even without it.

The 3^d Article which puts all the Councils of great Britain under the direction of one & the same parliament, was what I thought & still think one of the most essential parts of the Union. I never cou'd conceive the least good opinion of seperat parliaments & what they called a Federal union. For in all parts of the World, where an absolute power is not lodged in a sovereign prince there must be one supreme court, convention, council or parliament which must preside over all the nations or countries that comprise the union of any great state whether a Kingdom or a Republick.

The 4th Article which establishes a free and full communication of Trade between the Two Kingdoms will, I suppose, be allowed by every body to be the Basis of all the commertial happiness of Great Britain. Before the union, as I have already noticed the Scots were excluded from the benefites and advantages belonging to England in any part of the World 'tho purchased & secured by the English at a very great expence of Time Blood & Treasure.

The 5th Article which relates to the ships of Scotland, at the commencement of the union, was absolutely necessary, in order to entitle her ships to the same privileges and advantages of Trade which belonged to the English by the Act of Navigation in the 12th of King Charles the 2[d].

The 6th Article which appoints the same Regulations of Trade to take place over all the united Kingdom, was no doubt, for the general advantage of Trade—for I know few or no duties that affect our Exportations or importations but what have been wisely calculated for the benefite of our natural products or manufactories. Such for instance are the duties which affect French Wines & Spirits, soap paper Linnen and all forreign goods whatsomever. Happy had it been for the people of Scotland, if all these duties had been paid & all the Regulations on Trade had been punctually observed, but such was the perverseness & Avarice of many both in England & Scotland that called themselves Merchants, as to carry on no other Trade than what tended to defraud the publick Revenue and utterly destroy these advantages which the Law had entituled the produce of our Country & Manufactories to over these of strangers and hence it came that French Wines & Brandies with a great multitude of other goods have since the union, been imported into Scotland to the unspeakable hurt & Loss of this whole Island.

The 7th Article which settles the Excise in Scotland, seem'd to me, to be founded on justice and Equity. For a High Excise in England and a Low Excise in Scotland had put the two nations, on such an unequal footing with regard to Trade that no Union cou'd possibly have subsisted between them. All nations must trade on easy or hard terms in proportion to their ordinary expense of living, those who live dear, or which is the same thing, those who pay high duties for the common necessaries of Life must expect to be undersold & ruined in their Trade and manufactories by those who can support themselves at a less expence. But here I must notice that this Article of the union suffered a great alteration by the parliament of Scotland, from what had been agreed to in England. The Scots Commissioners took it for granted that what in Scotland was called Tipeny ale or Two penny Ale wou'd after the union be charged only with the small-beer duty which took place in England. But the parliament of Scotland unwilling to trust this explanation of the Article to any officers of Excise, added the express condition that such Ale brewed in Scotland should only pay 2 sh[s] ster: upon the 34 Gallons English measure or 12 Gallons Scots measure, but I have had many reasons to think that it had been much better for Scotland that the Article had continued as it was concerted in England viz: that all parts of the united Kingdom be for ever and after the union Liable to the same Excise on all Exciseable Liquors and the Excise settled in England on such Liquors when the union commences take place through the whole united Kingdom.

If this Article had continued to stand as it was at first concerted many of the people of Scotland had given over the idle custom & bad habite they have

fallen into, in spending their time & money in tipling the lowest kind of Malt
Liquors called twopenny Ale—a little Ale of a better quality, had done their
bodies more service and the small beer or Ale had served for their common &
ordinary drink. There was not the least reasone to be affraied of oppression
from the Officers of Excise, since the payment of the civil Establishment was
chiefly to depend on this branch of the publick Revenue. It behoved to be
paid as this best could be collected & therefor if the people had been unwilling
to pay a higher duty for twopenny Ale than they paid before the union they
wou'd have drunk the less of it & consequently been the less burdened, or
otherways, the officers of Excise behoved to have rated it as small Bier and
exacted payment of the duties accordingly. It had been a very easy matter for
the justices of peace who are the chief judges in matters of Excise to have
adjusted all the disputes that cou'd arise from this Article, yet such was the
fondness of some of the common people for their Tippeny Ale, that in some
places, particularly at Drumfrise, the Articles of the union were burnt & such
disturbance given that the parliament of Scotland was oblidged to make the
above-mentioned alteration for ascertaining and securing the duty on
Twopenny Ale as it then stood.

The 8th Article which relates to the duties on salt, received some alterations,
from the parliament of Scotland & not at all for the better.

The 9th Article which settles the Cess or Land Tax of Scotland will be always
esteem'd highly beneficial to her, especially in time of War. This will appear
very evident from comparing the proportion which a Tax of 4 shillings in the
pound bears in England to 8 moneths cess or 48000 lib ster: in Scotland I am
only a little difficulted how to reconcile this proportion to that reasonable
Equality of publick burdens which ought to be observed amongst the subjects
of an united Kingdom; however, this is very certain that the people of England
do not in reality pay 4 shillings in the pound which wou'd be a 5th of their
yearly incomes & 'tho the quota of Land Tax which is mentioned in this Article
namely 1997763 lib comes nearer to the real rent of England than 48000 lib
does the real rent of Scotland, yet it must be considered that Scotland in the
Infancy of its Trade manufactories and improvements and lying at a great
distance from the Center of Government cannot bear a real & true proportion
of the publick burdens of Great Britain. A small sum of money carried out of
Scotland does more prejudice in the necessary circulation, than five or six times
the like sum raised in England.

The 10 the 11th 12th & 13 Articles contain all the abatements of duties and
publick burdens which the people of England cou'd admit of at that time. They
were only temporary to certain limited periods & the parliament of Great
Britain might renue or discontinue them as should be thought most proper for
the circumstances of both nations, but whatever was exacted by these duties

or was afterwards exacted by their renewal and continuance was all expended for the benefite of Scotland for I can assure my Reader that all the Cess customs Excise Crown Revenues and other duties and burdens which affected Scotland seldom or never answered the Exigencies of the Government of this Country viz. The payment of the draubacks & premiums allowed upon the Exportations of the produce and Manufactories of Scotland, the payment of the civil Establishment of such Troops and Garisons as were necessary for the defence of this part of Britain. It is true, that sometimes there were considerable Remittances made to the Treasury of Great Britain at London, yet it is no less true that greater Remittances were made back to Scotland. For it was impossible that the Troops & Garisons in Scotland cou'd be supported by the ordinary annual Cess which in times of peace was no higher than 24000 lib, for this quota according to the Article varied proportionately, as 2 or 3 or 4 Sh^s was imposed on England as the Land Tax of that part of Britain.

The 14 Article which relates to duties that might happen to be imposed by the parliament of England, before the union should take place & declares them not to be chargeable on Scotland, needs no explanation or defence. It received no alteration from the parliament of Scotland save that no duty on Malt should take place during the War we then had with France. To have been perpetually exempted from it, wou'd have made too great an inequality between the two nations.

The 15 Article specifies several sums that were to be paid to Scotland as Equivalents or reimbursements for such parts of the Revenue of this Kingdom as should be applied towards satisfying the Debts of England. And in the first place, mention is made of the sum of 398085 lib 10 Sh^s as what was to be paid to Scotland for such parts of her Revenue of Customs & Excise as with the like duties in England were to be appropriated for the English debts. No fewer than six able Accomptants and amongst those, the Learned Doctor Gregory professor of Mathematicks in Oxford, were emploied to make the calculations necessary for ascertaining the s^d sum. Many were so ill natured, at that time, both in England & Scotland as to call this the price of the union, but it will appear otherways from the calculations that are to be found in the Minutes of the Commissioners of both Kingdoms. Justice it self, required it, and besides, there were two particular Reasons of great weight which inforced it. One was that England might do justice to Scotland for the injury done her in abandoning the Colony of Darien above mentioned to the fury of the Spaniards which occasioned the loss of the greatest part of the stock of the Scots company to Africa and the Indies. The other was that as part of the Customs & Excise in England was applied for payment of the publick debts of that Country so in like manner, the publick debts of Scotland should be paid out of the 398085 lib 10 Sh^s aforementioned. As to the Company of Scotland concern'd in the settlement of Darien I have already taken notice that nothing cou'd have been worse projected for the Advantage of Scotland yet since a vast sum of money was sunk by it, the English were willing by this Article that the same should be made up to the Adventurers. There was likeways a certain political reasone which pled strongly for the advancement of the s^d sum to the Scots, viz: they were so impoverished, as was generally thought, that unless they were put in Cash or credite, they cou'd not cooperat with the English in the advantages of Trade proposed by the union. However I may venture to affirm that the s^d sum was so far from being an incitement to the Scots to enter into the union, that on the contrary, the Generality of them wou'd willingly have contributed for as great a sum to have got free of it. And besides, I knew very few at the time of the union who wou'd ever be persuaded that the money was really to be paid. As to the two reasons above suggested for granting the aforementioned sum to Scotland, they never entered into the publick deliberations of the Commissioners of either Kingdom but were frequently talked of in a privat way especially amongst the Queens Ministers. With the same views provision was made in this Article for other Equivalents that might fall due to Scotland in case of any farther applications of her Revenue towards payment of the Debts of England.

And in order to the right disposal of such arising Equivalents, care was taken in this Article for the improvement of the Fisheries and manufactories of Scotland the good effects of which are every day more & more apparent. But before I dismiss this Article I must take notice that the parliament of Scotland made some few Additions to it, one was a provision of 2000 lib yearly for 7 years to be imploied for the benefite of the proprietors of the coarse wool of Scotland, in the several shires that produced the same, because upon the union there cou'd be no Exportation of coarse wool which 'tho a mismanagement of the wool of Scotland, had obtained for many years past. This sum, after the union was annually set aside till it made a capital of 14000 lib & the interest thereof was at last applied for encouraging the woolen manufactories.

Another Addition was a faculty referred to the parliament of setling the way or manner of payment of the African Company for extinguishing the publick debts of Scotland. And accordingly two Acts passed in the same session of parliament, the one is entituled Act *concerning the payment of the sums out of the Equivalent to the African Company. The other* is, Act *concerning the publick debts* both these Acts were very properly concerted & obviated many frauds & difficulties that might have been committed. I need not add any more to this important Article but refer my reader to Defoe's History of the union in folio from page 83 to page 100 & from page 146 to 151.

The 16 Article which relates to the uniformity of the coyn of Great Britain, was thought absolutely necessary & had a very good effect as will be afterwards shewn.

The 17 Article, in like manner, provides for an uniformity or equality of Weights & measures in both Kingdoms. It was no less acceptable to the parliament of Scotland than the former but to this day nothing was put in Execution save that standards were regularly sent down from England to be keept in such Royal Burghs as were appointed formerly in Scotland to have the custody of the like weights & measures, however, I must here by the bye take notice that the weights & measures even of England at the time of the union were very different & continue in the same state to this day. These indeed are upon a worse footing in Scotland but it is in the power of the justices of peace in both parts of the united Kingdom to make this Article of the union effectual.

The 18 Article which relates to the reservation of the Laws in both Kingdoms, was agreable to the humours & inclinations of the people, however, it is a great happiness to Great Britain that they are not like the Laws of the Medes and Persians that were unalterable. Our Laws are subjected to the parliament of Great Britain. Some of them have been altered, and many of them ought to be altered, particularly where privat Rights interfeer with publick Advantages. Entails are of this nature for all the subjects of Britain ought to be upon the same foot of credite. All crimes ought likeways to be equally punished in both parts of Britain, it being very rediculous that, for instance, one guilty of the same crime should in England meet with the punishment of Manslaughter and in Scotland be condemned to death as a murderer. Executions for Debts ought likeways to be the same in both Countries and All the decrees & sentences of all our soveraign Courts should be equally extensive & effectual. We suffer under the name of these & other Regulations which I hope may in time be set right by the Parliament of great Britain.

The 19 Article continues all the Courts of judicature in Scotland on the same footing except the Court of Exchequer which behoved to be setled in a great measure, according to the Rules and Regulations which obtain'd in the Court of Exchequer in England, in regard, the several Laws made with relation to Trade required such a conformity. But of this, I shall say a little more hereafter when the Union took place & this part of the Article came to be put in Execution.

I might here notice that the parliament of Scotland made some additions to the Article in relation to Advocats principal Clerks of the Session & Writters to the Signet who were to be capable of being made Lords of the Session but these things being agreable to what I suppose was the sense of the Projectors at that time need neither explanation nor Appology from me.

As to the 20th Article which continues all Heretable offices and jurisdictions for Life; I have no occasion to observe any thing, save that the parliament of Scotland thought fit to add, what the Commissioners for the Treaty of Union had a good mind to have keept out, namely the continuation of all superiorities as they were at the time of the union & without any subjection to the parliament of Great Britain, some of these superiorities in Scotland are dangerous to the Government therefor ought to have been left under the Authority of our Legislature or put on the same footing with these which are exercised by the Lords of Manours in England. But to go a little farther back; it had been happy for Scotland if they had never entered into the Systhem of her Laws, & that the Goths had keept their feudal constitutions to themselves. The Greek & Roman Laws as they stood at first had been sufficient for us.

The 21 Article which provides for the continuation of the privileges of the Royal Burghs in Scotland, like the former, is not so beneficial to these Burghs as they are commonly believed to be, especially as they are at present by many of them, exercised, however, the Commissioners thought fit to make this condition a part of the union because it was wished for & expected by the Royal Burrows—'tis certain that some of these privileges are hurtful to them, particularly such as restrict the freedom of the Citizens within certain bounds and limits in which they can exercise their Trades & occupations. For 'tho it may be true that there are few considerable Burghs in this Island, but which enjoy some restrictive privileges, yet it has been found that the less they made use of them it was so much the better. The Glory Richess Trade & prosperity of every city depend on the multitude of its Inhabitants, but which will never be attained in the way of exclusive privileges.

The 22^d Article provides for the number & Election of the 16 peers & 45 Commoners to sit in the parliament of Great Britain. This was a much smaller number, than I wished for but after a good deal of strugle by the Commissioners for Scotland it was all that cou'd be obtained. And with relation to the peers I was far from thinking the number sufficient but those peers who were Commissioners having agreed to it, I who was a Commoner had little or no concern in it, however, I must here declare what I knew to be the true reasone of their coming so easily into this condition. Most of them had promises made to them that the restriction of their number to sit in parliament needed be no ob[ject]ion to them for that most of them wou'd be after the union created a new, peers of Great Britain with the privilege of siting in the House of Peers & that by degrees all the noble Families in Scotland wou'd be received into the full Enjoyment of the peerage of Great Britain. I know that such promises were made by the Queen and her chief Ministers at that time and in pursuance of which the Duke of Queensberry who had the chief hand in bringing about the union was made Duke of Dover. The same Honour was likeways conferred on the Duke of Hamiltone he having been created Duke of Brandon and both of them sat in the House of peers. They were admitted indeed, under a protestation taken by those who thought that by the conception of the Article of union they had no right to the privilege of siting in parliament exclusive of the sixteen peers then chosen for Scotland and therefore they were afterwards excluded by a vote of the House of peers—however, those who represent those Dukes think they have still a good right, as being agreable to what they had reasone to believe was the sense of those peers who were commissioners & Representatives of the peers of Scotland at the Treaty of Union. As to the number of 45 Commoners, I own I judged it sufficient, considering the inability of Scotland for sending a greater number, and indeed it is such as will always be sufficient to support the Interests of Scotland against any prevailing party from bearing too hard upon her. But this is what I am persuaded will never happen, it being the great Interest of the Legislature and Government to treat all the subjects of Britain with equal tenderness and lenity.

The 23^d Article which relates to the privileges of the 16 peers, needs no observations to be made upon it, by me. The conditions stipulated were agreable to themselves and no alterations were made by the parliament of Scotland.

The 24 Article which relates to the Great Seal, & other seals in Scotland, was likeways acceptable to the parliament and received only an addition to this effect that the Crown Scepter and sword of State should remain in Scotland as they were at the time of the union and likeways that all the Records of parliament and all other Records whatsoever should be keept and preserved as they were in that part of Britain & in all time coming. These additions I think were not amiss, but no neglect wou'd have appeared in these matters.

By the 25 Article it is declared that all Laws and Statutes inconsistent with the union shall cease and become voide, and indeed this great Transaction cou'd conclude no otherways.

Few amendments, as I have noticed before, have been made to these Articles by the parliament of Scotland and some of these that were made had done as well, if they had been overlookt. Now it remains that I should say something with regard to the Establishment & Security of the Episcopal church in England and the presbyterian Kirk of Scotland, this being to be understood in both nations as a perpetual and fundamental Article of the union. But all I need say shall be comprehended in a very few words. This Establishment of the two church Governments, was agreable to the humurs of the people for the time, but how long; posterity must determine; for as in many other things, so in Religious matters we have been remarkable for fickleness and inconstancy.

We have made sad work of Religion 'tho one wou'd be inclined to think, that of all human concerns it should be the most fixed and invariable. Yet even in this we are not more unsteady than many others in Europe. There are differences all the World over both in the Essentials of true Religion and in the forms of church Governments, so that the best way is for wise civil Governments to bear with lesser differences in Religious matters provided fundamental points be keept sacred & inviolable and provided that those who call themselves the Ministers & servants of God behave on all occasions with that regard to Civil Society which becomes them.

Liberty of conscience & a freedom of worshiping God, in what manner people think reasonable, has been found to conduce very much to the prosperity of every Kingdom and State. Here in Britain by the Establishment of two church Governments there is no more done than a Liberty of Conscience settled as a fundamental Article of the union. Both these churches may & I hope will perpetually exist in the manner they have been managed now for 38 years past. None of them pretend to encroach upon one another but subsist with that unity which becomes Christians. In former times, they contended frequently for dominion and prehemenency, and these contentions brought the two Kingdoms once to ruine, and frequently into very great dangers, but these Misfortunes will, I hope, never happen again. The union will be found the soveraign Remedy by the help of Trade & industry to cure all our little soul-distempers. As idleness and Laziness dissipat amongst our people, Enthusiastick Turns of mind will vanish by degrees & that peace & Unity of Sentiments, that Brotherly Love and Charity for one annother will succeed which ought always to be the ornaments of a Christian people.

As to that Act of the parliament of Scotland entituled Act settling the manner of Electing the 16 peers and 45 Commonners to represent Scotland in the parliament of Great Britain; I do believe that most things contain'd in it, were both reasonable and necessary at that time, however, there is no necessity for me to enter upon any disquisition about them. The Commissioners for the Treaty of Union were no farther concerned in them than the rest of the Members of the Parliament, were. Party differences, as in most publick Councils continued to run very high amongst them, and some vestiges of these, may still appear in this Act as well as others, relative to the Union but nothing that ought to disturb our publick Tranquillity.

Now with regard to the management of the Affaires of Scotland subsequent to the union down to this present year 1744 I shall shortly touch at a few things that seem to me of any considerable weight or importance, not so much to act the part of an Historian as to justify my self in any concern I had in them. *Egotisms* in my case, will I hope, be excusable, it being the design of this paper to state my self as it were, a panel before the great judicature of posterity to be justified or condemned as they think proper. If I have erred in any thing I confess I have erred voluntarily but still according to that light of Reasone which God has given me.

I was chosen in the last parliament of Scotland as one of the 45 Commoners who were to represent her in the first parliament of Great Britain conform to the power lodged in the said parliament of Scotland by the 22 Article of the union. In this quality therefor I was not only an Eye witness but particularly concern'd in the first settlement of the Affaires of Great Britain. But in the mean time I cannot pass over in silence the humurs and prejudices of the people of Scotland after the ratification of the union in both parliaments.

The several parties & Factions in Scotland who had been against the union, were in the first place, extreamly divided amongst themselves and acted very contradictory inconsistent parts—however, all of them seem'd to agree in one thing, namely, to rail at the union and those who had been concerned in it.

The Whigs who composed the greatest part of the nation were satisfied with the settlement & security of the protestant succession in the Electoral House of Hannover but still were angry at the establishment of Episcopacy in England, without reflecting what an equivalent they had by the security given to the presbyterian Government in Scotland.

The Jacobites[1] & those who favoured the Interests of the Late King James were irreconcilable Ennemies to the union, and indeed they cou'd Act no other part, considering the advantages which the Whigs had gained over them in the settlement of the aforementioned succession.

Merchants, who of all others ought to have favoured the union most were far from being pleased with its success, for the many of them had attained their favourite point in view, the Liberty of the plantations yet as most of them dealt in Dutch & French commodities, they saw that after the 1 of May next following they behoved either to run all their goods with extream hazard of losing them by seizurs or otherways, to be subjected to all the high duties that took place in England. But amongst all this medley of humurs & Inclinations one prevail'd exceedingly amongst all Ranks and degrees of people 'tho in my opinion worse founded than any one thing in all the Anti-union schemes. This was what they called the loss of the Soveraignity and Independency of Scotland. As to this Soveraignity, I own I could never conceive in what it consisted, I knew that England by the strength & number of her Ships of War had a just claime to the Soveraignity of the seas. I knew that she by the expence of much blood and Treasure for a long time past was soveraign of most of the

---

1   Clerk's marginal note: 'N.B. These jacobites acted as they thought by a principal of justice for the lineal succession but the circumstances of Scotland required our compliance with the Schems of England for things may be just which are not always convenient in political Schems and there was nothing more just than that the general good of our country should have been the Rule of all our actions.'

northerly Colonies & plantations of America. That she acted as one of the potentats in the East Indies by the great Trade carried on to these countries and that she had a real claime to the Soveraignity of Ireland with a Titulary one to France but I was a stranger to the Soveraignity of Scotland, except within her own confines. And as to her Independency it was at best a meer shadow and an empty name as before has been observed for 'tho upon the Restoration of King Charles the 2^d she was disjoined from that Republick of England, which Oliver Cromwell had established, and was restored again to her Liberty and Independency yet this was only a jugle of state to please the people. Her Government was altogether precarious and her publick Councils were entirely under English influence. But to proceed After the parliament rose, the privy Council of Scotland took care of the Affaires in this part of Great Britain and continued to act as before tho in a much less arbitrary way. In Aprile the Duke of Queensberry who had been her Majesty's High Commissioner in the Union parliament set out for London with a great Equipage and was waited upon by most of the nobility and gentry to Dunbar. I was not only of his retenue but had an invitation from him to attend him to London in one of his coaches which I accepted of.[1] I can therefore bear testimony that he was quite otherways treated in England than he had been in Scotland. Here he had many times been in perril of his Life from an unruly Mob which had been daily instigated against the union & all its wellwishers, wheras in England he was every where caressed and received with great acclamations of joy. At Berwick Newcastle, Durham & other cities, as he passed, he was waited on & complemented by the chief Magistrats in their Formalities. Every where the people running together testified their joy on the happy Event in which he had been so instrumental. All the Scots in his retinue were likeways treated with the outmost civilities, so that all of us had the greatest reasone imaginable to expect success in the transaction we had just come from finishing. At Barnet Highgate and other places within 20 miles of London all the Queens ministers, all the peers commons of parliament waited upon him in their coaches so that I am persuaded there never was so great & so joyful a concourse of people seen, since the Entry of King James the 6th of Scotland on the union of the Crowns.[2] The parliament of England was then sitting. Both Houses had by a vast Majority ratified the union so that the Duke's Reception was in proportion to the great Services he had done by accomplishing a thing so desirable as the union of the two nations. He was no less acceptable to the Queen who after the union took effect, made him one of the Principal Secretaries of State both for Forreign & Domestick Affaires and created him Duke of Dover with all the privileges of A peer of England as has been already noticed. He was to have

1   Clerk's marginal note: 'N.B. He always treated me as if he had been my parent.'
2   In *History*, 4, fo. 2, Clerk describes the welcome given to James as 'generally feigned'.

been one of the sixteen peers for Scotland in the parliament of great Britain but on this new Creation his seat became vacant for he had been already chosen in the last parliament of Scotland & before the meeting of the British parliament another was chosen to supply his place.

As he was a persone of great parts, great temper and affability he became more and more a Favourite of the Queen 'tho he had been for a long time past in a greater degree of Interest with her and her Royal Consort prince George of Denmark than any Scotsman. Great court was therefor made to him by all degrees of Men & in the new Establishment of the Kingdom of great Britain nothing was done but what was agreable to him nor any preferr'd to Offices but by his recommendation.

In the mean time, that matters were preparing in London for the new Government of Great Britain, all the Merchants of interprising Heads and selfish views not only in Britain but in all Forreign parts, laid schems for gaining great advantages to themselves by the difference of Dutie in Merchandise which took place in England and Scotland before the union. On which account, great Quantities of Wines & Brandies from France & Spain and all kinds of Goods were imported into Scotland and entered at the low duties which were received there between the rising of the Parliament of Scotland and the commencement of the union on the first of May ensuing. Leith Port Glasgow and other ports were crouded with ships from all parts and even the English Merchants themselves contributed not a little to the Trick which was to be put on their own Revenues for these goods were after the union to be imported into England with a view to the benefite Scotland was to receive by the free communication of Trade between the two nations which was provided by the 4 Article of the union. The Mobb of Scotland was exceedingly pleased with this great appearance of shiping, as they took it to be the happy effects of the union, but the Ministry and the House of Commons in England were terribly alarmed at it, wherefor this Resolve past in that House 'That the importation of goods and merchandizes of the growth and produce of France and other forreign parts into Scotland in order to be brought from thence into England, after the first of May and with intention to avoide the payment of the English duties will be to the damage & ruine of the fair Traders, to the prejudice of the Manufactories of England, a great loss to her Majesty's Revenue of the Customs and a very great detriment to the publick.' Upon this Resolve a Bill past in the House of Commons for preventing & discouraging such fraudulent practises, but the House of peers thought fit to reject it least any interruption to the communication of Trade stipulated between the two Kingdoms should be declared a Breach of the union. Thus the importations into Scotland went on without interruption till the first of May, 1707.

That day, when the union of the two Kingdoms began to take place, was solemnized at London with great Rejoicings particularly by a solemn Thanksgiving at the church of St Paul with all the splendour and magnificence of Ceremonies used in the church of England. Her Majesty & both Houses of parliament went there in a very August manner. All the Forreign Ambassadors then at Court & of the Reform'd Religion All the Magistrats of London Sheriffs justices of peace & others of note accompanied her. In the Galery on her right hand sat all the Bishops and peers of England who cou'd be present and all those peers of Scotland who were come up to Court. And on her left hand sat all the Commons of parliament and amongst the rest some of us who had been chosen in the parliament of Scotland amongst the 45 Commoners who were to be members of the House of Commons in the first parliament of Great Britain.

Her Majesty and many of the English present shewed great Devotion on this occasion. The joy was universal & indeed the English nation had never better reasone having been delivered from the terrible fears and Apprehensions they were under from Scotland, for in this Kingdom they evidently saw that all things tended to a Rupture & the calamities of a civil war. The parliament of England was before that day adjourned but still with an intention that in conjunction with 16 peers from Scotland and 45 commoners in the terms of the union, it should compose the first parliament of Great Britain, however, as the Government of the Kingdom of England was understood from the s^d first day of May to be dissolved, the Queen & her Ministry laboured dayly in modeling the new Government of Great Britain but with as few alterations as was possible.

The first thing that occurred, was the management of the Revenue of Scotland, either by a deputation from the boards of Customs & Excise in England sent down to Scotland or by seperat commissions. The first was thought unacceptable to the people there & therefor Two Commissions were appointed, in each of these were nominated three English Men & Two Scots. A majority was given to the English because new Laws & Regulations were to take place in Scotland to which All there were justly supposed to be entire strangers.

The next thing which came under consideration was to appoint Commissioners for the management of the Equivalent-money conform to the 15 Article of the Treaty of union. The number was 24 amongst whom were 4 Merchants in London who were Directors of the Bank of England. The Ministry negotiated the Affair by this Bank who in Agust after the union took effect, sent down the money in this manner 100000 lib in silver & 298085 lib in Exchequer Bills which the Bank of England was oblidged to circulat as ready money. I had been appointed one of the Commissioners and therefor came down to Edinburgh before the money arrived. The silver-species was brought in Twelve wagons guarded by a small body of Horse, the whole way, for as we were at war with France & the coast infested by pyrats, the Bank wou'd not venture to send the money by sea. When it came it was carried directly to the Castle of Edin & with the Exchequer bills deposited in a vault there.

Immediatly after this, the Commissioners above named, went upon the payment of the African Company conform to the directions of the said 15 Article, but people being unwilling to take the Exchequer Bills, the species of silver was soon exhausted & 50000 lib in Gold was sent down by the Bank.

When this affaire was going on in Scotland the Ministry of England took the best care they cou'd to discourage the importations from Scotland of these Goods that had been entered there with a view of defrauding the Revenue. The Merchants concern'd in these projects lost very deservedly the great Advantages they expected. However, vast quantities of such Goods escaped the hands of the Customhouse officers and the Revenue sustained a very great loss for two or three years after.

But to remedy the like evils & lay the first foundation of the Kingdom of Great Britain The Queen finally resolved to call a parliament conform to the power reserved to her in the 22 Article of the Union to consist of those who had composed the last session of the parliament of England in both Houses & those 16 peers and 45 Commoners who had been chosen in the last session of the parliament of Scotland and accordingly they met at Westminster in November thereafter.

I was to have gone up to the parliament at that time but the Exchequer Bills of which I had a part of the care as one of the Commissioners of the Equivalent, fell into a discount of 4 or 5 per cent therefor I and three more were intrusted by the Bank of England with a credite of about 100000 lib to keep up the circulation of these Bills. So soon therefor as any of them were presented to us we received them at par & gave our Bills for the valew payable by the Bank on demand. These Bills were punctually Honoured & in February 1708 which was the soonest we cou'd get this affaire brought to a conclusion I carried up the Exchequer Bills that had been brought in to the Equivalent office amounting to about 60000 lib and delivered them to the Directors of the Bank. I had their sincere thanks for the service I had done them and indeed it was a piece of very good service since they had applied for their own benefite the premium of 3 or 4 per cent given by the Government for circulating these Exchequer Bills.

As to the distribution of the rest of the Equivalent-money, it was afterwards carried on in the precise terms of the 15 Article of the union without the defalcation of one farthing except what was annually allowed to the Commissioners and these were restricted to such a number that no body had the least reasone to complain of Injustice or the expence of the Commission.

In the first parliament of Great Britain the two following Acts were of the greatest consequence to Scotland.

The first was An Act for rendering the union of the two Kingdoms more intire and complet. And in this it was appointed that after the first of May 1708 there should be but one Privy Council in Great Britain, & that justices of peace should be named by her Majesty her Heirs & successors under the great seal of Great Britain in all the shires stuartries and Burghs of Scotland with the same powers as they have been appointed in England.

That circuit courts of justitiary should be annually kept in Scotland according to an Act of parliament made there in the Reign of King Charles the second intituled Act concerning the Regulation of the judicatures. And That a certain and uniform methode should take place for electing & returning Members of parliament as is prescribed in this Act.

And here I shall only observe that by the appointment of one privy Council in Great Britain, the seperat privy Council which had continued in Scotland since the commencement of the union was to be dissolved after the s^d 1 of May 1708. However I cannot think but that this measure was at least premature for tho it was true that the privy Councils of Scotland had formerly been guilty of many arbitrary things yet it was very useful for the first year after the union took effect and might have been so regulated in subordination to the privy Council of Great Britain as to have kept up a better face of Government and order in the Affaires of Scotland than I have hitherto observed. For the justices of peace who were by the above Act to have supplied the place of the privy Council of Scotland neither understood their duty nor were willing to execute their offices as was expected. They were in a good measure strangers to the Laws by which they were chiefly to Act and in some shires of Scotland they seldom or never met.

The other Act of any consequence to the north part of Great Britain was that which constituted the Court of Exchequer upon the present footing it has now been for 36 years past. I had the honour conferr'd upon me of being one of the Barons, but how I have acted in this station, I must leave it to others to decide. All I shall say for my self is that I never made this office a *sine cure*. I attended duely and acted for most of my time, as the head of the Court in the absence of our Chief Barons. I did the best I could to discourage smugling & prevent all kinds of frauds of the like kind, for on this I was persuaded, depended the Advancement & success of all the Trade & Manufactories of Scotland. I had perhaps in this the ill will of all the Fraudulent Traders but I always took this as the greatest mark of Honour and respect that possibly cou'd be put upon me.[1]

But to return to the privy Council of Scotland in which I was interested as a Commissioner of the Equivalent even after I was a Baron of the Exchequer. It did great service before its expiration, in reducing the coyn of Scotland to the valewe & standard of the coyn in England. Several very profitable orders and regulations were from time to time made in this arduous affaire. The Forreign coyne which was then current & extended to above 150000 lib was without order or compulsion called in & recoyn'd in the Mint of Edin and the proper coyn of Scotland fell likeways under the same Regulation. The Loss was made up to the proprietors of every kind of coyn & particularly of English coyn for all the species of this coyn such as crowns half crowns and shillings were current between 8 & 9 per cent above their true valew. And all this was done without the least detriment to Trade or without any remarkable stop or defect of the species of money. The Bank of Scotland by their Bills & other persones in their several stations contributed greatly to this advantageous schem according to the 16 Article of the Treaty of union.

The Total sum of the current species of Gold and Silver then in Scotland was estimated at least to a Million sterling upon which I cannot but observe that a few years before the union of the Kingdoms there were great complaints by the people of Scotland for the want of money to transact their necessary affaires & for this reasone in the parliament of Scotland held in 1705 a Commitee was appointed to bring in a Report by what means the defect of species cou'd be properly supplied. I my self was one of the Commitee. Several overtures were made to us—one for raising the valew & denomination of our species one by a certain Doctor Chamberlain & Mr William Law for a kind of Land Bank—the first was absolutely rejected & the second was submitted to the parliament but being dangerous, never took effect. This was very near the same project which Mr Law had the interest some years after to set up in France under the designation of the Mesisippi Company, very much to the detriment of the Trade and Manufactories of that Country. The above mentioned Commitee in Scotland was far from having any opinion of it & mighty glad that their Country had been delivered from so great a snare.

As to the management of publick affaires relative to the union I have nothing to observe save that both the English & Scots seem to have been treated with great Equality and without these national distinctions and preferences which were expected. For if at any time Englishmen have been preferred to Scotsmen in any offices or stations of Life, such preferences were visibly oweing to other

---

1   Clerk's marginal note: 'N.B. The late general Resolutions in all the shires and Brughs in this Country are a sufficient approbation of my conduct but after so many losses in Trade I fear these Resolutions came too late.'

reasons than meerly that the Candidats were English, for either their natural
or acquired qualifications or a nearer access & better opportunities of addressing themselves to the Favourites of the Court gave occasion for them.[1] The
Scots have not only had their Advancements in the Fleets and Armies of Great
Britain without distinction but they have already been Governours of almost
all the plantations & colonies in America & the East Indies 'tho these were
advancements, of all others they least expected about the time of the union.
We have had likeways our share in profitable & Honourable Embassies to
Forreign Countries, so have not had the least cause to complain. In the mean
time, I cannot pass over in silence the attempt which was made about six years
after the union to dissolve the same. The Queen hapned to have her heart
alienated a little from the succession of the House of Hannover and for that
end gave way to the groundless complaints of some peers both of the English
& Scotch nation who were about that time about her. The last raised a clamour
against the duties which then took place in Scotland & some of the peers of
England, none of the best Friends to the Government, thought the 16 peers a
burden on their House & that they sometimes intercepted too many of the
Royal favours. But this project vastly displeased the House of Commons and
therefor was let fall before it came to any considerable height.

As to the success of the Revenue of Customs & Excise upon the foot of
some of the Regulations which obtain'd in Scotland after the constitution of
the Court of Exchequer I saw evidently a detriment to Trade & Honesty by
the oaths which Merchants were oblidged to take at the entry of their Goods
and by the determinations of juries. It did not belong to the Barons of
Exchequer to alter these Regulations which took place in England but I often
regretted them and tho juries were thought in England to conduce very much
not only to justice, but to the preservation of the Liberties of the people yet I
cou'd not help being of a different opinion with regard to the Trade and
Manufactures of Scotland. In England there is a vast multitude of people and
but little connexion between the Traders and the juries wheras in Scotland it
is very difficult to find a jury so little interested in persons & causes before them,
hence many bad consequences hapned & I have been often tempted to wish
that the determinations in the Court of Exchequer had been as formerly before
the union and as is practised in the Court of Session in all civil cases.

I am now to leave Scotland in the full possession of her proper share of all
the soveraignities Honours and dignities all the Trade shiping and manufactures that any way belonged to England before the Union. I leave her in great
peace and unity with her nearest nighbours and doubt not but my Country
will be always happy if this union be supported and cultivated as it ought by

1   Brown ('Modern Rome and ancient Caledonia', 40) remarks that in reality Clerk 'suffered and resented
     discrimination', having 'hoped for years to be Lord Chief Baron of the Exchequer'.

all succeeding Monarchs and parliaments of great Britain. The old maxim of *vis unita fortior* can never be better applied than in our case therefor sooner ought the old Heptarchy of England, to be restored, & the antient Kingdoms of the Scots & picts again divided, than the union of England and Scotland dissolved. It has met with so much opposition at various times that nothing but the Influence of Heaven cou'd have carried it on & I hope the same Influence will protect and defend it, for ever.

This Memorial consisting of forty three pages was written by me in September 1744 & sign'd at pennicuik house the 4th of Octob^r in the same year John Clerk

pennicuik 18 jan 1747

As it has been my Fate to survive an unhappy Rebellion, which broke out in july & Agust 1747[1] it may be fit for me to make a few observations on it, with regard to the union of the two British nations.

My first observation, is, that by the pretender's declaration & his sone's proclamations at Edin: it was intended to dissolve the union & put things on the same foot they were, upon the restoration of King Charles the 2^d. This was done, I suppose, to satisfye the Ambitious views of some of his Followers who by a dissolution of the union, expected higher offices of trust than they thought they cou'd attain to, in an united state. But however resolved the pretender & his son might be at first they were afterwards oblidged to alter their schem & give out that the continuation of the union should be submitted to a parliament, but whether this was to be the parliament of Great Britain or not, was uncertain. The reasone of this last resolution was, it seems, that the pretender & his followers discovered that the Merchants in Scotland wou'd oppose the dissolution of the union as a schem that wou'd deprive them of the priviledges in the West Indies & of a free communication of Trade with England.

2° I had sufficient grounds to observe that if the union had not taken place, the protestant succession in the house of Hannover had, in all probability, been overturn'd, for it is very probable that the Legislative Authority in Scotland had authorised the Rebellion on account of former disputes & grudges at the people of England. The Scots had probably tried to set up a seperat Kingdom from England, tho the attempt must have been vain & fruitless and ended at last in a bloody civil war between the family of Hannover & the House of Stuart.

I may here likeways take notice that one of the pretences for the last years trubles was to relieve the two nations of the publick debts, but this was likeways given up when the pretender & his Friends found that these debts were for the

1   Sic. Ainsley in his copy emends to 1746.

most part oweing to our selves & that no Man can with any propriety of speech be said to be in debt to himself. It is true that what we owe to Forreigners must receive a different consideration but the people of Great Britain will be in no hazard of turning Bankrupt on that account 'tho the sum was three times greater than it is. And as to the takeing off the duties on forreign goods such as French Wines & Brandies & most of all the Dutch commodities, it is impossible to do it, without destroying our Manufactories & the ballance of our Trade.

                                                                          J:C

INDEX

—

1

SCOTTISH HISTORY SOCIETY

OFFICE-BEARERS AND COUNCIL
1992-93

President
DR G.G. SIMPSON

Chairman of Council
DR JEAN MUNRO

Honorary Treasurer
MR W.W. SCOTT
Flat 3, 16 Parkside Terrace
Edinburgh EH16 5XW

Honorary Secretary
DR E.P.D. TORRIE
The Haining, North Queensferry
Fife KY11 1HE

Honorary Publication Secretaries
DR JULIAN GOODARE   DR MICHAEL LYNCH
Department of Scottish History
University of Edinburgh
17 Buccleuch Place
Edinburgh EH8 9LN

Honorary Membership Secretary
DR ALAN MACINNES
Department of Scottish History
University of Glasgow
9 University Gardens
Glasgow G12 8QH

COUNCIL

DR ALAN BORTHWICK
DR JANE DAWSON
DR DAVID DITCHBURN
MR IAIN FLETT
DR IAIN HUTCHISON
DR JAMES KIRK

DR FARQUHAR MACINTOSH
MR W.A. MACKAY
DR ATHOL MURRAY
MRS MAIRI ROBINSON
MR W.D.H. SELLAR
DR IRENE SWEENEY

Corresponding Members of Council
PROFESSOR MICHEL DE BOÜARD, *France*
PROFESSOR MAURICE LEE, JR, *USA*

MEMBERSHIP

*Membership of the Scottish History Society
is open to all who are interested in the history of Scotland.
For an annual subscription of £15.00
members normally receive one volume each year.
Enquiries should be addressed to
the Honorary Secretary, whose address
is given overleaf.*

SCOTTISH HISTORY SOCIETY

106th ANNUAL REPORT
*Presented to the Annual General Meeting
by the Council, 12 December 1992*

The fourth volume of the Fifth series, *The Calendar of Fearn: Text and Additions, 1471-1667*, edited by Professor Robin Adam, appeared in late November. All paid-up members should have received it as the 1991 volume. It contains an obituary notice of Professor Ian Cowan, the long-serving Treasurer of the Society, written by Dr John Durkan. Progress on the volume edited by Dr Ian Levitt, *The Scottish Office: Depression and Reconstruction, 1919-1959*, has continued steadily. Members may be interested in a special lecture, organised by the Society in collaboration with the Department of Scottish History and the Unit for the Study of Government in Scotland of the University of Edinburgh, which will be given by Dr Levitt on the general subject of his forthcoming volume on 3 December 1992. Progress on the volume edited by Dr Joseph Donnelly, *The Black Book of Coldingham, 1298-1430*, has been delayed somewhat due to unforeseen circumstances; the typescript and disks are now expected to be in the hands of the publication secretaries in the new year. The volume edited by Dr Douglas Duncan, *The History of the Union of Scotland and England* by Sir John Clerk of Penicuik (consisting of translated extracts from a history of Anglo-Scottish relations from early times written in Latin in the 1720s, with particular attention devoted to the Scottish parliament's debate on the Union of 1707), has advanced significantly, with the text now virtually complete.

The Society's immediate financial position has continued to be healthy for the reasons mentioned in the 1991 report. The Society is also benefiting from a generous donation towards the cost of the *Calendar of Fearn* by the Glenmorangie Distillery Coy., an internationally known malt whisky company with strong links with the area of Easter Ross. This assistance is gratefully acknowledged.

Professor Donald Watt's term of office as President of the Society is coming to an end. His last presidential address will be given at the Annual General Meeting on 12 December. Council thanks Professor Watt for his scholarly, and entertaining, addresses over the last four years. Council is pleased to put to the Annual General Meeting its nomination of Dr Grant G. Simpson to serve as President for 1993-1996.

The three members of Council to retire by rotation this year are Dr Charles Munn, Mrs Virginia Wills and Mr Ian Maciver. To replace them Council recommends the election by the Annual General Meeting of Mr W.A. Mackay, Dr David Ditchburn and Ms Irene Sweeney. Any other nominations made by at least two other members of the Society should reach the Honorary Secretary not less than seven days before the Annual General Meeting.

The membership of the Society now stands at 476 individual and 207 institutional members.

5

ABSTRACT ACCOUNT OF THE CHARGE AND DISCHARGE OF THE
INTROMISSIONS OF THE HONORARY TREASURER

1 October 1991 to 30 September 1992

CHARGE

			£
1	Cash in Bank at 1 October 1991		
	a	Sum at credit of Premier Account with Bank of Scotland	40494.57
	b	Sum at credit of current (Treasurer's) account with Bank of Scotland	10894.78
			51389.35
2	Subscriptions received		9944.21
3	Past publications sold		577.60
4	Interest on Premier Account		3526.15
5	Interest on Current (Treasurer's) Account		1067.32
6	Income Tax refunds (1989-90 & 1990-91)		1095.32
7	Miscellaneous		201.90
8	Sums drawn from Bank Premier Account		5500.00
9	Sums drawn from Bank Current Account		14736.75
			67802.45

I

DISCHARGE

		£
1	Subscriptions refunded	28.50
2	Cost of publications during year	13977.47
3	Editorial expenses	254.93
4	Costs of insuring stock of unsold books	60.00
5	Costs of AGM	142.50
6	Costs of postage re AGM	128.90
7	Office bearers' expenses	144.45
8	Sums lodged in Bank Premier Account	3526.15
11	Sums lodged in Bank Current Account	18386.95
		14736.75
12	Funds at close of this account	
	a Sum at credit of Premier Account with Bank of Scotland	38520.72
	b Sum at credit of Current (Treasurer's) Account with Bank of Scotland	14544.98
		67802.45

STIRLING, *2 November 1992.*

I have audited the Account of the Honorary Treasurer of the Scottish History Society and certify that I am satisfied that proper records appear to have been kept and that the above Account is a correct statement of the transactions recorded during the year.

H.D. PEEBLES
Auditor

SCOTTISH HISTORY SOCIETY
LIST OF MEMBERS
1992-93

INDIVIDUAL MEMBERS

ABBOT, D.M., Scottish Record Office, HM General Register House, Princes Street, Edinburgh EH1 3YY.

ADAM, Prof. R.J., Easter Wayside, Hepburn Gardens, St Andrews KY16 9LP.

ADAMSON, Duncan, 39 Roberts Crescent, Dumfries CD4 27RS.

AITCHISON, Ian M., 20 Gorse Way, Freshfield, Fromby, Liverpool L37 1PB.

ALDERSON, J.J., Havelock, Victoria 3465, Australia.

ALLAN, Norman, FRCOG, Glenbrae, 2 Campbell Street, Banff AB4 1JR.

ANDERSON, Hugh D., 12 Stanley Drive, Ardrossan, Ayr KA22 8NK.

ANDERSON, I.G., Cribton, Irongray, Dumfries DG2 0YJ.

ANDERSON, J. Douglas, FSAScot, 74 Kirkcaldy Road, Pollockshields, Glasgow G41 4LD.

ANDERSON, Mrs Marjorie O., West View Cottage, Lade Braes Lane, St Andrews KY16.

ANDREW, H., Strone Aline, Colintraive, Argyll PA22 3AS.

ANGUS, Rev. J.A.K., TD MA, The Manse of Crathie, Crathie by Ballater, Aberdeen AB3 5UL.

ANNAND, James K., 173/314 Comely Bank Road, Edinburgh EH4 1DJ.

ARMSTRONG, Campbell, Tarras, 1 Almond Place, The Grange, Kilmarnock, Ayr KA1 2HS.

ARMSTRONG, Murdo, 5 Quebec Avenue, Tain, Ross.

ARNOTT, Mrs H. Lynne, BA, 133 Redford House, Edinburgh EH13 0AS.

ASPLIN, P.W., University Library, University of Glasgow, Glasgow G12 8QQ.

AULD, Mrs Joan, University Archives, University of Dundee, Dundee DD1 4HN.

BAIRD, Gerald, 3 West Grange Street, Monifieth, Angus DD5 4LD.

BALLANTYNE, J.H., 6 Mansfield Place, Edinburgh EH3 6NB.

BANKS, Noel, Wolverton, Stratford on Avon, Warwick CV37 0HG.

BANNERMAN, Dr John, Dept. of Scottish History, University of Edinburgh, 17 Buccleuch Place, Edinburgh EH8 9LN.

BARCLAY Rev. Iain C., MA BD, The Manse, Tighnabruich, Argyll PA21 2DX.

BARROW, Prof. G.W.S., DLitt, Dept. of Scottish History, University of Edinburgh, 17 Buccleuch Place, Edinburgh EH8 9LN.

BAXTER of Earlshall, The Baron & Baroness, Earlshall Castle, Leuchars, St Andrews KY16.

BAYNE, George P.L., 115 Laurel Drive, Greenhills, East Kilbride, Lanarkshire G75 9JG.

BEATON, Duncan M., 77 Back o'Hill, Houston, Renfrew PA6 7LE.

BEECK, Karl Hermann, DPhil, Linde 27, 5600 Wuppertal 2, West Germany.

BELL, Gilbert T., 129 Wedderlea Drive, Glasgow G52 2SX.

BENNETT, Miss J.M., 91 Victoria Road, Dunoon PA23 7AD.

BERNARD, K.N., BA FSAScot, Chapel Style, 3 MacLeod Drive, Helensburgh, Dumbarton G84 9QS.

BIGWOOD, Mrs A.R., 38 Primrose Bank Road, Edinburgh EH5 3JF.

BORTHWICK, Alan R., 9 Corrennie Drive, Edinburgh EH10 6EQ.

BORTHWICK, Charles Stuart, Netherbarns, The Street, Stradishall, Newmarket, Suffolk CB8 8YW.

BOWIE, J.C., MB, 219 Ferry Road, Edinburgh EH6 4NN.

BOYLE, Dr I.T., B.Sc MB ChB, University Dept. of Medicine, Glasgow Royal Infirmary, Glasgow.

BOYLE, Rev. Hugh N., STL PHL, 1 Kelvinside Gardens, Glasgow G20 6BG.

BRASH, J.L., MA, Dept. of History, University of Western Australia, Nedlands, WA 6009, Australia.

BROADIE, Prof. A., Dept. of Philosophy, University of Glasgow, Glasgow G12 8QQ.

BROOM, Andrew M., MA LlB, Scottish Record Office, HM General Register House, Princes Street, Edinburgh EH1 3YY.

BROWN, Robert, 34 Mayfield Avenue, Stranraer, Wigtown.

BROWN, Prof. Stewart, BA MA PhD, Dept. of Ecclesiastical History, University of Edinburgh, New College, Mound Place, Edinburgh EH1 2LX.

BROWN, David J., MA PhD, Scottish Record Office, HM General Register House, Princes Street, Edinburgh EH1 3YY.

BROWN, Margaret, PhD, 27 Woodend Drive, Aberdeen AB2 6YJ.

BRUCE, Iain, 2a Charles Street, Oxford OX4 3AS.

BRUCE, Fraser F., MA LlB, 1 Hazel Drive, Dundee DD2 1QQ.

BRYCE, Arthur, FLA FSAScot, 17 Pinedale Terrace, Scone, Perth PH2 6PH.

BRYDON, G.W.M., BA, 53 Addison Gardens, London W14 0DP.

BUCHANAN, Prof. W. Watson, Medical Centre, McMaster University, 1200 Main Street W., Hamilton, Ontario, Canada.

BURNS, Right Rev. Mgr. Charles, Archivio Segreto, Citta del Vaticano, Italy.

BURNS, David M., MA, 5 Great Stuart Street, Edinburgh EH3 6AP.

BURNS, Prof. J.H. & Mrs Yvonne M.Z., 6 Chiltern House, Hillcrest Road, Ealing, London W5 1HL.

BURNS, Murray A., 50 Ann Street, Edinburgh EH4 1PJ.

BURNS, R.J., BA LlB, 4 Spylaw Avenue, Edinburgh EH3 0LR.

BURRELL, Prof. Sydney, 43 Walker Lane, Needham, Mass. 02192-1436, USA.

BUTE, The Hon. The Marquess of, Mount Stewart, Rothesay, Isle of Bute PA20 0OL.

BYRNE, Mrs Maureen A.J., Cornagowna Home farm, via Rossinver, Co. Leitrim, Eire.

CADELL, Patrick, BA, 11a Tipperlinn Road, Edinburgh EH10 5ET.

CAIRD, Prof. J.B., Dept. of Geography, University of Dundee, Dundee DD1 4HN.

CAIRNS, John, LlB PhD, Dept. of Scots Law, University of Edinburgh, Old College, South Bridge, Edinburgh EH8 9YL.

CALDER, Dr Angus, Open University in Scotland, 60 Melville Street, Edinburgh EH3 7HF.

CAMERON, The Hon. Lord & Lady, 28 Moray Place, Edinburgh EH3 6BX.

CAMERON, Mr A.D., 3 Dalfoil Court, Ralston, Paisley PA1 3AH.

CAMERON, Alexander D., 14 Esplanade Terrace, Edinburgh EH15 2ES.

CAMERON, Mrs Elspeth, Morar Dale, Fassifern Road, Fort William PH33 6QX.

CAMPBELL, A.G., 5 Wickens Street, Beckenhorn 6107, Western Australia, Australia.

CAMPBELL, Alastair, Inverawe Barn, Taynuilt, Argyll PA35 1HU.

CAMPBELL, Colin, PO Box 9106, Belmont, Mass, 02178, USA.

CAMPBELL, Prof. R.H., Dept. of Economic History, University of Glasgow, 4 University Gardens, Glasgow G12 8QH.

CAMPBELL, Russel, c/o Loch Ness Lodge Hotel, Drumnadrochit, Inverness IV3 6TJ.

CAMPBELL, W.D., Gate-End, Stenton, Dunbar EH4 1TE.

CAMPBELL of Canna, Dr J.L., Isle of Canna, Inverness.

CANT, Dr R.G., 2 Kinburn Place, St Andrews, Fife KY16.

CAUTHIE, Mr R.B., 3804 Eleventh Street, SW Calgary, Alberta, Canada T2T 3M4.

CHALMERS, Trevor, MA, Public Record Office, Chancery Lane, London WC2A 1LR.

CHAMBERS, J.W., BSc MB ChB, 14 Woodburn Road, Glasgow G43 2TN.

CHEYNE, Rev. Prof. A.C., 12 Crossland Crescent, Peebles EH4 8LF.

CHRISTIE, Stephen J.A., BA MA, 33 West Mains Road, Edinburgh EH9 3GB.

CLANCHY, Michael D., LlB, 35 Wellshot Drive, Cambuslang, Glasgow.

CLARK, S. Aylwin, BA, 18 Queens Gardens, St Andrews, Fife.

CLARK, Lt. Col. Victor E., Jr., USAF(ret) BS FSAScot, 142663 Southern Pines Drive, Dallas, Texas 75324, USA.

CLARKE, Tristram, 29 Cumberland Street, Edinburgh EH3 6RT.

COCKBURN, R.W., 31 Ellen Street, Whitburn, West Lothian EH47 0HJ.

COHEN, Mrs M.C., The End House South, Lady Margaret Road, Cambridge CB4 0BJ.

COLLINS, Dennis E., MA LIB, Stirling House, Craigiebarn Road, Dundee DD4 7PL.

COSH Miss Mary, MA, 63 Theberton Street, London N1.

COVENTRY Charles S., MA ALA, 27/1 Jamaica Mews, Edinburgh EH3 6HL.

COWAN, Prof. Edward J., MA, Dept. of Scottish History, University of Glasgow, 9 University Gardens, Glasgow G12 8QH.

COWPER, Miss A.S., BA, 32 Balgreen Avenue, Edinburgh EH12 5SU.

COX, Ms Eileen E., Blackhill, Dunkeld, Perth.

COYLE, Edward, 10 Ingram Place, Kilmarnock.

CRAWFORD, Ian A., Christ's College, Cambridge CA2 3BU.

CRAWFORD, Mrs P.S., Brenchoille Farm, Inveraray, Argyll PA32 8XN.

CRIPPS, Miss Judith, 62 St. Ronan's Drive, Peterculter, Aberdeen AB1 0RJ.

CUMMINGS, Andrew J.G., BA, Dept. of History, University of Strathclyde, McCance Building, 16 Richmond Street, Glasgow G1 1XQ.

CURRIE, David, 3 Marine Road, Dunbar, East Lothian EH42 1AR.

DACRE of Glanton, Rt. Hon. the Lord, The Old Rectory, Didcot OX11 7EB.

DAICHES, Prof. David, 12 Rothesay Place, Edinburgh EH3 7SQ.

DALGLEISH, George R., MA, 104 Montgomery Street, Edinburgh EH7 5HE.

DALTON, Mr Anthony D.F., Maolachy House, Lochavich, by Taynuilt, Argyll PA35 1HJ.

DALYELL, Tam & Mrs Kathleen, The Binns, Linlithgow EH49 7NA.

DARRAGH, James, MA, 103 Deakin Leas, Tonbridge, Kent.

DAVEY, Christopher J., BA, Dept. of Modern History, University of Dundee, Dundee DD1 4HN.

DAVIDSON, Nimmo C.M., MA BMus, 72 Auldhouse Road, Glasgow G43 1UR.

DAWSON, Jane, PhD, Dept. of Ecclesiastical History, University of Edinburgh, New College, Mound Place, Edinburgh EH1 2LX.

DEARNESS, Mr J.W.S., Whistlebrae, Sanday, Orkney KW17 2AZ.

DEVINE, Prof. T.M., Dept. of History, University of Strathclyde, McCance Building, 16 Richmond Street, Glasgow G1 1XQ.

DIACK, William G., 41 Middleton Circle, Bridge of Don, Aberdeen AB22 8LF.

DICKIE, Ms Agnes, 10 Strathfillan Road, Edinburgh EH9 2AG.

DICKSON, Mr Paul, 2 Bramble House, Deeham Road, Reepham, Norwich NE10 4LD.

DILWORTH, G.M., The Abbey, Fort Augustus, Inverness-shire PH32 4DB.

DITCHBURN, David, MA PhD, Dept. of History, University of Aberdeen, Taylor Building, Old Aberdeen AB9 2UB.

DOCHERTY, Rev. Henry, MLitt, General Secretariat Bldg., 64 Aitken Street, Airdrie ML6 6LT.

DONALD, Rev. P.H., MA PhD BD, Leith St. Serf's Parish Church, 1 Denham Green Terrace, Edinburgh EH5 3PG.

DONALDSON, Rear Admiral Vernon D., 19 Collingwood Court, Melbourn Road, Royston, Herts SG8 7BY.

DOUGLAS, Dr Elma P., 4 Dowanhill Street, Glasgow G11 5HB.

DOUGLAS, Mr Gordon D., 3390 Norman Drive, Reno, Nevada 89502, USA.

DREXLER, Miss Marjorie, PhD, RD2 Box 2430,'Middleburgh, Vermont 05753, USA.

DROCHOCKI, Mr Marshal, FSAScot, 260 Paisley Road West, Glasgow G51 1BN.

DRUMMOND-MURRAY, P., 67 Dublin Street, Edinburgh EH3 6NS.

DUFF, Mr Alan, 10 Paragon Grove, Surbiton, Surrey KT5 8RE.

DUFF, Huisdean A.M., MA MLitt, 182c Gilmartin Road, East Fulton, Linwood, Renfrew.

DUN, M.D. & Mrs, 59 Dalhousie Road, Broughty Ferry, Dundee.

DUNBAR, John G., MA, FSA, Hon.FRIAS, Patie's Mill, Carlops, by Penicuik, Midlothian EH26 9NF.

DUNCAN, Prof. A.A.M., FBA, Dept. of Scottish History, University of Glasgow, 9 University Gardens, Glasgow G12 8QH.

DUNDAS-BEKKER, Mrs A., Arniston House, Gorebridge, Midlothian EH32 4RY.

DUNLOP, Rev. A. Ian, 59 Meggatland Terrace, Edinburgh EH14 1AP.

DUNNETT, Mrs Dorothy, 87 Colinton Road, Edinburgh EH10 5DF.

DURHAM, Mrs Jane M.S., Scotsburn, Kildary, Ross IV18 0PE.

DURIE, Dr Alastair J., Dept. of Economic History, University of Glasgow, 4 University Gardens, Glasgow G12 8QH.

DURKAN, John, DLitt, 37 Earlsburn Road, Lenzie.

EDWARDS, Owen Dudley, BA, Dept. of History, University of Edinburgh, William Robertson Building, 20 George Square, Edinburgh EH8 9JY.

EGGERER, Elmer W., CandPhil, Fuggerstrasse 6D-8058 Erding, Germany.

ELLIOT, Lady Margaret R., BA, 39 Inverleith Place, Edinburgh EH3 5QD.

EWING, Mrs Elsie, 6 Rullion Road, Penicuick, Midlothian EH26 9HT.

EWING, Mrs Winifred, MEP LlB, 52 Queens Drive, Glasgow G42 8BP.

FENTON, Prof. Alexander, CBE MA, School of Scottish Studies, University of Edinburgh, 19 George Square, Edinburgh EH8 9LU.

FERGUSON, Miss Joan P.S., 21 Howard Place, Edinburgh EH3 5JY.

FERGUSON, Dr William, Dept. of Scottish History, University of Edinburgh, 17 Buccleuch Place, Edinburgh EH8 9LN.

FFORDE, Mrs K., MA, Allt Darach Bhlaraidh, Glenmoriston, Inverness IV3 6YH.

FINDLAY, Donald R., QC LlB, 26 Barnton Park Crescent, Edinburgh EH4 6EP.

FINDLAY, William, BA, 36 Firpark Road, Bishopbriggs, Glasgow G64 1SP.

FINLAY, Mr J., 3 Cowden Grove, Dalkeith, Midlothian EH22 2HE.

FISHER, Ian, BA, RCAHM (Scotland), John Sinclair House, 16 Bernard Terrace, Edinburgh EH8 9NX.

FLETCHER, Ernest McD., BA, Clan Donald USA, 1314 North 9th, Temple, Texas 76501, USA.

FLETT, Iain E.F., MLitt, Archive & Record Centre, City Chambers, City Square, Dundee DD1 3BY.

FORD, John D., MA LlB LlM, Gonville & Caius College, Cambridge CB2 1TA.

FORREST, Alfred D.A. & Mrs Catherine, Burn Wynd House, 47 Lade Braes, St Andrews KY16 4DA.

FORRESTER, Rev. Ian L., The Manse, Inverkeilor, by Arbroath, Angus DD1 5GA.

FORSYTH, Alexander, BSc MPS, Golf Course Road, Granton-on-Spey, Moray PH26 3HY.

FOSTER, Linda, RR#4, Cambridge, Ontario, Canada.

FOTHRINGHAM of Grantully, H. Steuart, Grantully Castle, Aberfeldy, Perth PH15 2EG.

FRANCIS, James Y., MA LlB, 33 Worsley Crescent, Crookfur, Newton Mearns, Glasgow G77 6DW.

FRASER, Mrs Jean, Dept. of History, University of Strathclyde, McCance Building, 16 Richmond Street Glasgow G1 1XQ.

FRASER, Alexander, Parkgrove, Gladstone Road, Bishopton, Renfrew PA7 5AU.

FRY, Mr M.R.G., MA, 15 Rothesay Place, Edinburgh EH3 7SQ.

FULTON, Dr Henry L., Dept. of English, Central Michigan University, Mount Pleasant, Michigan 48859, USA.

FURGOL, Dr Edward & Mrs Mary T., 1340 County Ridge Drive, Germantown, Maryland 20874, USA.

FYFE, Ronald, Northern College of Education (Aberdeen Campus), Hilton Place, Aberdeen AB9 1FA.

GALBRAITH, D.A., BA MEd, 9 Fernbourne Close, Sheffield, Walsall, W. Midlands WS4 1XD.

GALBRAITH, James D., MA MLitt, Scottish Record Office, HM General Register House, Princes Street, Edinburgh EH1 3YY.

GELLATLY, Michael C., 33 Thorndene, Elderslie, Johnstone, Renfrew PA5 9DB.

GIBSON, Dr J.A., MD DRCOG MRCGP, Foremount House, Kilbarchan, Renfrew.

GIBSON, John S., 28 Cramond Gardens, Edinburgh EH4 6PU.

GILFILLAN, John B.S., Tigh-na-Leven, Dunmore, by Tarbert, Argyll PA29 6XZ.

GILLIE, Judge William T., BA JD, 26 Nottingham Road, Columbus, Ohio 43214, USA.

GILLIES, Prof. W.M., MA, Dept. of Celtic, University of Edinburgh, David Hume Tower, George Square, Edinburgh EH8 9JX.

GIMSON, G.S., BSc LlD, 11 Royal Circus, Edinburgh EH3 6TL.

GLEN, F.J., York Cottage, 1b Drummond Road, Inverness IV6 4NA.

GOLDBOURN, Robert, The Latch, Ranfurly Place, Bridge of Weir, Renfrew PA11 3DR.

GOODARE, Dr Julian, Dept. of Scottish History, University of Edinburgh, 17 Buccleuch Place, Edinburgh, EH8 9LN *(Honorary Publication Secretary)*.

GORDON, Prof. W.M., LlB PhD, Dept. of Legal History, University of Glasgow, Glasgow G12 8QQ.

GORRIE, D.C.E., MA, 54 Garscube Terrace, Edinburgh EH10 6BN.

GOSLETT, Ruth V., BA, 24 Capri Road, Lower Addiscombe, Croydon, Surrey CR0 6LE.

GRAHAM, Miss Barbara, MA FSAScot, 42 Annanhill Avenue, Kilmarnock, Ayr KA1 2LQ.

GRAHAM, Hugh F., MA, 324c Hagden Lane, Watford, Herts WD1 8LH.

GRAHAM, Sir Norman W., The Steading, Chesterhall, Longniddry, East Lothian EH32 0PQ.

GRAHAM, Thomas, MA PhD, University Library, University of York, York.

GRANT, I.D., Scottish Record Office, HM General Register House, Princes Street, Edinburgh EH1 3YY.

GRANT, Miss Margaret W., 3 Ben Bhraggie Drive, Golspie, Sutherland.

GRANT, Ruth Ellen, 40 Pilmuir Road, Forres, Moray IV36 0HE.

GREIG, Robert F.B., MA, 42 Albany Street, Edinburgh EH1 3QB.

GRIEVE, Miss Hilda E.P., BEM BA, 153 New London Road, Chelmsford, Essex CM2 0AA.

GROVES, William W., 5 Staikhill, Lanark ML11 7PW.

GRUBB, Rev. George D., BA BD, 22 Belgrave Road, Edinburgh EH12 6NF.

GUESSEGEN, Achim, MA, Hauptstrasse 86D-6360 Friedberg 1, Germany.

GUILD, Ivor R., 16 Charlotte Square, Edinburgh EH2 4YS.

GUNN, Colin, MB ChB, 12 Abbots Walk, Kirkcaldy.

HAGGART, Craig, 31 Cairnview Road, Milton of Campsie, Stirling G65 8BN.

HAIG, Mrs Eve, 1 Orchard Court, East Linton, East Lothian EH40 3EG.

HALFORD-MACLEOD, J.R.S., Balfour, Shapinsay, Orkney Isles KY7 2DY.

HALL, Sir John, Bt., MA, Inver House, Lochinver, by Lairg, Sutherland.

HALL, John N.S., MA, Glenaladale, 9 Lochpark, Doonfoot, Ayr KA7 4EU.

HALLIDAY, James, 15 Castleray Cresecent, Broughty Ferry, Dundee DD5 2LU.

HAMILL, Mrs Chantal, 128 Gowanbank, Livingston, West Lothian EH54 6EW.

HAMILTON, Matthew, 10 Westland Gardens, Paisley, Renfrew.

HAMILTON, Dr D.N.H., FRCS, 18 Kirklee Crescent, Glasgow G12.

HANHAM, Prof. H.J., PhD, University of Lancaster, The Croft, Balrigg Lane, Balrigg, Lancaster LA1 4XP.

HARDIE, Rev R.K., MA BD, Manse of Stenhouse & Carron, Church Street, Stenhousemuir, by Larbert, Stirling FK5 4BU.

HARGREAVES, Prof. John D., Dept. of History, University of Aberdeen, Old Aberdeen AB9 2UB.

HARTMAN, Barry W., FSAScot, Lieut. to Maclaine of Lochbuie, 4744 Casper Drive, Roanoke, Virginia 24019, USA.

HAWES, Lionel, BA, 50 Kingsacre Road, King's Park, Glasgow G44 4LP.

HAWES, Timothy L.M., 8 Keswick Road, Cringleford, Norwich NR4 6UG.

HAWORTH, John C., PhD, 519 Witherspoon Drive, Springfield, Illinois 62704, USA.

HAWS, Dr Charles H., MBE BA PhD, PO Box 7590500, Lexington Avenue, New York, NY 10163, USA.

HAY, Frederick G., MA, Dept. of Political Economy, University of Glasgow, Glasgow G12 8QQ.

HESKETH, Lady, Pomfret Lodge, Towcester, Northamptonshire NN12 7HT.

HILDEBRAND, Prof. Reinhard, Institut fur Anatomie, Universitat Munster, Vesalius 2-4, D44009, Munster, Germany.

HILTON, Miss Margaret, BA, 22 Mardale Crescent, Edinburgh EH10 5AG.

HODGSON, Leslie, DipArch, 5 St Stephens Place, Stockbridge, Edinburgh EH3 5AJ.

HOGG, James C.T., MA ALD, 13 Grindlay Street, Edinburgh EH8 9AT.

HOOD, Daniel, MA LlB, 12 Braehead Drive, Carnoustie DD2 7JX.

HOPE, George A., Luffness, Aberlady, East Lothian EH32 0QB.

HORN, Miss B.L.H., Scottish Record Office, HM General Register House, Princes Street, Edinburgh EH1 3YY.

HOUSTON, Prof. George, Dept. of Political Economy, University of Glasgow, Glasgow G12 8QQ.

HOWAT, Mrs Marjory M., 44 Craigie Road, Perth PH2 0BH.

HOWATSON, Mr & Mrs William, Rosefield, Beach Road, St Cyrus, Kincardine DD10 0BJ.

HOWELL, Roger, Jr., MA PhD, Dept. of History, Bowdoin College, Brunswick, Maine 04011, USA.

HUME, Mr & Mrs J.B., 2/9 Succoth Court, Edinburgh EH12 6BZ.

HUNTER, Alexander, 35 Hambeldon Drive, Greasby, Wirral, Merseyside L49 2QH.

HUNTER, Bruce, Graham Hunter Foundation, Restenneth Library, Restenneth Priory, Forfar.

HUNTER, Mrs Jean, The Old Police House, Port Charlotte, Islay PA48 7TL.

HUTCHISON, Iain G.C., MA PhD, Dept. of History, University of Stirling, Stirling FK9 4LN.

HUTCHISON, H., MB ChB DRCOG, 228 Dundee Street West, Trenton, Ontario K8V 324, Canada.

HYDE, Dr E.D., 12 Douglas Crescent, Edinburgh EH4 5BB.

IGOE, Luke J., MA, 40 Summerside Place, Edinburgh EH6 4NY.

IIJIMA, Keiji, BLitt, 4-34-8 Yayoi-cho, Nakano-Ku, Tokyo, Japan.

IMRIE, John, CBE LlD, 41 Bonaly Crescent, Edinburgh EH13 0EP.

INGRAM, Mrs & Mrs David B., 76 Granite Street, Foxborough, Mass. 02035, USA.

INNES of Edingight, Sir Malcolm, Court of the Lord Lyon, HM Register House, Princes Street, Edinburgh EH1 3YT.

INNES, T.L., BComm, 1116 Cloverbrae Crescent, Mississauga, Ontario, Canada.

JOHNSON, Mr Paul E., 35B Rothesay Road, Luton, Beds. LU1 1QZ.

JOHNSTON, James J., BA MA, PO Box 65, Marshall, Ark. 72650, USA.

JOSEPH, A.T.T., WS, 53 East High Street, Forfar, Angus DD8 2EL.

KEILLAR, Ian J., 80 Duncan Drive, Elgin, Moray IV30 2NH.

KENNEDY, A., Craigmullen, Dundrennan, Kirkcudbright DG6 4QF.

KIRK, David C., 15 Apsley Road, London SW18 2DB.

KIRK, Russell, BA MA DLitt, PO Box 4, Mecasta, Michigan 29332, USA.

KIRK, James, PhD DLitt, Dept. of Scottish History, University of Glasgow, 9 University Gardens, Glasgow G12 8QH.

LAMBIE, Brian, 113 High Street, Biggar, Lanarkshire ML12 6DL.

LAW, Dr John, Dept. of History, University College of Swansea, Singleton Park, Swansea SA2 8PP.

LAWRIE, Peter, BSc MBCS, 95 Pitkerro Road, Dundee DD4 7E.

LAWRIE, Mrs Caroline G., MA, Fair Fields, Newton Port, Haddington EH41 3LZ.

LAWSON, H., BSc, 7 Lynedoch Place, Edinburgh EH3 7PX.

LAWSON, William M., The Old Schoolhouse, Northton, Harris PA85 3JA.

LECKIE, S.H., BSc, Auchengarroch, 16 Chattan Road, Bridge of Allan, Stirling FK9 4DX.

LEE, Prof. Maurice, Jr., Douglass College, Rutgers University, New Brunswick, NJ 08903, USA.

LEIPER, Mr James G., 13 Muirpark Way, Drymen, Glasgow G63 0DX.

LEVITT, Ian, MA PhD, Dept. of Applied Soc. Studies, Plymouth Polytechnic, Plymouth PL4 8AA.

LILBURN, Alistair J., BSc, Mains of Coul, Aboyne, Aberdeen AB3 4TS.

LOCKHART, Ms Kate, Diabig, Balmachie Road, Carnoustie DD7 7SR.

LOGUE, Kenneth J., 24 Sheridan Drive, Bangor, Co. Down, Northern Ireland.

LOLE, Mr & Mrs F.P., 5 Clayton Avenue, Didsbury, Manchester M20 0BL.

LYNCH, Dr Michael, MA PhD, Dept. of Scottish History, University of Edinburgh, 17 Buccleuch Place, Edinburgh EH8 9LN *(Honorary Publication Secretary)*.

LYTHE, Prof. S.G.E., 45 Aytoun Road, Glasgow G41.

MACARTHUR, D., Ards Cottage, Connel, Argyll PA37 1PT.

MACAULAY, James H., MA PhD, 11 Kirklee Circus, Glasgow G12 0TW.

McCAFFREY, John, PhD, Dept. of Scottish History, University of Glasgow, 9 University Gardens, Glasgow G12 8QH.

McCONNELL, John W., BA FSAScot, 102 Orchards Lane, Winters, California 95694, USA.

McCOSH of Huntfield, Bryce K., Quothquan, by Biggar, Lanark ML12 6NA.

McCOWAN, David B., BASC RR, 19 Monarchwood Crescent, Don Mills, Ontario M3A 1H3, Canada.

McCRAW, Ian, 27 Pitcairn Road, Downfield, Dundee DD3 9EE.

MACDONALD, Miss Christina A., 36 Glasgow Street, Glasgow G12 8JR.

MACDONALD, D., 10 Pearce Avenue, Corstorphine, Edinburgh EH12 8SW.

MACDONALD, Hector, MA PhD, National Library of Scotland, George IV Bridge, Edinburgh EH1 1EW.

MACDONALD, Miss Kathleen R., MA MLitt, 43 Chatton Road, Bridge of Allan FK9 4EF.

MACDONALD, Ranald C., Swiss Cottage, Post Office House, Barcaldine, by Oban, Argyll.

MACDONALD, Robert, BA, 12 Orchard Terrace, Edinburgh EH4 2HA.

MACDOUGALL, Dr Norman A.T., Dept. of Scottish History, St Katherine's Lodge, University of St Andrews, St Andrews KY16 9AL.

McEWEN, Ewen, DSc, 45 Pearce Avenue, Poole, Dorset.

MACFARLANE, L.J., FSA, 43 The Spittall, Old Aberdeen AB2 3HX.

MACFARLANE, William A., BSc, 9 Grange Valley Crescent, Ballyclare, Northern Ireland BT39 9AY.

McFAULDS, John, 89 Anstruther Street, Glasgow G32 7BB.

McGLASHON, Peter, Pinewood School, Hoe Lane, Ware SG12 9BP.

McGOWAN, Ian D., BA, National Library of Scotland, George IV Bridge, Edinburgh EH1 1EN.

McGREGOR, Miss Sheila A., ClanGregor Centre, 44 St Patrick's Square, Edinburgh EH8 9ET.

MACGREGOR-HASTIE, Roy, BA MEd, Via Trento, 40 Tuenno (TN), Italy.

MACINNES, Dr Allan I., MA PhD, Dept. of Scottish History, University of Glasgow, Glasgow G12 8QQ *(Honorary Membership Secretary)*.

MACINTOSH, Farquhar, CBE MA DLitt, 12 Rothesay Place, Edinburgh EH3 7SQ.

MACINTOSH, Malcolm, MA, 21 Ravendale Avenue, London N12 9HP.

McINTYRE, Ms M., Dept. of History, University of Guelph, Guelph, Ontario N1G 2W1, Canada.

MACINTYRE, Robert D., MA ChB, 8 Gladstone Place, Stirling.

MACINTYRE, Prof. Stuart, Dept. of History, University of Melbourne, Parkville, Victoria 3052, Australia.

MACIVER, I.F., MA, National Library of Scotland, George IV Bridge, Edinburgh EH1 1EW.

MACKAY, A.D., MA, Dunviden, Bridgend, Ceres, by Cupar, Fife.

MACKAY, Rev. Hugh, MA FSAScot, The Manse, Duns, Berwickshire.

MACKAY, Miss Inez W., 25a Inverleith Terrace, Edinburgh EH3 5NU.

MACKAY, James S., Lianag, Barcaldine, by Oban, Argyll.

MACKAY, Rev. P.H.R., Clola, 1 Direlton Road, North Berwick EH39 5BY.

MACKAY, William A., MA BSc, 34a Inverleith Terrace, Edinburgh EH3 5NU.

MACKAY, William R., 1 Howe Hall Cottages, Littlebury Green, nr. Saffron Waldon CB11 1XF.

MACKECHNIE, Donald, Schoolhouse, Bridge of Douglas, Inveraray, Argyll.

MACKENZIE, C.W.T., MA, c/o Seet plc, Essex Hall, Essex Street, London WC2R 3JD.

MACKENZIE, Robert, BA, Drummuie Cottage, Golspie, Sutherland.

MACKENZIE, Ross, MA, The Reps Cottage, Culloden Moor, Inverness IV1 2ED.

McKERROW, Mr N.A.H., c/o Macdonald & Muir Ltd., PO Box 211, Macdonald House, 186 Commercial Street, Leith, Edinburgh EH6 6NN.

MACKICHAN, N.D., MA MB BChir, Aros, Towerside, Whittingham, Alnwick, Northumberland NE66 4RF.

McKINLAY, Mrs Isabella, 11 Laburnam Road, Methil, Fife KY8 2HA.

McKNIGHT, G., ARICS, Nirvana, 26 Harburn Road, West Calder, West Lothian EH55 8AH.

MACLACHLAN, G.S., BA FSAScot, Dunadd, 4 Dean Place, Crosshouse, Kilmarnock, Ayr KA2 0JZ.

McLAUCHLAN, Miss Elise R.M., BL, 511/173 Comely Bank Road, Edinburgh EH4 1DJ.

MACLEAN, A.J., LlB, Dept. of Scots Law, University of Edinburgh, Old College, South Bridge, Edinburgh EH8 9YL.

MACLEAN, Alexander, Aird, Bhearnasdail, Skye.

MACLEAN, Donald F., 5787 Ogilvie Street, Halifax, Nova Scotia 33H 1C3, Canada.

MACLEAN of Dochgarroch, Mrs L.M., Hazelbrae House, Glen Urquhart, Inverness IV3 6TJ.

MACLEAN, Mrs Mary, 59 Society Street, Nairn IV2 4NL.

MACLEAN-BRISTOL, Major Nicholas, Breacachadh Castle, Isle of Coll, Argyll PA78 6TB.

McLEISH, Mrs Mary E., 7 Friday Avenue, Direlton, North Berwick, East Lothian EH39 3DY.

MACLEOD, Innes F., MA, Dept. of Adult Education, University of Glasgow, 57-59 Oakfield Avenue, Glasgow G12 8LW.

MACLEOD, Miss Iseabail, 11 Scotland Street, Edinburgh EH3 6PU.

McMAHON, George I.R., MA BLitt, Homerton College, Cambridge CB2 2PH.

McMILLAN, N.W., George House, 36 North Hanover Street, Glasgow G1 2AD.

MACNEIL of Barra, Ian R., BA LlB, Kismull Castle, Castlebay, Isle of Barra PA17 80.

McNEILL, Sheriff Peter G.B., 31 Queensferry Road, Edinburgh EH4 3HB.

McNIE, R.W., MA MEd, 34 Fountainhall Road, Edinburgh EH9 2LW.

MACPHAIL-GREEN, Mrs Marjorie, MA, PO Box 66D, Gibraltar.

MACPHERSON, Roderick A., BA FSAScot, Hollybush Villa, Langside, Glasgow G42 9VH.

MACQUARRIE, Dr Alan, MA PhD, 173 Queen Victoria Drive, Glasgow G14 9BP.

MACQUEEN, Hector L., LlB, Dept. of Scots Law, University of Edinburgh, Old College, South Bridge, Edinburgh EH8 9YL.

MACRAE, Iain A., MB BSc, North Farm, Murton, Seaham, Co. Durham.

McTYRE, Raymond M., 3987 Indian Lakes Circle, Stone Mountain, GA 30083, USA.

MAKEY, W.H., MA PhD, 3/2 Chessels Court, Edinburgh EH8 8AD.

MAPSTONE, Sally, DPhil, St. Hilda's College, Oxford OX4 1DY.

MARCHBANK, Mrs Agnes, 28 Belhaven Terrace West, Glasgow G12.

MARSHALL, Miss Rosalind, PhD, 11 St. Clair Terrace, Edinburgh EH10 5NW.

MASON, Roger, MA PhD, Dept. of Scottish History, St Katherine's Lodge, University of St Andrews, St Andrews, Fife KY16 9AL.

MATTHEW, Mrs Irene, Oakbank, Kilchrenan, by Taynuilt, Argyll PA35 1HD.

MATTHEWS, Henry McN., 120 East End Avenue, New York, NY 10028, USA.

MAXWELL, Stuart, FSAScot, & Mrs Ailsa, 16 Dick Place, Edinburgh EH9 2JL.

MAXWELL STUART, Peter & Mrs F., Traquair House, Innerleithen, Peebles EH44 6PW.

MEGAW, B.R.S., 11 Merchiston Gardens, Edinburgh EH10 5DD.

MENZIES, George M., 5 Gordon Terrace, Edinburgh EH16 5QH.

MILLER, Jonathan, Wellcraig, Tayport, Fife.

MILNE, Mrs Margaret P., DipCom, 10 Balfron Crescent, Hamilton ML3 9UH.

MITCHELL, Brian, 30 Trinity Road, Brechin, Angus DD9 6BJ.

MITCHELL, Miss Rosemary, MA, 24 Alexandra Place, Oban, Argyll.

MITCHISON, Prof. Rosalind, Great Yew, Ormiston, East Lothian EH35 5NJ.

MOFFAT, Mrs Elizabeth, MA BA, 13 Tyler's Acre Road, Edinburgh EH12 7HY.

MOODIE, William T., BSc MIMechE, 141 Wood Lane, Handsworth Wood, Birmingham B20 2AQ.

MORRISON, Andrew G., 8b Overdale Avenue, Barnston, Wirral, Merseyside L61 1OB.

MUNN, Charles W., BA PhD, Institute of Bankers, Scotland, 19-20 Rutland Square, Edinburgh EH1 2DE.

MUNRO, D.J., MA, 65 Meadowcroft, St Albans, Herts AL1 1UF.

MUNRO, Dr Jean, 15a Mansionhouse Road, Edinburgh EH9 1TZ *(Chairman of Council)*.

MUNRO, R.W., 15a Mansionhouse Road, Edinburgh EH9 1TZ.

MURDOCH, Alexander, BA PhD, Dept. of History, Northampton Polytechnic, Northampton.

MURDOCH, Mrs S.M., Seaview, Shore Street, Gairloch, Ross IV21 2BZ.

MURISON, David, 14 Dennyduff Road, Fraserburgh, Aberdeenshire.

MURRAY, Dr Athol L., LlB, 33 Inverleith Gardens, Edinburgh EH3 5PR.

MURRAY, Miss Elizabeth S., MA MSc, 3 Westbank Quadrant, Glasgow G12 8NT.

MURRAY, Murdoch D., MRCVS, 3 Gardiner Grove, Edinburgh EH4 3RT.

NAIRN, Dr Stuart A., MB ChB, & Mrs Ruth G., Tigh na Faoillinn, Lochinver, by Lairg, Sutherland.

NASH, Robert P., 2715 North 53rd Street, Omaha, Nebraska 68104, USA.

NEWTON, Norman S., BA MA ALA FSAScot, 11 Lochend Street, Campbeltown, Argyll PA28 6DL.

NICHOLSON, C.B. Harman, Lenbrook Square, 16083747 Peachtree Road, Atlanta, Georgia 30319, USA.

NIMMO, Mrs A.E., 9 Succoth Gardens, Edinburgh EH12 6BR.

NOBLE, R. Ross, MA, Highland Folk Museum, Kingussie, Inverness PH21 1JG.

NOWAK, J.J., 90 Buckstone Loan, Edinburgh EH10 6VG.

O'BRIEN, Patrick, The School House, Dull, by Aberfeldy, Perthshire.

ORAM, Dr Richard D., Rosevalley, Mid Street, Hopeman, Moray IV30 2TF.

PAGE, Mr Ronald A., 1 Jupiter Hill, Glenrothes, Fife KY7 5TH.

PALMER, Kenneth W., 4 Cumin Place, Edinburgh EH9 2JX.

PATON, Douglas Mark P., BSc MSc, 57 Cargill Road, Earlsfield, London SW18.

PEDEN, Prof. G.C., MA PhD, Dept. of History, University of Stirling, Stirling FK9 4LA.

PHILLIPSON, N.T., Dept. of History, University of Edinburgh, William Robertson Building, 30 George Square, Edinburgh EH8 9LP.

POWELL, Mr S.J., Flat 5, 36 Canning Row, East Croydon, Surrey.

PREBBLE, John, FRSL, Hill View, The Glade, Kingswood, Surrey KT20 6LL.

RAY, Angus J., PO Box 397, Barrington, Il 60011, USA.

REID, Prof. W. Stanford, Apt. 906, 19 Woodlawn Road East, Guelph Ontario N1H 7B1, Canada.

RICHARDSON, G.D., OBE MA, 16 Eriskay Road, Inverness IV2 3LX.

RILEY, P.W.J., BA PhD, 2 Cherry Tree Cottages, Meal Street, New Mills, via Stockport, Derbyshire.

RITCHIE, Alexander, Glenlora, 15 Ladysmith Avenue, Kilbarchan, Renfrew PA10 2AS.

RITCHIE, Donald B., 9 Farrow Drive, Corpach, Fort William, Inverness PH33 7JW.

RITCHIE, James S., MA, 42 Dudley Gardens, Edinburgh EH6 4PS.

ROBERTSON, The Hon. Lord, 13 Moray Place, Edinburgh EH3 6DT.

ROBERTSON, Mrs Christina H., FSAScot, 1c James Street, Musselburgh, Midlothian EH21 8PZ.

ROBERTSON, F.W., PhD, 17 Sinclair Terrace, Wick, Caithness.

ROBERTSON, James J., LlB, Faculty of Law, University of Dundee, Dundee DD1.

ROBERTSON, John, BA DPhil, St Hugh's College, Oxford OX2 6LE.

ROBERTSON, John L., LDS BDS, Westerlea, 11 Deroran Place, Stirling FK8 2PG.

ROBERTSON, Lewis, CBE, & Mrs Elspeth, 32 Saxe Coburg Place, Edinburgh EH3 5BP.

ROBERTSON, Mr Peter, 19 Wynyards Close, Tewkesbury, Glos. GL20 5QZ.

ROBINSON, Mrs Mairi, MA, 23 Dundas Street, Edinburgh EH3 6QQ.

ROSIE, Ms Alison, Scottish Record Office, HM General Register House, Princes Street, Edinburgh EH1 3YY.

ROSS, Ian S., Dept. of English, University of British Columbia, Vancouver, British Columbia V6T 1W5, Canada.

ROSS, Rufus M., LDS BA, 34 Eastwood Avenue, Giffnock, Glasgow G46 6LR.

ROSS, Rev. Anthony, OP STL, Queens Drive, Langside, Glasgow.

ROWAN, Miss Elizabeth I.S., 59 Park Gardens, Kilbarchan, Renfrew PA10 2LR.

SANDERSON, Miss Margaret H.B., PhD, 28 Highfield Crescent, Linlithgow, West Lothian.

SCOTT, David, & Mrs Hester, MA, Glenaros, Aros, Isle of Mull, Argyll PA72 6JP.

SCOTT, J.G., 10 Abbotsford Court, 18 Colinton Road, Edinburgh EH10 5EH.

SCOTT, Ms Margaret, MA, 22a Mildmay Grove, London N1 4RL.

SCOTT, P.H., 33 Drumsheugh Gardens, Edinburgh EH3 7RN.

SCOTT, Roderick F., BA LlB, & Mrs Linda, 89 Cottenham Park Road, London SW20 0DS.

SCOTT, W.W., Thornleigh, Kippford, Dalbeattie DG5 4LJ *(Honorary Treasurer)*.

SEFTON, Rev. H.R., PhD, Dept. of Church History, King's College, University of Aberdeen, Aberdeen AB9 2UB.

SELLAR, W.D.H., Dept. of Scots Law, University of Edinburgh, Old College, South Bridge, Edinburgh EH8 9YL.

SHAND, Margaret H., BA, 52 Rio Vista Boulevard, Florada Gardens, Broadbeach Waters, Queensland 4218, Australia.

SHARP, Brian J., 12 Shelley Drive, Bothwell, Glasgow G71 8TA.

SHARP, Buchanan, BA MA PhD, Dept. of History, College VUC Santa Cruz, Santa Cruz, California, USA.

SHAW, Very Rev. Duncan, PhD, 4 Sydney Terrace, Edinburgh EH7 6SL.

SHAW, Miss Frances J., PhD, Scottish Record Office, HM General Register House, Princes Street, Edinburgh EH1 3YY.

SHEAD, N.F., 8 Whittlemuir Avenue, Muirend, Glasgow G44 3HU.

SHEPHERD, James P., MA, & Mrs Doreen, 14 East Fettes Avenue, Edinburgh EH4 1AN.

SIMPSON, Eric J., MA, 27 Briarhill Avenue, Dalgety Bay, Dunfermline, Fife KY11 5UR.

SIMPSON, Grant G., PhD FSA, Dept. of History, University of Aberdeen, Old Aberdeen AB9 2UB *(President)*.

SIMPSON, John M., Dept. of Scottish History, University of Edinburgh, 17 Buccleuch Place, Edinburgh EH8 9LN.

SINCLAIR, Iain M., Flat 16, 365 Byres Road, Glasgow G12 8QU.

SKINNER, Miss Gillian, Bank House, Drumnadrochit, Inverness IV3 6TJ.

SLADE, H. Gordon, TD ARIBA, 15 Southbourne Gardens, London SE12.

SLAVEN, Prof. Anthony, Dept. of Economic History, University of Glasgow, 4 University Gardens, Glasgow G12 8QH.

SLIMMINGS, Sir William, MM CBE, 62 The Avenue, Worcester Park, Surrey KT4 7HH.

SLOAN, A.W. & Mrs Sheila M., 4 Rockville Terrace, Bonnyrigg, Midlothian EH19 2AG.

SMALL, Mr Gillean P., 3 Princes Gardens, Hyndland, Glasgow G12 9HP.

SMART, Mrs Aileen, MA, 64 Essex Drive, Glasgow G14 9LU.

SMITH, Mrs Annette, PhD, 9 Lade Braes, St Andrews, Fife KY16 9ET.

SMITH, Sheriff David B., MA LlB, 72 South Beach, Troon, Ayrshire.

SMITH, J.A., BEd, 108 Queen Victoria Drive, Glasgow G14 9BL.

SMITH, J.A.B., CBE MA BSc, Callune, 33 West Hemming Street, Letham, Angus DD3 2PU.

SMITTEN, J.R., Dept. of English, Utah State University, Logan, Utah 84322-3200, USA.

SMOUT, Prof. T.C., PhD, Dept. of Scottish History, St Katherine's Lodge, University of St Andrews, St Andrews, Fife KY16 9AL.

STEELE, Ms Margaret, MA, 13 Amundsen Crescent, Kanata, Ontario K2L 1A6, Canada.

STEVENS, T.E.R., 247 Viewfield Road, Tarbrax, by West Calder, West Lothian EH55 8XE.

STEVENSON, Prof. David, BA PhD, & Mrs Wendy B., Dept. of Scottish History, St Katherine's Lodge, University of St Andrews, St Andrews, Fife KY16 9AL.

STEVENSON, Mrs Stephanie B., BA DPhil, Johnston Lodge, Anstruther, Fife.

STEWART, Miss Anne, 1 Pleasance Court, Falkirk FK1 1BF.

STEWART, Archibald Ian B., Askomel End, Campbeltown, Argyll PA28 6EP.

STEWART, Miss Marjorie A., Airlie Cottage, 7A Hawkcraig Road, Aberdour, Fife KY3 0XB.

STIRLING of Garden, James, Garden, Buchlyvie, Stirlingshire.

STRACHAN, M.F., CBE FRSE, Glen Lighton, Broughton, by Biggar ML12 6JF.

STRAWHORN. John, PhD, 51 Connel Crescent, Mauchline, Ayrshire.

STRINGER, Keith, MA PhD FSA, Dept. of History, University of Lancaster, Lancaster.

STUART-MURRAY, Gaenor, 10 Abbey Road, Kelso, Roxburgh TD5 7JI.

SUNTER, J.R.M., MA PhD, Dept. of History, University of Guelph, Guelph, Ontario N1G 2W1, Canada.

SURRY, Andrew, 116 Old Hale Way, Hitchin, Herts SG5 1XT.

SUTHERLAND, The Countess of, House of Tongue, by Lairg, Sutherland.

SUTHERLAND, Mrs Margaret C., BA FSA, 2 Glen Road, Bridge of Allan, Stirling FK9 4PP.

SUTHERLAND, Norman A., MA, 55 Argyle Way, Dunblane, Perth FK15 9PX.

SWEENEY, Dr Irene, Dept. of Scottish History, University of Glasgow, 9 University Gardens, Glasgow G12 8QQ.

SZECHI, D., BA DPhil, Dept. of History, Auburn University, 7030 Haley Centre, Auburn, Alabama 36849-5207, USA.

TAYLOR, David, FSAScot, 39 Ashley Drive, Edinburgh EH11 1RP.

TAYLOR, W., PhD, 25 Bingham Terrace, Dundee.

THOMSON, Alan J.R., 2 Parkhill Place, Northmuir, Kirriemuir, Angus DD8 4TA.

THOMSON, Prof. Derick S., MA BA FRSE, 263 Fenwick Road, Giffnock, Glasgow G46 6JX.

THOMSON, J.A., Summerhill House, Annan, Dumfries.

THOMSON, J.A.F., DPhil, Dept. of Medieval History, University of Glasgow, 10 Univeristy Gardens, Glasgow G12 8QQ.

TODD, J.M., Redbourn House, Main Street, St Bees, Cumberland.

TORRANCE, Donald R., BSc, 1 Strathfillan Road, Edinburgh EH9 2AG.

TORRIE, Dr E.P.D., The Haining, Ferryhills, North Queensferry, Fife KY11 1HE *(Honorary Secretary)*.

TROUP, J.A., St Abbs, 34 Hillside Road, Stromness, Orkney.

TURNBULL, John G., c/o Garcia, 42–26 81st Street (Apt 5G), Elmshurst, Queens, NY 11373, USA.

VOUSDEN, D.H., 132 Earl Street, Glasgow G14 0BW.

WALKER, Charles T., Flat A5, 8 Caldecott Road, Kowloon, Hong Kong.

WALKER, Bruce, BA, Dept. of Architecture, University of Dundee, Dundee DD1 1BR.

WALKER, David M., CBE QC PhD LlD, Dept. of Private Law, University of Glasgow, Glasgow G12 8QQ.

WALLACE, Ms Veronica, BSc, 48 Findhorn Place, Edinburgh EH9 2NS.

WARD, Mrs Anne, 1A South Hamilton Road, North Berwick, East Lothian EH39 4NJ.

WATSON, T.A., MA, 8 Melville Terrace, Anstruther, Fife.

WATT, Prof. Donald E.R., 43 Hepburn Gardens, St Andrews, Fife KY16.

WEBSTER, A. Bruce, FSA, 5 The Terrace, St Stephens, Canterbury, Kent.

WEIR, The Hon. Lord, QC MA LlB, 9 Russell Place, Edinburgh EH5 3HQ.

WEIR, Thomas E., USNR BD PhD, PO Box 642, Riverdale, Maryland 20737, USA.

WHATLEY, C.A., BA PhD, Dept. of Scottish History, St Katherine's Lodge, University of St Andrews, St Andrews, Fife KY16 9AL.

WHITE, Mrs C.A.E., 228 Coldington Road, Bedford MK40 3EB.

WHITEFORD, Rev. D.H., QHC BD PhD, 3 Old Dean Road, Longniddry, East Lothian EH32 0QY.

WHYTE, Donald, 4 Carmel Road, Kirkliston, West Lothian EH22 9DD.

WIGHT, John H., MA, 146 Rowanhill Place, Kilmarnock KA1 1ON.

WILKIE, A., Cruachan, Dalnavert, Kincraig, Inverness.
WILLOCK, Prof. I.D., Dept. of Law, University of Dundee, Dundee DD1.
WILLS, Mrs Virginia, Glentyne, Sheriffmuir, Stirlingshire KFK15 0LN.
WILSON, Miss Isabel J.T., 2 Segton Avenue, Kilwinning, Ayr KA13 6LQ.
WILSON, Mr A.G., Little Carbeth, Killearn G63 9QJ.
WILSON, John B., MD FRCPE, The Whins, Kinnelbanks, Lochmaben, by
Lockerbie, Dumfries DG11 1TD.
WISEMAN, William George, 33 Burnton Road, Kendal, Cumbria LA9 7LT.
WITHERS, Charles W.J., MA, College of St Paul & St Mary, The Park,
Cheltenham, Glos. GL50 2RH.
WITHRINGTON, D.J., MEd, Dept. of History, University of Aberdeen, Old
Aberdeen AB9 2UB.
WOODHOUSE, Miss Unity N.R., BA, Bruce Lea, Lumphanan, Kincardine AB3
4QJ.
WORMALD, Jennifer M., MA PhD, St Hilda's College, Oxford OX4 1DY.
WRIGHT, Mrs Hilary J., Tighvallich, Dunkeld Road, Bankfoot, Perth PH1 4AJ.
WRIGHT, W.C., Rinnes, 4 the Pillars, Dornoch, Sutherland.

YOUNG, Mrs E.M., MA FRGS, Beechwoods, Kittishaws Road, Dalry, Ayr KA24
4LL.
YOUNG, Kenneth G., LlB WS, Mansfield, Auchterarder, Perth PH3 1DB.
YOUNG, Miss Margaret D., 1 Craiglockhart Gardens, Edinburgh EH14 1ND.
YOUNG, Mrs Margaret D., 73 Kingslynn Drive, Glasgow G44 4JB.
YOUNG, R.M., Rustlings, 38a Cross Lane, Congleton, Cheshire CW12 3JX.
YOUNG, William N., Bellenden, Buccleuch Street, Melrose, Roxburghshire.

ZULAGER, R., PhD, 1262 Fry Avenue, Lakewood, Ohio 44107, USA.

SUBSCRIBING LIBRARIES AND INSTITUTIONS

Aberdeen Family History Shop
Aberdeen Public Library
Aberdeen University Library
Adelaide University, Barr Smith Library, Australia
Adelphi University, Swirbul Library, NY, USA
Alabama University Library, USA
Alberta University Library, Edmonton, Alberta, Canada
Allen County Public Library, Fort Wayne, Indiana, USA
Argyll & Bute District Library, Dunoon
Ayr Carnegie Public Library

Bayerische Staatsbibliothek, Munchen, Germany
Bibliothèque Nationale, Paris, France
Birmingham Central Libraries
Birmingham University Library
Blackfriars (Order of Preachers), Edinburgh
Boston Athenaeum, Mass., USA
Boston Public Library, Mass., USA
Boston University Libraries, Mass., USA
Bowdoin College Library, Brunswick, Maine, USA
Bristol University Library
British Columbia University Library, Canada

Calgary University Library, Alberta, Canada
California University at Berkeley Library, Ca., USA
California University at Los Angeles Library, Ca., USA
California University at Riverside Library, Ca., USA
California University at San Diego, Ca., USA
California University Library, USA
Cambridge University Library
Chesters College, Glasgow
Chicago University Library, Ill., USA
Cincinnati University Library, Ohio, USA
Clan Donald Centre, Skye
Cleveland Public Library, Ohio, USA
Coatbridge Public Library
Columbia University Library, NY, USA
Copenhagen Royal Library, Denmark
Cornell University Library, NY, USA

Dalhousie University Library, Nova Scotia, Canada
Dartmouth College Library, NH, USA
Delaware University Memorial Library, USA
Dublin University College Library, Eire
Duke University Library, Durham, NC, USA
Dumbarton Public Library
Dumfries, Ewart Public Library
Dundee Public Library
Dundee University Library
Dunfermline Public Library
Durham University Library

Ealing Central Library, London
East Lothian District Library, Haddington
Edinburgh Central Public Library
Edinburgh City District Council
Edinburgh New Club
Edinburgh University Library
Edinburgh University, Scottish History Library
Edinburgh University, Scottish Studies Library
Episcopal Church of Scotland Theological Library, Edinburgh
Essex University Library
Exeter University Library

Falkirk Public Library
Flinders University of South Australia, Australia
Folger Shakespeare Library, Washington DC, USA
Forfar Public Library
Free Church of Scotland Library, Edinburgh
Fukushima University, Tokyo, Japan
Georgia University Library, USA
Glasgow University, Baillie's Library, Scottish History Department
Glasgow University Library
Goteborge Universitetsbibliotek, Sweden
Grangemouth Victoria Public Library
Guelph University Library, Ontario, Canada

Harvard College Library, Mass., USA
Hope Trust, Edinburgh
Houston University Libraries, Texas, USA
Hull University, Brynmor Jones Library
Huntingdon Library and Art Gallery, San Marino, Ca., USA

Illinois University Library, USA
Indiana University Library, USA
Inverness Divisional Library
Iona Foundation, Philadelphia, Penn., USA
Iowa State University Libraries, USA

John Donald Publishers Ltd., Edinburgh
Johns Hopkins University, Peabody Library, Baltimore, Md., USA
Jordanhill College of Education, Glasgow

Kilmarnock Public Library
Kirkintilloch, William Patrick Memorial Library

Lancaster University Library
Leeds City Libraries
Leeds University, Brotherton Library
Leicester University Library
Library of Congress, Washington DC, USA
Liverpool University Library
London City Libraries
London Library
London University, Institute of Historical Research Library
London University Library
Los Angeles Public Library, Ca., USA

McGill University Libraries, Montreal, Quebec, Canada
McMaster University, Mills Memorial Library, Ontario, Canada
Manchester Public Library
Manchester University, John Rylands Library
Maryland University, McKeldin Library, USA
Miami University Library, Alumni Library, Oxford, Ohio, USA
Michigan State University Library, USA
Michigan University, Hatcher Library, USA
Midlothian District Libraries, Roslin
Minnesota University Libraries, USA
Missouri University General Library, USA
Mitchell Library, Glasgow
Moray House College of Education, Edinburgh

National Library of Australia, Canberra, Australia
National Library of Canada, Ottawa, Ontario, Canada
National Library of Scotland, Edinburgh
National Library of Scotland, Lending Division, Edinburgh
National Museum of Scotland, Edinburgh
Nebraska University Libraries, USA
Netherlands Royal Library, The Hague, The Netherlands
New England University Library, Armidale, NSW, Australia
New South Wales Library, Sydney, NSW, Australia
New York Public Library, NY, USA
New York State Library, NY, USA

New York State University at Buffalo, NY, USA
New York University Libraries, NY, USA
Newberry Library, Chicago, Ill., USA
Newcastle University Library
Newcastle-upon-Tyne Public Library
Newfoundland Memorials University, Queen Elizabeth II Library, Newfoundland,
Canada
North Carolina University, Wilson Library, USA
North East Scotland Library Service, Aberdeen
Northern College of Education, Aberdeen Campus
Northern College of Education, Dundee Campus
North Western University Library, Evanston, Ill., USA
Notre Dame University Library, Memorial Library, Ind., USA
Nottingham University Library

Oregon University Library, USA
Orkney County Library, Kirkwall
Oxford University, All Souls College Library
Oxford University, Balliol College Library
Oxford University, Bodleian Library
Oxford University, Worcester College Library

Paisley College of Technology
Pennsylvania Historical Society, Pa., USA
Pennsylvania State University, Patee Library, Pa., USA
Pennsylvania University Library, Pa., USA
Perth and Kinross District Library
Pontifical Institute of Medieval Studies, Toronto, Ontario, Canada
Presbyterian Theological Hall, Melbourne, Victoria, Australia
Princeton Theological Seminary, Speer Library, NJ, USA
Princeton University Library, NJ, USA
Public Record Office, London

Queen's University Library, Belfast

Reading University Library
Renfrew District Libraries, Paisley
Rochester University Library, NY, USA
Royal College of Physicians Library, Edinburgh
Rutgers University, Alexander Library, New Brunswick, NJ, USA

St Andrew's College of Education, Bearsden, Glasgow
St Andrews, Hay Fleming Library
St Andrews University Library
St Andrews University, Scottish History Library
St Benedict's Abbey, Fort Augustus
St Francis Xavier University Library, Antigonish, Nova Scotia, Canada
Saltire Society, Edinburgh
Scottish Catholic Archives, Edinburgh
Scottish Genealogy Society, Edinburgh
Scottish Record Office, Edinburgh
Scottish Reformation Society, Edinburgh
Sheffield University Library
Shetland Archives, Lerwick
Signet Library, Edinburgh
Society for Promoting Knowledge, Belfast
Society of Antiquaries, London
Society of Australian Genealogists, Sydney, NSW, Australia
Society of Genealogists, London
Southern California University, Doheny Library, Los Angeles, Ca., USA
Speculative Society, Edinburgh
Stanford University Library, Green Library, Ca., USA
Stewart Society, Edinburgh
Stirling District Library
Stirling University Library
Stockholm Royal Library, Sweden
Strathclyde Regional Archives, Glasgow
Strathclyde University, Andersonian Library, Glasgow
Sydney University, Fisher Library, NSW, Australia

Texas University at Austin, USA
Toronto Metropolitan Central Library, Ontario, Canada
Toronto University Library, Ontario, Canada
Trinity College Library, Dublin, Eire
Tweeddale Society, Peebles

Uppsala Royal University Library, Sweden

Vanderbilt University, Jean and Alexander Heard Library, Nashville, Tenn., USA
Vaticana Biblioteca Apostolica, Vatican City, Italy
Victoria State Library, Australia
Victoria University of Wellington Library, New Zealand

30

Virginia State Library, USA
Virginia University, Alderman Library, USA

Washington University Libraries, St Louis, Mo., USA
Washington University Libraries, Seattle, Wash., USA
Western Australia University, Reid Library, Australia
West Highland Museum, Fort William
Wisconsin University General Library, USA

Yale University Library, Conn., USA

Zetland County Library, Lerwick

Copies of the Society's publications are also presented to the British Library, London, and to the Carnegie Trust, Edinburgh.

31

SCOTTISH HISTORY SOCIETY

PUBLICATIONS

A full list of publications from 1886 onwards will be found in *Acts of the Lords of the Isles, 1336-1493* (1986). The following volumes are still in print and may be obtained from the Honorary Treasurer.

THIRD SERIES

16. REGISTER OF THE CONSULTATIONS OF THE MINISTERS OF EDINBURGH, VOL. II, 1657-1660. Ed. W. Stephen. 1930.

17. MINUTES OF THE JUSTICES OF THE PEACE FOR LANARKSHIRE, 1707-1723. Ed. C.A. Malcolm. 1931.

19. THE WARRENDER PAPERS, VOL. II, 1587-1603. Ed. A.I. Cameron, with introduction by R.S. Rait. 1932.

21. MISCELLANY OF THE SCOTTISH HISTORY SOCIETY, VOL. V. 1933. (Miscellaneous charters, 1315-1401. Bagimond's Roll for the archdeaconry of Teviotdale. Letters from John, earl of Lauderdale, and others, to Sir John Gilmour, president of Session. Letters to John Mackenzie of Delvine from the Rev. Alexander Monro, 1690-1698. Jacobite papers at Avignon. Marchmont correspondence relating to the '45. Two fragments of autobiography, by George Keith, 10th Earl Marischal.)

23. CALENDAR OF SCOTTISH SUPPLICATIONS TO ROME, 1418-1422. Ed. E.R. Lindsay and A.I. Cameron. 1934.

24. EARLY CORRESPONDENCE OF ROBERT WODROW, 1698-1709. Ed. L.W. Sharp. 1937.

25. WARRENDER LETTERS: CORRESPONDENCE OF SIR GEORGE WARRENDER, LORD PROVOST OF EDINBURGH, 1715. Ed. W.K. Dickson. 1935.

26. COMMENTARY ON THE RULE OF ST AUGUSTINE, BY ROBERTUS RICHARDINUS. Ed. G.G. Coulton. 1935.

31. THE JACOBITE COURT AT ROME, 1719. Ed. H.A. Tayler. 1938.

32. CHARTERS OF THE ABBEY OF INCHCOLM. Ed. D.E. Easson and A. Macdonald. 1938.

FOURTH SERIES

3. LETTERS OF JOHN RAMSAY OF OCHTERTYRE, 1799-1812. Ed. B.L.H. Horn. 1966.

5. MINUTES OF EDINBURGH TRADES COUNCIL, 1859-1873. Ed. I. Macdougall. 1968.

8, 9. PAPERS ON SUTHERLAND ESTATE MANAGEMENT, 1802-1816. Ed. R.J. Adam. 2 vols. 1972.

11. PAPERS ON SCOTTISH ELECTORAL POLITICS, 1832-1854. Ed. J.I. Brash. 1974.

12. CALENDAR OF PAPAL LETTERS TO SCOTLAND OF CLEMENT VII OF AVIGNON, 1378-1394. Ed. C. Burns. 1976.

13. CALENDAR OF PAPAL LETTERS TO SCOTLAND OF BENEDICT XIII OF AVIGNON, 1394-1419. Ed. F. McGurk. 1976.

14. SCOTTISH INDUSTRIAL HISTORY: A MISCELLANY. Ed. R.H. Campbell. 1978. (Introductory Essay. Journal of Henry Kalmeter's travels in Scotland, 1719-1720. Journal of Henry Brown, woollen manufacturer, Galashiels, 1828-1829. The North British Railway inquiry of 1866. The beginning and the end of the Lewis chemical works, 1857-1874, by D. Morison.)

15. PAPERS ON PETER MAY, LAND SURVEYOR, 1749-1793. Ed. I.H. Adams. 1979.

16. AUTOBIOGRAPHY AND CORRESPONDENCE OF JOHN MCADAM, 1806-1883. Ed. J. Fyfe. 1980.

17. STIRLING PRESBYTERY RECORDS, 1581-1587. Ed. J. Kirk. 1981.

18. THE GOVERNMENT OF SCOTLAND UNDER THE COVENANTERS, 1637-1651. Ed. D. Stevenson. 1982.

20. A SCOTTISH FIRM IN VIRGINIA: W. CUNINGHAME AND CO., 1767-1777. Ed. T.M. Devine. 1984.

21. THE JACOBEAN UNION: SIX TRACTS OF 1604. Ed. B.R. Galloway and B.P. Levack. 1985.

22. ACTS OF THE LORDS OF THE ISLES, 1336-1493. Ed. R.W. and J. Munro. 1986.

FIFTH SERIES

1. GOVERNMENT AND SOCIAL CONDITIONS IN SCOTLAND, 1845-1919. Ed. I. Levitt. 1988.

2. LETTERS OF GEORGE LOCKHART OF CARNWATH, 1698-1732. Ed. D. Szechi. 1989.

3. MISCELLANY OF THE SCOTTISH HISTORY SOCIETY, VOL. XI. 1990. (Plea roll of Edward I's army in Scotland, 1296. Letters of John Graham of Claverhouse. Some late seventeenth-century building contracts. Correspondence relating to Millburn Tower and its garden, 1804-1829.)

4. THE CALENDAR OF FEARN: TEXT AND ADDITIONS, 1471-1667. Ed. R.J. Adam. 1991.

5. THE SCOTTISH OFFICE: DEPRESSION AND RECONSTRUCTION, 1919–1959. Ed. I. Levitt. 1992.

6. HISTORY OF THE UNION OF SCOTLAND AND ENGLAND, BY SIR JOHN CLERK OF PENICUIK. Ed. D. Duncan. 1993.

FORTHCOMING PUBLICATIONS

SCOTTISH MIGRATION, 1740–1920. Ed. A. Macinnes and M. Storey.

MISCELLANY OF THE SCOTTISH HISTORY SOCIETY, VOL. XII. (Three thirteenth-century charters. 'Dialogue of the twa Scottish wyfeis', 1570. Letters of Lord Balmerino to Harry Maule, 1710–1713, 1720–1722. Strike bulletins from the General Strike, 1926. Various other documents.)

THE BLACK BOOK OF COLDINGHAM, 1298–1430. Ed. J. Donnelly.

THE BRITISH LINEN COMPANY, 1745–1775. Ed. A. Durie.

CLAN CAMPBELL, 1550–1583. Ed. J. Dawson.

FRENCH MILITARY AND FINANCIAL DOCUMENTS CONCERNING SCOTLAND DURING THE REIGN OF HENRI II. Ed. E.A. Bonner.

MINUTES OF MID AND EAST LOTHIAN MINERS' ASSOCIATION, 1894–1914. Ed. I. MacDougall.